THE LOONY-BIN TRIP

Kate Millett

THE
LOONY-BIN
TRIP

UNIVERSITY OF ILLINOIS PRESS

Urbana and Chicago

The author gratefully acknowledges permission to reprint a portion of the lyrics from the following:

"All That You Have Is Your Soul" by Tracy Chapman © 1989 EMI April Music Inc. and Purple Rabbit Music. All rights controlled and administered by EMI April Music Inc. All rights reserved. International copyright secured. Used by permission.

"Me and Bobby McGee" by Kris Kristofferson and Fred Foster © 1969 Temi Combine Inc. All rights controlled by Combine Music Corp. and administered by EMI Blackwood Music Inc. All rights reserved. International copyright secured. Used by permission.

"Ticket to Ride" by John Lennon and Paul McCartney. © 1965 Northern Songs Ltd. Rights for the U.S., Canada, and Mexico controlled and administered by EMI Blackwood Music Inc. Under license from ATV Music (MACLEN). All rights reserved. International copyright secured. Used by permission.

"Planxty's Older Version of Yeats's Sally Gardens" from "The Rambling Boys of Pleasure" by Planxty. Reprinted with permission from Tara Records, Dublin, Ireland.

Library of Congress Cataloging-in-Publication Data
Millett, Kate.
The loony-bin trip / Kate Millett.—1st Illinois pbk. ed.
p.   cm.
Originally published: New York: Simon and Schuster, © 1990.
ISBN 0-252-06888-2 (pbk. : acid-free paper)
1. Millett, Kate—Mental health.
2. Psychotherapy patients—United States—Biography.
3. Antipsychiatry.
I. Title
RC464.M53A3   2000
616.89'0092—dc21   00-036488
[B]

P 5 4 3 2 1

Even though this is a work of nonfiction
and the author has endeavored to be accurate,
some of the names have been changed.

FOR THOSE WHO'VE BEEN THERE

"Hunger only for a taste of justice,
Hunger only for a world of light,
'Cause all that you have is yourself."
—Tracy Chapman

PREFACE TO THE
ILLINOIS PAPERBACK

I am enormously glad to see this book back in print. So will a great many readers to whom it has been useful over the years, those who have experienced official psychiatry and found it abusive or oppressive. When *The Loony-Bin Trip* first appeared, I was deluged with letters, letters from those who had been there themselves, their relatives and friends. There was a great need to communicate, explain, and understand what had been a traumatic and tragic experience: even to admit to this event took great courage. All people stigmatized with this diagnosis—and it is a vast number of people—until recently had only *The Cuckoo's Nest* and this book to rely on as argument against the treatment they received. To question or criticize psychiatric treatment was unthinkable then and largely remains so today.

Two more books have since emerged that describe depression brilliantly, William Styron's *Darkness Visible* and Kay Redfield Jamison's *Unquiet Mind,* though the latter derives from a conventional psychiatric point of view, and the former offers no explanation at all, merely the experience itself. A new book by Sarah Payne Stuart, *My First Cousin Once Removed,* an account of Robert Lowell and a number of other "crazy" relatives, has added humor and some perspective to the subject. I have wanted to do the same in my own case and to admit to the moments when the darkness returns and a small prophylactic dose of lithium seems a sensible precaution. Susanna Kaysen's *Girl Interrupted* has just provided insight on the issue of confinement for another generation.

Meanwhile, a movement for patients' rights and the claims of psychiatric survivors against abuses by the system grows. The German group Irren

Offensif staged a theatrical event cosponsored with the Free University of Berlin in May of 1998 whereby psychiatry was "put on trial" for human rights abuses: involuntary incarceration, forced drugging, four-point restraint, and electroshock. What was crucial to psychiatry's "conviction" after days of debate was its insistence on the use of force. Without coercion and police power, it claimed it could not operate and refused to relinquish them. This dialogue over human rights in the face of psychiatric abuse will surely continue and be an important issue in our time. There are psychiatric survivors forming nongovernmental groups on the model of Amnesty International to bring such issues to the attention of the United Nations. There is also the question of how the concept of "mental patient" and the legal implications of "substituted judgment" create a category of person, as it were, outside human rights' protection. Finally there is psychiatry's role in social control through the vast network of civil and government agencies and powerful pharmaceuticals.

PREFACE TO THE 1990 EDITION

This is an account of a journey into that nightmare state ascribed to madness: that social condition, that experience of being cast out and confined. I am telling you what happened to me. Because the telling functions for me as a kind of exorcism, a retrieval and vindication of the self—the mind—through reliving what occurred. It is a journey many of us take. Some of us survive it intact, others only partially survive, debilitated by the harm done to us: the temptations of complicity, of the career of "patient," the pressures toward capitulation. I am telling this too in the hope that it may help all those who have been or are about to be in the same boat, those captured and shaken by this bizarre system of beliefs: the general superstition of "mental disease," the physical fact of incarceration and compulsory drugs, finally the threat of being put away and locked up forever, or if released, stigmatized throughout the rest of one's life. A fate, after all, held before all of us through the whole course of our lives, the notion of "losing one's mind." An eventuality I once would have regarded as absurd, impossible, someone else's bad luck but not mine.

I already had a glimpse of the nether regions or at least the first circle of this dark landscape early in life: I had a summer job in St. Peter's Asylum in southern Minnesota when I was eighteen. Knowing already how terrible such places were, it never occurred to me that I would be delivered into one as an adult, when I was independent, established, a published writer. When it happened, in 1973, I was bemused and saw it as a fluke, a shameful incident, an error and misunderstanding among family members, the product of naïvete. Following my release I became profoundly depressed, my confidence broken by confinement; despite the fact that I had won my freedom through the intercession of civil rights lawyers and a trial—unusual in itself—it was accepted by those around me that I was "crazy," so I might just as well be. Moreover, there was the ominous diagnosis of manic depression, a professional scientific verdict of insanity. I began to crumble in fear and loneliness. Desperate to keep from killing myself—which seemed the logical next step, an execution I was bound by circumstances to carry out—I turned frantically to what seemed my only other option to save my life, my body anyway, and surrendered my mind, the spirit, the self: I sought "help," became a lithium patient and lived thereafter a careful existence. An unsound mind like mine must be tranquilized and occluded with a drug; left to itself it was tainted, unstable.

For seven years I lived with a hand tremor, diarrhea, the possibility of kidney damage and all the other "side effects" of lithium. Then, in the summer of 1980, I decided to go off lithium, thereby severing the control of an authority I had never entirely believed in and had reason to resent. The decision to go it on my own was a gamble for my own reason. For in accepting lithium as a remedy for depression caused by incarceration and diagnosis, I was accepting the validity of both, together with the pronouncement of my incompetence and degenerative insanity; I was confessing to an illness whose other treatments lead to the loss of one's freedom and dignity through confinement. I had been fortunate that my loss was temporary. But I had seen thousands of persons for whom it had been permanent. I dared to refuse the stigma, challenge the ascription itself. If I had kept my own counsel, maybe nothing would have come of the decision. But I imagined I was safe. This is what happened.

PART ONE

The Farm

1

At the farm in Poughkeepsie just before dinner the first evening light is soft and almost violet. Sophie and I cross the grass in the circle drive by the big locust, the gravel drive stretches just before us and beyond it the farmhouse lawn where the tables are laid for dinner under the trees. We are going to see the coop which Sophie has just fixed up as her studio. A barren New England shed, a chicken coop—she has transformed it. It is the South now, nearly tropical, "Like a New Orleans whorehouse," I say, and we laugh. "But it's perfect." I pace the room, admiring it, remembering how they called them sporting houses, places of the afternoon. The last passionate fullness of day, Sophie's straw mats and bamboo hangings filtering the light. "How clever you are." The look between us grows into a suggestion. A quickie? "Do you suppose there's time before dinner or will the apprentices catch us in the act?" she asks. We smile and look around the room at the spectacle of light, the dark gleam inside, the light outside building, massive as water, brilliant by contrast, overwhelming like the sea around a boat.

The beauty of what Sophie has created in a few casual hours takes my breath away. I have known this place for years at nearly every hour of the day, even worked here, yet I've never seen the room in this light; Sophie has enchanted the place. This amazing woman, her intelligence, her knack, her whim and instinct conceptualized, then realized. It's genius, the way the light is caught and held by her hangings, the bamboo blinds placed at just the right junctures to filter and direct the light as it floods in at the big openings in the wall to the front of the coop on the southern and western sides. There's the old camera from her family in Canada mounted on its tripod as if in explanation, as if the camera had taken a picture and we were in it. Oceans of light in the lens of the eye opening to the masses of color in the fervent July sunset beginning now just out of reach beyond the far western wall, all the refracted yellows and reds defused in the air around us—the room has become a camera. How brilliant she is, this is beyond anything she has shown me before. Bending over me, courting me, taking me, seducing me—the whole structure a seduction, the most outrageous compliment that someone would create this and then pay me the homage of showing it as a private exhibition that would end in bedding me. The soft of her skin, her bare shoulder against my lips, the pristine blue sheets under us, cobalt, their color and the color of the golden light around us, one does not wish to close one's eyes, miss it.

And then they burst in on us, pirates of noise, Kim and Libby stumbling in the door, laughing, knowing full well what they would displace. Somehow their presence is a compliment to our love, just as they prevent it they also validate and applaud. We look at each other and cannot find resentment. "Aha, we know just what you're up to, but you're too late, the food is on the table." "Really on the table?" "Really. We give you two minutes, exactly two minutes." They both laugh. "To make yourselves decent." How they love it, being young and so full of sex themselves, its energy, its ripe invitation; sexual appetite is a presence in the room, its apprehension here is a celebration.

For they love us, as we love them, every day more so, friendship becoming a drunkenness becoming love, a love none of us define, so we call it the farm or the colony, as if it were merely an idea, an ideology of a communal something politically correct. Through it, rapturously happy. Because of how we live? Because of who we are? Sophie and I say it's because this year's bunch of apprentices is wonderful, they're treasures. Calling them the kids, though we know they are young women, young but already women.

Life has never been so good. The apprentices, the farm, the summer still ahead, only half over, spreading already to a richness, a perfection, like a peony in full bloom. Or the loosestrife around the pond. And

Sophie. All, I have everything. I am even off the lithium. With no ill effect. It is six weeks now we have been keeping check on the experiment, and if it works I am whole. Either I was never crazy or I have recovered and can be sane henceforth. To be whole, not a cracked egg, not an imperfect specimen, not a deformed intellect or a mental defective—but whole. It's working, I'll make it.

"Hey, come on, you guys, the cook will have a fit." We look at each other, face to face in the circle of bodies in this wonderful light; they are by the door, between the door and the bed, their shapes already darkened against the light; leaning on an arm, you can smile up at each of them, in love. With them, with the place, with Sophie. "Come on, you're already late." Discovered now and on our way to dinner, crossing the grass with Sophie, I see the rest of them standing at the table to toast, their glasses raised, the red wine in the glasses, the last light cleansing and sparkling the glasses and plates along the straw place mats, the different, warmer light of kerosene lanterns on the wooden boards of the table, and their long brown arms above their heads, raised to toast with the pleasure of clinking glasses. "They're a wonderful bunch," I say again to Sophie as we cross the grass. "The best we ever had," she says nodding. This is the happiest summer of my life.

2

Another morning and I wake up uneasy beside her. Something is going wrong with us. This new bickering, this vexation. A monstrous quarrel is growing between us: Sophie is unraveling the thing connecting us, that bright beauty of the early days, our bodies white in the light of dawn, the mist coming up from the pond, the insatiable greed of our lust, our love, our tenderness, our rutting tenderness. We were unable to stop, one gratification only calling for another, the wildest improvisations, the never-finished copulation, franker and more animal than with any lover I'd ever known. Fond of the same pleasures, fond of all pleasures, an infinite variety of subtle clitoral stimulation, hard vaginal fucking, anal invention, breasts, eyes, the never-satisfied mouth; how easy and endless the going down, the coming up to rest on a nipple or a kiss or a look—the highest trust, the secret between us, the billy goat lust of our perfect shamelessness, all borders passed, transcended— utterly given to each other, in league.

All those mornings that made our love, forged before those great windows onto the water, the little willow tree framed in them. The willow, the bed, the drawing table just above and to the right if you stand before the big casement windows and look through them to the pond below. At that big table I drew her. Over and over a thousand times, sketches and then finished drawings with a Japanese brush, then poems in them, then silk screens of them. Sophie Sophie Sophie, the lines of ink making her body, the words so many kisses along its flesh, that sweet slender mass, the lines of the brushstroke trying as for salvation to imitate hers, merely imitate the so perfect life before me in the light of summer, the green beyond the pond and the willow, the waving grass beyond the white of her haunch, her belly, her buttock, her breast, the so difficult and tender shoulder.

All unraveling now. We no longer make love, or if we do it is only a reminder of how things have degenerated that were once so magnificent. When the memory of before sweeps over me it mocks, humiliation colors orgasm; you get off to get it over with. Light a cigarette, trying to forget, wanting to get up rather than linger: have breakfast, start working, anything rather than linger, anything to replace this knowledge, the dead certainty of it. For a while one could say it changes, love changes, settles, becomes daily no longer paradisical but solid, the living with rather than the falling in love, the marriage not the wedding. But it is not that now, because I have known that with Fumio and it was good.

This is not that; instead it is some mock marriage, some soap opera of quarrels and jealousy frightening me. Terror and losing and apology in me. Shrewishness and accusation and declaration in her, the harsh voice going on annihilating me as I sputter. Hours of this, and I break my rule and finally raise my voice. I don't want a wife, for Christ's sake; we are not some grotesque married couple, the nineteenth century or the divorce court or television. We are lovers, friends. Those two things. But when we are not lovers, we seem unable to be friends.

Maybe it's my fault for the notion of doing a will, making her my heir, giving her the farm. Perhaps she was right to reject the idea. Yet somehow, past her good instinct, another impulse has been unleashed and given its head. The lady of the manor, which I thought was only gallantry—we could go about in long dresses and be ladies both, some evening when we're not quite so busy—some whimsical view of ourselves and the place, a fantasy to play with, like the fantasy of woodswomen, tractor drivers. The fantasy of living in the south of France in our banquets of lanterns and wildflowers. Good God, it was playing.

But I have now a termagant not a lady, or a lady affronted, more superior than High Church. I cannot bear that voice. Mostly I cannot bear that sound of British scorn. Where did she learn that tone, that knife in the tongue? She with her once soft Canadian accent, the bonny burr of Scots honey in it when moved, when talking long-distance, when whispering beloved obscenities. So pure in her lust—the utter cleanness of spirit that could play at slut and wanton. Randy, horny, and always the fine good of the white of her skin, arms, thighs, hip, her silly knobby feet, the one imperfection that fascinated me, held me too. However rank we were, there was always this still purity at the center, this untouched individuality, this excellent personhood that maintained itself entire days in bed; when the phone rang, when it was time to have still another cup of coffee in the big bedroom in the farmhouse, the fire glowing past the little marble-topped table that held the breakfast china and the coffee cups. Laughing at the rumpled sheets, the wonder of her self-composure, lady and woman, adult and something of a girl, who went to England early, ran away from home, had every adventure, and was alone, for all the sad and funny stories of poverty or screwing around or being screwed over by this or that figure in a tale—business partners who cheated her out of a house, or a guy whom she jilted and never married. The ordeal of coming apart with Ellen, who is still her best friend. Through all of it she had arrived in this room untouched. Till now, till I touch her and we unlock in each other the most surprising and munificent congruity of sexual energy. That would last a lifetime, that would build the farm. And look what we have made of it already.

The years I labored here alone are nothing to the dreams and fairy tales Sophie and I have built in bed: greenhouses, the conversion of the carriage house, the lavender barn, into an exquisite house—when we're done, we'll put big tubs of lavender flowers in front under a balcony— just so, she says. And we laugh and conspire and solve the insoluble problem of the staircase. We can do anything, we are geniuses of architecture, plumbing, carpentry, electricity, design and decoration. Money is no object—if there isn't any, we can't let a thing like that stop us, ingenuity and our own labor and the "how to" books will see us through. But most of all, the wonderful inventiveness of her mind. How blessed I am to have a mate who loves this place. Not to carry the whole weight of it alone any longer but to have a fellow conspirator in making it paradise to share with our friends, with the apprentices, with the artists to come here someday when the cottages are built for them. All the mad maps of the crops, how many trees will be in the ground in nine years, how many harvested in ten? How the first crop can build the first cottage, how the thing can go on forever. Even when I die, for I will die first: she could steward it, make it go on, run it as a farm that supported all the rest, the colony.

But now she is shifting in her towering British arrogance, delivering ultimatums. She has other fish to fry. She ought to make some prints and try to get exhibited; she has to do it this moment. Or perhaps she'd like to draw. Maybe this is the exact moment when she should sit down and finish her unfinished manuscript—do I care nothing for her book, for God's sake?

"Your life—I am sick of your life!" she shouts at me. "I am embroiled in your goddamned life, I am up to here with it. Your show, your fucking farm, your bloody apprentices, your leaky faucets and running toilets. I am sick to death of your life, I want a life of my own." It's my fault; I see it now. The toilet does run. And the Sunset plumbing book makes it all so easy and sensible to do this stuff ourselves. But she's right, there are a million things wrong with this place which I either cannot afford to fix or haven't got to yet, or fix only to have them break down again. I must be doing a terrible job—burdening her with what I thought was such enormous happiness to us; such an adventure, learning how to print photographs, build a darkroom, make drawings together and apart in the third-floor studio on the Bowery, Sophie's clever delightful pictures, her miniature sculptures, her neat drawing table, the pencils arranged with her meticulous style and care. Sophie drawing at one table, I at another. Sophie, who taught herself the darkroom doing the photos from Iran, teaching me how to print now, looking at my results, printing a better print to show me how.

Sophie and Susan Ryan, one of last year's apprentices and a professional photographer. "You're not going to show that . . ." Susan says, looking at that pair of prints that became the ferocious cunts. "Yup," I say, trembling that she finds the printing too amateur. "My God," Susan laughs. "You're out of your mind—this is wonderful." "Want a drink? It's closing time." The gin of evening on the third floor, later a fire in the Franklin stove on the fifth floor in the living loft, and a hilarious dinner around the low table before the fire, high talk about our painting and photography, images and words; the feasting of friendship and gratitude. The doorbell rings and another face looks up from the pavement down on the Bowery, another crony or Dakota herself, our best photographer; the sock is thrown down with a key in it, there's another bottle of wine in the rack, we can even stretch this little chicken over four people, why not. The fun and activity, the friends, and all the talk and work of those times, the work done. Even the nights you come upstairs so tired from standing on the cement floor of the darkroom, which is really only a toilet. A large toilet with wooden boxes lined with plastic for your chemicals; develop, stop fix—then rush around the corner to a kitchen sink for the wash, heady chemicals in an unvented toilet so riotous you are dizzy. But with all that—all the work that was done those months, all the learning. And this is my life that is overwhelming her, strangling her. I hadn't known it. The news is like a blow on the head. Surely she loved it too, I know it.

But now I see what she means, my projects, my comings and goings, my two places—the Bowery and the farm—my books, perhaps even my by no means overwhelming achievements. . . . I have written my first book, and published it. And many more after that: one bookcase in the loft is full of my books, editions in different languages. And it is big, about eight feet high and maybe seven feet long, and though I was far too casual storing these books so close to a sunny window since they fade at a great rate, I was proud of it. Now I am rather ashamed. The loft and the farm become onerous today—they are a stone around her neck. Should I have come to her with nothing? How can I give her what I have without divesting myself of it utterly? How can you share what you have without giving it away so that you then have nothing?

There is a quality in her I have begun to mistrust. It began with the deeding of the farm. At first she refused both the temptations and the obligations of property. "It's better I should have nothing. I'm better off that way, it's how I arrived when we first met." I am puzzled. "And I have had property in my capitalist phase"—her usual ironic reference to the time in London when she renovated and speculated in real estate and was done out of a house. "It wasn't good for me, it didn't agree with me."

But then—as if she had thought the matter over and changed her mind yet could not go back—she has undertaken a different sort of ownership. In running me. Every morning during those coffee sessions in the barn before the big windows, little confabulations where we usually talk about the day's tasks, a discussion that ends up in a list. They are a nightmare now. She is the boss, I am her gardener receiving orders. She makes every decision, is responsible for every item on the list. And perhaps I could live with that if it were not for the tone; she is brilliant, I think, if only she did not speak to me in that contemptuous, superior way—full of anger, scorn, bullying. The sessions go fast now, composing the list of tasks, since they are no longer discussed or weighed, just issued—the rest of the time is left for rebuke. "Surely you must realize you can't paint that siding in the sun." "When will you ever make up your mind what to do with the hill field?" "I told you not to send Libby out into that bog—how are you going to get the tractor out now?" It is all my fault. I sit there and realize it with flaming cheeks: I am utterly unfit to run this farm, only she is fit. Why doesn't she do it, then, just tell me what to do since I am so incompetent, must be hauled back after each foolish run at things—my stomach turns to water—why not restrain me first?

Actually, I don't remember sending anybody into that bog. Lauren and Libby managed to get the tractor stuck all by themselves. My perception. But it vanishes under her scolding—how persuasive she is, how devastating. "Are you going to call Ed?" I groan inside, hating to bother my neighbor again. Poor patient guy, the man who sold me the tractor and has come to our rescue seemingly a thousand times, how awkward to call him again, to wait while this man who lost his farm and now drives a truck—his voice tired with ten hours of driving—looks at his beer bottle, thinking about these damn silly women driving that tractor which he loves and understands and still owns in the sense of knowing far more than we do or ever will. And then contains his fatigue and impatience and says he'll come over as soon as he can. It may be days, it could be a few moments. I want to weep with futility, beg him to have a bath, eat his dinner, watch some TV, play with his kids, even just tell me over the phone what to do and I'll give it a try. "To get it out of a swamp you drive it in fourth gear, maybe fifth—don't even rock it; just bust it out of there—a tractor's not like a car, the higher gears are for power." But with all the other problems, things are often obscure, dark, the machine so complicated, the book open before me to the page on the generator, the pages on the wiring, the page with the condenser, the page with the lubrication system, oily gnarled pages, for the book goes out into the field each day. Somewhere in a high meadow Libby and Lauren rewired the entire machine, studying it like medicine, having a field day, heroic in the heat. But they never removed the old wiring, and used one color for the whole job so there is no color coding; most of the wire did not even need to be replaced. And the machine was down for two weeks.

"They are here to learn," Sophie says. "I have a tractor in order to mow," I say, "the season is passing us by, there are only ninety days we can farm as a group, and we have thirty acres of fields.'' ''It's hopelessly overgrown and you are working the machine too hard in that heat.'' ''I have to.'' ''Then learn not to have tantrums when it breaks down.''

I have put my last dime into this farm, it's all I own—I have even paid for it—but now I can hardly afford gas and oil for a twenty-year-old tractor. I would like to strike her, to slap the godforsaken snobbery out of her self-righteous tone. I would also like to kiss her face, to take her in my arms, to make all this past twenty minutes of bruising gall disappear—to heal us. Without that how can anything succeed, farm, colony, all?

''You run this place like a nitwit,'' she tells me. ''You have no idea what you're doing.'' Even agreeing with her—I am only learning to farm, so for that matter is she—but even agreeing with her, I hear in her voice the ring of foreclosure, of one who would sell up. I had wanted her to have the farm with me so that it would never be sold, so that the colony could go on. ''If I had this place I'd run it for a profit, I'd live off it.'' I close my eyes and wonder how you live off something with taxes and insurance so high they are not covered by renting the cottage in winter, how you live by selling Christmas trees that are only eight inches high so far and will not be a crop for ten years.

''If you had a mortgage you could get machinery; your machinery is ridiculous,'' Sophie lectures. ''Sure it is. But having no income, I cannot take on a mortgage, that's clear, isn't it?'' ''Everybody else does, lives on credit, it's how business works.'' ''I can't. Call me an Irish peasant, I can't risk it. I cannot lose this place.'' She gives me a withering look reserved for Irish peasants. I want to scream at the unfairness of it, the absurdity of her coming into my life penniless and expropriating it, given everything only to call me a cheapskate. Part of me is also intrigued by her fearlessness, her proclaimed mastery of the mysteries of finance, her ruthlessness, her awesome blind pride, obdurate, awful. How can anyone so lord it over another? I wonder, marveling at it. Not the lady of the manor, not even old Scarlett at her most obnoxious; this is the seigneur, the rapscallion, the bully gigolo. God, have I given my heart to a confidence man?

''And start taking that lithium again. You're acting very odd. Watch it or you're going right off the deep end.'' ''Are you saying you think I'm getting crazy?'' The blaze in her eyes, defying mine. ''Put it that way if you like. You're making a fool of yourself and ruining this place. Don't forget your list.'' I had forgotten it.

In the spinning horror of what is happening to us, what is falling apart between us, in the terror of what is happening to me, my hands shake again but not from lithium, the dizzying humiliation of this half hour affecting me so that I cannot face them at breakfast, cannot bring my unsteady legs across the lawn. Fool and moron—yes, you had forgotten your list.

3

"You better cool it in there or they're going to drop you and you won't be able to insure anything," Sophie calls out. "But you won't believe this!" "Sure I will." "Look, the people in New York who always insure the loft are offering to insure both the loft on the Bowery again, which they've never seen, and now the farm too, which they will not even get around to looking at for a month or two." "So, let 'em." "But I could be living up here in a corncrib and playing with matches." "Let 'em, their price is better." "No, what I want is for my insurer up here to give in and cover both places. They're real, they're local, I've dealt with them for years."

"You're not going to much longer if you don't leave that woman alone." "All I said was didn't she think it was outrageous that an artist's studio can't get insurance, didn't that constitute discrimination?" "She is not interested in answering that sort of question." "She won't answer anything, just this same old jazz all the time about the head office. So I gave her Mom's line about complaining to the commissioner of insurance for the State of New York. Let's see what she says this time—this must be her calling back."

And it is. She will give me liability insurance for the loft; the head office has relented, reconsidered, made an exception, looked up a ruling or whatever it does. And the price is right too; I knew I'd get a better rate if I hung on. I have saved three hundred dollars, real live money to run the farm on. "It has taken you all afternoon to do this—why don't you go swimming now?" Sophie says.

Alas, there are still all the bills to pay and the checks to write. Writing in the confusion of entry and exit from the three rooms that give onto this one, the sounds of the kitchen, the radio and the phonograph accompanying apprentice labor on the next set of French windows, which are being dressed down with paint remover on the front lawn, bits of yellow paint and the vicious chemical that has dissolved it now mixed with bits of grass and tracked over the front porch. From my desk in the front hall I must apprehend each fleet set of tennis shoes seeking lemonade or the toilet, or they will track this gunk over the rugs as well. And these two Persian rugs happen to be my treasure, paid for with the first big show I ever had in California; imagining I had earned twice the money I actually did, I took it right over to Omar Khayyam, my man in Berkeley, and spent seven hours buying two rugs. I am livid at the prospect of their being harmed, insisting, pleading, begging—whatever—that they be seen not as bourgeois objects to be despised and disrespected but as works of art women have made over months of time, underpaid and unrecognized. "You would not track paint remover over a canvas, would you?" "No." The bored look; they have heard about these rugs so damn many times. Because, of course, I am at their mercy, they must know it by now; their malice, conscious or unconscious, could destroy anything in this house and I would still be forced to play the good hostess and say that's all right, don't worry about it. Today it's all too much for me; whenever I'm on the phone someone comes in wanting me to write a check to H. G. Page, our building supply, for turpentine or sixpenny nails, and where are the car keys? While writing the check I am interrupted by four other issues: Where are the screwdrivers? "Where they always are." "We can't find them." "Do you want me to go find them for you?" "Yeah." Then it's the saw, then it's shall we take the fittings off the doors? "Yes, would you put them in an envelope so they won't get lost?" "Where is an envelope?" I am still writing the check I began ten minutes ago. And look down to find that I have miswritten it. And explode.

I sit by the pond feeling like an awful person, one who explodes. Now you have made the apprentices hate you. They will see you as a bully for blowing up and shouting at them, they will never understand how impossible it has been to concentrate for the last two hours, for days now. Because you have made bad arrangements, you can't work at a desk in the middle of a traffic pattern that involves all those rooms: living room, dining room, front porch, the staircase up to the second floor—Grand

Central Station. Maybe you should move over to the cottage next door, the oldest section of the farmhouse; no one uses the ground floor there. Maybe you could have a real office, get something done, have room for all those files spilling around on the floor.

But I have alienated them. When I wanted to be their friend, see the light of admiration in their eyes. It is so easy to go from big sister to old bag. I too am a little sister, I know what it's like. Sitting by the pond and nursing the wounds of big and little sisters, I decide to give my own big sister a call. Elder, the Lawyer out in Nebraska. I'll tell her about my insurance difficulties; I'll amuse her with this geometric proof that when they refused to insure my loft because it's an art studio I got the goods on a giant corporation and material for a theoretical little case of discrimination.

"Hi, Sally, I have the funniest thing to tell you. How's this for a new civil rights angle—how about artists—would you believe that the insurance business won't touch an artist's studio for theft or fire?" "Are you taking your medicine?" What the hell does this have to do with anything? I wonder. Though it is not the first time I've called her or Mother with some joke or something to crow over and been hit in the face with this inquiry. "Yeah. Are you interested in what I have to say?" But the fun has gone out of it; in fact this moment has been like being a child again and getting slapped. And however bravely I claw back to the adult level—my self-conscious attempt to play amateur legalist to her actual prairie lawyer—I cannot manage it. Her voice is steely with patience: "Are you taking your lithium?"

Suddenly it all comes back, the last time, the loony-bin trip, the shame, the terror of being locked up. It was she who put me there—a thing I can forgive but not quite forget, though it was forgotten until the line: "Are you taking your medicine?" like a bullying sergeant, like an order, like a prison guard in those prisons I thought I had left forever. I realize that if she were to know I have gone off the stuff, she might be out here in no time, might even have me busted with a few phone calls. Meaning well—they always mean well. And they always win: by the time you are busted you are crazy, certified and incompetent, marked to the extent of having a record, broken by the bust and, when the depression comes down, contrite and crumpled and only too willing to crawl to the psychiatrists, take what they will give you; the arrival of depression proving you were manic too at the moment when they cornered you.

I will not be cornered again. This call was a mistake, the wrong number, the very opposite of what I want to evoke. It was hubris to have done this; I've opened the very doors of my doom. What false and self-defeating impulse was this?—you can never prove anything here. "You're getting out of line," she says. "Sally, really . . ." "Is Sophie there?" Is Sophie a guard, a keeper of sanity? "She's outside, probably having a go in that little boat of hers out on the pond." "What?" As if the little boat were proof of hallucination. Speaking up, I say: "We have a little plastic boat here. Sophie's afraid of the pond because of the leeches. She insists on sitting in her boat." "Listen, are you taking your medicine?"

Should I lie? Or should I tell her of the experiment? How Sophie is part of it, how we will stop if anything goes wrong, how there's a doctor in the neighborhood who is doing tests, will check for any damage the drug may have done, and can be relied on if something is wrong; failing that, there is Foreman, the lithium doctor, if I have to go back on it. It is over six weeks now and we perceive no ill effects at all. So why involve Sal in this?

It was Sally's idea after all to have me seen by a doctor at Highlands Hospital in Oakland. It was July then too, seven years ago, in California. The first bust. Detained on a seventy-two-hour observation hold, I was transferred at once from Highlands to Herrick Hospital in Berkeley. When the three days were up at Herrick, Sally had me transferred to Napa, where the clock began again.

Sally had decided Napa would be cheaper. And the law could be stretched by moving me from Highlands to Herrick and then to Napa so that the seventy-two hours—not counting court holidays, weekends, and the Fourth of July—came to some ten days in the end. And a few more for good measure, to look like a good sport while bargaining for my freedom with a shrink at Napa, a man who didn't need trouble and now could no longer hold me against my will. Since I seemed to be a stickler for legality—whether I was crazy or not I obviously had a penchant for civil liberties. Playing the good fellow and cleaning off his end of the action, he promised me my freedom—if I said I'd been hospitalized voluntarily. The price both a lie and a gamble. It was a document I hardly remember: Thorazine and fright; the entire maneuver a risk I scarcely understood. But I would have signed anything to get out of there and into daylight again.

A week later I arrived in St. Paul, stopping off to visit my mother on my way to the farm, and she had me committed to the Mayo wing of the University of Minnesota. That same morning the word went around among the social workers, and by afternoon civil liberties lawyers arrived at my side to demand a hearing to challenge commitment. We won our trial ten days later. I was free again. And came here to the farm to spend August, happy to be alone, alive and well. Freedom was everything after the hells I had seen stretching away into an eternity I glimpsed as a college girl with a summer job as a psychiatric aide. St. Peter's Asylum, a snake pit in southern Minnesota. Things hadn't changed that much in twenty years; the joints where I was an involuntary patient, a prisoner, in California and Minnesota, were not very different. Solitary and the jacket still lurked about, but dope had replaced having to manage the inmates; drugged out, they managed themselves. At Napa we used to stay up late surreptitiously guzzling instant coffee to counteract the effects of Thorazine. Sitting up together, getting high, or rather normal though it felt high, we became comrades on contraband. But other nights in those places, television evenings, the crowded air around the long rows of beds, the eternal night of those wards where you hardly dare sleep lest you awake translated to some place worse than the dungeon you close your eyes on . . . will this be the rest of my life?

At St. Peter's commitment was for life; most of those deposited there, shrugged off by their relatives, had been parked ten, fifteen, twenty years ago. They would die there. Even at the newer places in California, at Napa for example, you'd turn and ask a very nice Belgian whose papers were not quite in order and he'd say four years already. How long had it been for that tall black undergraduate who loved to sail and studied literature at Berkeley, he of the lovely Braque-like drawings— have you saved the drawing he gave you? Have you forgotten them all, have you forgotten the guy with the battered cowboy hat, another black man, getting high on his coffee, the caffeine enabling us to talk at last, even to talk fast, rebel talk, a thing the Thorazine frustrated entirely? The bravado in that lovely hat, a gambler, a wit, our "dealer." The talk making us comrades, breaking down the solitude, the isolation, the fear and shame and despair; talking was organizing. And the poor stiff ones, have you forgotten them too, mute as the old ladies in St. Peter's, those blanked-out women at Napa who had forgotten how to write or talk, who only mumbled to themselves? While you sped on, busily writing letters on that humiliating ruled school paper, the regulation issue whose very look would undermine your credibility with a bank or a lawyer, whatever assistance you needed from the real world, a dead giveaway even without your address. Back at the farm, your address and your bank accounts straightened out nicely, the keys to your car and your front door firmly in hand, have you forgotten it, imprisonment?

I think so. But that tone in Sally's voice reminds me again. Yes, I took the lithium. All those years of forgiving those who imprisoned me, realizing they were perplexed and felt they had no option, forgiving them because they did not understand the consequences of their ignorance but still will never hear you when you try to explain.

But didn't they take one look and shudder, knowing they themselves would never consent to be locked inside there for an indeterminate period, a detention utterly at the behest and discretion of a doctor about whom they know nothing and over whom they now have no control whatsoever? He might as well be a cipher with a label on his chest, so superstitiously have they responded to his license, his function. A function, it now emerges, they do not comprehend and can no longer influence. At his pleasure one can have electroshock, psychosurgery, all manner of debilitating drugs, terms of incarceration of any length or duress, solitary confinement, "restraints."

Then why quit taking lithium? Six years of diarrhea. Six years of hand tremor in public places, on podiums, at receptions, at the moment one is watched and observed. Six years of it in private while trying to draw, only the greatest concentration stilling the Japanese brush to the perfect calm it requires. Six years of being on a drug that made one sluggish, the mind sedated, this suppressant. Rumors that it isn't good for you in the long run, the kidneys, the liver, maybe even the brain. Maybe the time had come to try living without it. You don't need it if you aren't a convicted manic depressive. I was convicted but never convinced. What if I could get possession of or even expunge my records? If not, this "take your medicine" thing is going to dog me the rest of my days, like parole. I will be at the mercy of anyone who knows my history and can invoke the authorities against me. A few months off lithium without freaking out might prove otherwise, establish my sanity. Absurd really, incapable of proof, but still to lift the judgment against me would be to have my selfhood again, absolved of the ever-present and proven charge of insanity. For which I can be made to do time at any moment. Not an "illness" but a crime; for in fact that's how it's seen. Lithium maintenance is only a suspended sentence. What if I were innocent altogether? Sane all along? Rather than the bearer of an incurable illness, a chronic recurrent disease, a rot in the very heart of the brain, a cancer of the mind?

Accusing me of mania, my elder sister's voice has an odd manic quality. "Are you taking your medicine?" A low controlled mania, the kind of control in furious questions addressed to children, such as "Will you get down from there?" At the end of my patience, I ask, "Will you ever stop bossing me around?" But I am already scared and at the moment I hang up I discover I am weeping.

As if by going off lithium I could erase the past, could prove it had never happened, could triumph over and contradict my diagnoses; this way I would be right and they would be wrong. It had always been the other way; they were right and I was wrong. Of course I had only to take the lithium in order to be accepted back. The ascription of madness was never lost, it could be pulled forth at any moment, but on lithium I would be "all right." Are you all right?—always their first question, intense with a very special intensity we both understood. We want you to be all right, they say, especially Mother, meaning it so earnestly, benevolently. But I am never all right, just in remission. If I could win this gamble. . . .

"The apprentices say you quarreled with your sister on the phone."

"For God's sake, Sophie."

"Do you feel all right?"

"I feel fine, except that I am so angry at Sally and so hurt. She went on and on about taking my lithium. In the most menacing way."

"You must have provoked her. Forget about it, go swimming; it will be dark soon. Kim and Libby have already gone in."

I look at the pond and do not want to go swimming. "Let's hope she doesn't have the white coats up here. Do you realize she could declare me incompetent?—it's that easy, you know. If they get a bee in their bonnet."

"Don't be paranoid."

"I'm not paranoid. It's the law. She could start on Mom. My sister Mallory's just down in the city, they could get her stirred up two hours away. And she's next of kin. If I were locked up, what about the farm?—they can make it so you don't even own your own property."

Sophie goes on, looking at me across the white wrought-iron table.

"Do you feel all right? You're not going off the deep end, are you? You have to tell me if you do; you know that was part of the deal in this experiment."

"It's just been an awful day. I can't get any work done at that desk—do you know how many times I get interrupted?"

"We'll have to do something about that, move you into the garage or something."

"How about the cottage?"

"I was thinking about that too. But look, do you feel different? You must tell me if you do. Anything that feels different."

I look at her: how fine she is to go along in this, to take this risk. "I really don't, I don't feel different at all."

But a differentness has begun, if not in me, then in those around me, in Sophie, in the apprentices, particularly those who love us most, love the farm most. For the farm seems threatened now, and their tenure insecure in this place toward which their feelings have become so proprietary. It's only two weeks before they're in love with the place. In another week they think they own it, we always say, joking about this phenomenon; the conquest of utopia by the utopians, you might call it, drinking bourbon on the porch late at night, someone blowing grass.

In the weeks past, there have been references, clues, discussion of psychiatry. A few of the apprentices know I have gone off lithium. Believers in health food and homeopathic medicine, they approve in a fuzzy way. But it was really supposed to be a private venture, something between Sophie and me. There was always the possibility of manic break, but that would be handled by the two of us, here at the farm. The intrusion of my family was not foreseen. The apprentices were safe and happy in the farm world, a utopia they have made and now love, a dream state consisting as much in each other's company as in mine, rather more in fact. They have been each other's entire society, staying up late becoming friends or lovers, having long talks, their poems, their pictures, their parties, the farm their whole world.

Suddenly a shadow has intervened. They could lose this dream. She could be crazy. And there are people out there, her relatives, who could invade the place, take it over, put an end to it all. She's got a history of this, flipping out, they put her away before, they could show up any time. Hmm, wonder what will happen. We don't want the colony to fall apart; we'd better talk to Sophie.

That night there is an air of ridicule about them at dinner, an insolence caught out of the corner of one's eye, a hint of their making fun of someone crazy. The teacher in me knows one is to ignore this, the way a lady pretends not to hear remarks by construction workers. Part of me is too hurt to believe it. They're sore at me over my exploding today while trying to write checks; it will blow over. The fact that you got busted for being crazy once and that your family had you incarcerated in a nuthouse is bound to be a little unsettling, you must remember how all that sort of thing gives people the jitters. It would be a good idea for you to be extremely quiet at dinner and let everybody else talk. A low profile, smile and be charming, but it would be just as well if you shut up tonight. There is coming to be a kind of danger around you. You have talked too much already—do you realize all this rumor is the result of your own error in calling Sally, letting others know what she said, or rather your interpretation of what she said? What she did in fact say was the old business they give you every time you call them up happy and with an idea of your own. It's all only the memory of the other time, the bust, and the threat you read into it—that and your own big mouth. You cannot live out your traumas naturally as they occur, now that you've gone off this stuff and are making a stand for your sanity and so forth—you cannot live all that out among nine people who have no interest in it and are here for something else. Learn a little discretion, cultivate a public manner here; this is not the family you thought it was, nothing can be that when it comes to this sort of thing: craziness. Remember how crazed with fear and loathing and apprehension people are in the face of that.

These kids are here to spend the summer with you—recover your dignity with them. Do the hardest thing now and be cordial, talk small talk, be kind. Overcome your shame and embarrassed reluctance and be what you are supposed to be to them, the companion disguising the teacher, the artist, the writer, other presences unacknowledged but still desired with a desire that will not condescend to speak its name. How hard always to be a teacher never permitted to teach, never accorded the place and position of teacher, that little perch without which it is so difficult to teach and not sound like an ass or a bore. Never mind, forgo pomposity and all your great designs upon the young; you're without a license here. Just be agreeable, recover the mood, cheer them and make them happy. Summon cheerfulness against the humiliation you feel. You cannot let this fail.

4

The first bust was like this. California. Berkeley, and Sacramento where I had a teaching job, temporary, but with a grand title nonetheless, Distinguished Visiting Professor. Berkeley was where I was busted; it was also where Sita lived, since she was a university administrator there. I had rented an apartment across the hall, planning to cut some film there over the summer, and done the place up—fireplace, Greek bedspread, flowers.

First I went back East for a visit which changed my life, irreparably as it turned out, by my getting involved in the case of Michael X, a black man from Trinidad, a writer and painter and civil rights figure now about to be hanged there. Michael had become a well-known leader in England but on his return to Trinidad offended the dictator, was perceived as a threat to him, and suddenly found himself framed for two murders which a study of the trial transcript convinced me he could not have committed. Michael was in the Royal Gaol in Trinidad awaiting execution; it looked like a long shot. But we had a good committee: William Kunstler for chief counsel, my peace activist friend Jon Hendricks to "run the office," John Lennon and Yoko, friends of Michael's, who, being friends of mine as well, first put me on the case. As Trinidad was then a British dominion, my job was to affect public opinion in England. Hard as that was to do, I came back to California having achieved something: the front page of the *New Statesman,* for one thing; a banner headline and a long article asked "Shall We Hang Michael?" It had at least become a question; when I went over, it was fiat—British racism was dying to swing Michael. It was difficult to move reporters but I had. There was the hope of an appeal in the law lords; no execution could take place without the signature of the Queen, and if we could generate and then maintain the pressure of public opinion . . . Tuesdays are hanging days in Trinidad; four years later, on a Friday and without the Queen's signature, Michael was pushed up the gallows steps. That was the end—this was only the beginning.

I returned to Berkeley full of this—it was the biggest civil rights assignment I had ever had. To stop a lynching, to prevent a hanging—both the American and the Irish in me were thrilled by this long narrow chance, a gamble against evil. And though I didn't know the man, I'd read him and liked him. His wife I knew by phone, and when you are talking to a woman who loves a man about to die, there is a great poignancy. They would not let her enter England, so she had appointed me her delegate. I was also William Kunstler's. It was all-absorbing.

It was not, however, all-absorbing to my friends. Sita tired of it early, probably deciding it was hopeless. And it wasn't women's liberation. Fumio, who was visiting me in California, tired quite soon as well. Joel Liebowitz, an old friend who had been our best man, was in Berkeley for an evening, stayed up late to warn me that I should concentrate on our marriage which was falling apart. I saw no special evidence of that yet, beyond Fumio's coolness, a wound I had lived with for nearly a year. Sita told me later that Fumio was about to discard me for another woman, but I would not have believed it then.

Meanwhile, in my happiness, I was with both mistress, Sita, and husband, Fumio, and had the prospect of two apartments, hers and mine, for comfort, convenience, privacy, and respectability. Sita was delighted to meet Fumio, Fumio less delighted to meet Sita but coming to like her; he had known about her for months. I had with each of them by this time a freer relationship, permanent without being confining. The theory. Into this enters my elder sister, Sally, called to their assistance by Sita and Fumio, who are nervous because I talk about Michael all the time and use a tape recorder and even talk back to the radio when the news is on. Sally went to college in California and welcomes any chance to return. She is married to a lieutenant colonel in the Strategic Air Command, has four young children, and still goes to Mass on Sundays. She lives in Nebraska. She has, however, at my urging started law school, or rather has applied and been accepted by the Jesuits of Creighton. Of course, I think it would be wonderful if she would give me a hand with the legal aspects of Michael's brief so that I can produce essays on his behalf—it is most urgent that things be published about him in order to get a stay of execution, mobilize opinion, and so forth. I spent thirteen weeks at Angela Davis's trial and observed publicity in action there.

Sally arrives and the four of us spend a very happy time; she is enormously sweet in an Irish misty way, speaking of the peace of our reunion, the sun of the evening in her eyes and our martinis as we sit on the cushions of Sita's very beautiful apartment, Fumio and Sita sitting before us. Naturally Sally loves Fumio, everyone does, all my family adores him; he is one of the most delightful people in the world. Sita is a great lady whom Sally liked at once; they had already met in Nebraska when Sita visited there on university business.

Dinner didn't go so well. I offended by wanting more butter. The serving was one puny pat, and that is hardly the thing for a girl from dairy country. My teasing the proprietor was regarded as unladylike, and from being the center of attention in a circle of beloveds, because of this incident I seemed demoted to an outcast. I began to feel the old breath of family wrath. Beyond Michael, *Flying* looms; no one has read it yet but there is already an uproar over the lesbian passages, shame made public. Soon the disgrace would be in print, irreparable. During the course of an unfriendly nightcap, Sally decided she would take over my apartment for the night, leaving Sita, Fumio, and me in Sita's apartment. Hardly a convenient arrangement. Husband and lover under one roof. This annoyed me so much I had another nightcap, rather uncertain of what to do, where to sleep. Sita will sleep in her own bed. Fumio will sleep on a heap of cushions in the living room. I can sleep with him or with her, but making the choice before their eyes is hardly good manners to either of them. I could sleep on the couch and be with neither. I think Sita—generous and tolerant, a woman of the world— expects me to sleep with Fumio.

Perhaps we should have had an orgy, all and sundry of us. Then perhaps what followed would never have followed; I used to contemplate the idea with a platonic distance when confined. Instead I committed a sin—that is also how I saw it when confined, perceiving it as the existential equivalent of sin and my confinement the poetic justice; indeed at the deepest psychological level, the only explanation of the things that happened afterward. I sinned by sleeping with Sita in her bed. Largely for the comfort of it, perhaps to some degree for the revenge of it, or the lesbian insistence of it, or the taunt that lying by her would provide to Fumio. Because he had rejected me for over a year now. I did not mean thereby to lose him, or even to hurt him, realizing it all only afterward.

I had been cruel and perhaps had hurt him, a thing I should never do in this world, and the idea of Fumio sorrowful or in pain in the living room took me to him where he lay like a stone, refusing to awake or to speak to me, and I knew I had indeed broken something in him, was broken in turn, lying next to him for hours of shame and regret under Sita's big cloak on the pile of cushions. Then I could suffer no more and got up to go to work at Sita's desk in the front room. Dialing Désiré in Trinidad for news and charging the call to my farm, writing some checks, paying bills, because my salary had just been automatically deposited with my friendly banker in Sacramento; so smooth things are out here, so efficient. How well organized my life is. All except for this awful thing I have done to Fumio. If he would only awake and forgive me, indeed if he will ever forgive me.

Then he seems glum and not that much different; Sita is cheerful and nervous, Sally like a bolt of thunder when she arrives from across the hall. She is talking to the others in the next room, which I ignore or pretend to, fearing it, not quite understanding it, and afraid of what I do understand. Sally goes out and returns. I am sitting on Sita's bed when Sally comes into the room; I am astonished by her and surprisingly afraid when she sits beside me. There is something punitive. I think of the night before, the way we live, Sally leaning toward me furious. "We are worried about you, kid." "I'm worried about Michael—why won't you help me with the brief while you're here?" "To hell with that crap." "We're talking life and death, Sal." "Nitwit, you're throwing money away, going to England, you're in way over your head." "What do you mean?" "I mean we're worried about you." "Worried" is suddenly the most ominous word I have ever heard; one has heard this stuff before, only so distantly, other unfortunates. "So?" I say. "I want you to come with me to a psychiatrist." "Sally, that junk." There is a long furious argument such as only siblings are capable of, and finally, with the ever-ready folly of a kid sister daring a mountain or a jail, I say, "Okay—I'll go to the damned shrink and let them decide who's right or wrong or crazy. Okay?" "Okay." And then the machine springs into action. They are ready with my car, who knows what else.

We were expected today in San Francisco across the bay at a party Flo

Kennedy is giving, and at first I imagine we are still going there; the shrink, once I have agreed, can surely wait; you have to make appointments with those people. It's someone Sal found through her Mills College connections, promised to be a woman.

Then as Sally drives I begin, slowly and in horror, to realize we are going to the appointment rather than the party. It's already past five; this is not just one of your lay citizen's office hours appointments. There is something possessed in Sal's driving, not even knowing the way. Sita has to give her instructions, reluctant as is Fumio, yet the two of them cooperative—more sickening awareness—if not as avid as she. This is her deal. My God, they are going to turn me in. The one occasion on which one's beloveds conspire with the state—the three of them, three of the people I love most in the world; only my younger sister and my mother are missing—this is my entire universe and they are now about to betray me utterly. To a place they have never been. I have. No one in the family ever listened to my descriptions of how hellish St. Peter's Asylum was. When I wanted to publish something in the St. Paul paper they discouraged me. They have no comprehension at all of what they do; they are the innocents.

I am to be the victim of that ignorance, and whatever rage each of them has for me—I'm in for it now. But to turn someone in to the state, to deliver a witch—shit, if I fucked the whole world and made you watch it, you have no right to do this to me. The car entering the gates . . . Dear God, what will they do to me, the long sad corridors of how long? What torments, shock, drugs, the waiting that goes on forever? No one I knew when I worked at St. Peter's ever got out alive and was not back a few months later—this is the labyrinth; the rest of my life I will wear this mark on my forehead if this is the place it seems. I open the car door. Later proof of my insanity, that I opened a car door while the car was moving. No one noticed that I opened the door of my own car and sat tight, having no intention of getting hurt, only aiming to make that damn sister of mine stop the thing so I could get out. "I agreed to go somewhere with you, Sal, but not a locked box, no way. Never. I was voluntarily visiting a psychiatrist, that was the deal. This is not a psychiatrist's office, this is a hospital, a mental hospital, an institution—iron gates."

"Get in this car. I promise you it's just a shrink." "How long does it take?" "An hour, that's all." "We could still make the party." I want passionately to go to this party—it is life. The moment I saw the bay and the bridge we never crossed, I felt cheated of life. It was there across the bay, it was the fun the four of us would have together at a party, friends again. Instead we are here. I am trembling with fright. "Trust me." "Trust her," Fumio says. "Yes," Sita says. Surely she would not betray me into that death. Or Fumio; he is unalterably opposed to the lesser American institutions—psychiatry is one of them. I rescued him from deportation; surely he is not going to turn me over to the state. No Japanese with a good leftist background would; nor Sita, after all she has suffered in America. Sally might be dumb enough to believe in these healers or even be insensitive to imprisonment, but they never would. Trust us.

And behind the first door there is a lock. A locked ward, a lunatic asylum, not a hospital, the place screaming with frightened people and cops. Like the circles of Dante's Hell floor after floor, each door locking behind. You do not dare to touch the bolt with your hand but you guess it, you feel it, still trusting them. They cannot have done this. Lie or deceive, bully yes, but not capture. The frail thread of hope and faith finding Sita's eyes—how she smiles to reassure me, how serious Fumio looks, as if he were my best friend forever and would protect me; what we have been to each other for ten years now, utter loyalty. Admissions, cops and ambulance drivers and the terrified mad who could not convince these bastards of their sanity no matter what composure they adopted.

But this will not be my case, of course not. I am here with these wonderful people who have exercised—as usual Sally has made a mess of this in her overconfidence—enough poor judgment to locate a shrink in this hellhole instead of some comfortable California office or some calm academic setting. From the choices she must have had, this has got to be the worst. On top of that it's not the woman we were promised. It appears the woman with whom Sally made the appointment couldn't keep it. "We'll come back, then," I say. "No, he'll be just fine," introducing me to this fat and evidently stupid Dr. McSomething—God, could this creep be Irish, I groan inside while politely shaking his hand, my own trembling, his eyes noting this with satisfaction. We were not meant for each other. Each question—for it is an interrogation not a consultation, still less therapy or anything like that—each question is posited from the given that I am nuts. "Madness in the family?" "Surely that kind of thinking isn't still around?" I demur, being a full professor in this state's university and comporting myself like one even to male authority, even in the heartless trap I have been ambushed into, realizing its full extent only by stages. Still trying to make this a conversation, still even wanting to know what this man's credentials are to interrogate me: where he studied, for example. No one condescends to answer. "What are his degrees?" "He's a doctor." "You said so, what sort?" "Psychiatrist." "Sure, but what stripe, what kind, what ideas—has he published?" They ignore me and talk over my head. "Who chose this man?" "I told you he was recommended to me." "No you didn't, you told me I would see a woman." He lights up then; as a women's libber, am I prejudiced? The question is cute, tangential. I doubt that I can explain how important it is to me that I was promised one doctor and provided with another. "I am here voluntarily, because my elder sister dared me, taunted me into seeing a psychiatrist."

"Your only mistake then was in trusting the people who brought you here." I will hear this remark for the rest of my life; it will echo along the walls of my mind until all sound stops for me.

It can happen again at any moment.

5

At the farmer's desk on the phone to Hudson River Psychiatric. A certain paranoia has overtaken me since I spoke with my sister; already I feel I am running, am on the run against capture. My friend Sheila, a member of the American Civil Liberties Union, has given me the name of a civil liberties lawyer who has an office right there in the heart of the joint. This lawyer will tell me my rights and I must memorize them, must have them by me like a litany. There is a sinking feeling in my gut as I dial. But my other object is to see if I can get legal access to my psychiatric records, records that function virtually like criminal records, records from Napa and Herrick in California, from the Mayo wing of the University of Minnesota hospital. I am eager to read what they say, even curious; are they not descriptions of myself, true or false, revealing or misleading? Why should I be forbidden to read them when they are open to any individual with pull within official channels?

The lawyer thinks it will be difficult to obtain psychiatric records, still more difficult to expunge them. The psychiatric profession is very powerful; they resent lawyers to such an extent it would be best to write for them through one's own private physician. And she goes on: "Since your records are in two different states and you are in a third, you actually might have a better chance. If your physician's good, that's better than going through a lawyer; it only gets their backs up, they stall, they take forever, they keep things back." "Like the CIA and FBI under the Freedom of Information Act?" "Same mentality. First let's work on getting your records. When you have them, we can see what can be done, if anything, about expunging them. Meanwhile, I'll see what precedents there are.''

"I have one more question: Could you give me the terms on forced hospitalization in the State of New York?'' "Do you feel in danger of that?'' "Well, no, probably not, but my family have done this in the past; I thought it would be a good idea to know the law and where I stand.'' "The criterion is danger to oneself or others. Of course, there are many ways to interpret that. But if you struck someone, for example, you'd be dead. Or if it could be proven that you took any chances with your physical safety, then it's suicidal tendencies. Civil Liberties has representatives now in almost every hospital, and you could be out a few days after you were forced to enter. Our policy is no forced hospitalization, which is guaranteed under the revised Mental Health Act; we have some agreement on it within the psychiatric profession, but it is by no means general. Most people, including family members, have no idea of the principle at stake, and they can generally get a psychiatrist to go along with them. Many hospitals aren't fussy either about forced admissions.'' "Is one safer up here in Republican country than in the city?'' "I would think so, if you own your house, if you're on your own land, yes. Your position should be very good. Just keep your temper. And remember your civil rights training. Let me know when you get your records—this could be a very interesting case.''

I look out the big farmhouse doors onto the green, remembering all the summers I have talked to New York from this vantage, feeling lucky while they sweltered in town. The prospect looks good in Dutchess County; property law is strong here; sit on your front porch and be mad as a hatter and they can't touch you. The troopers are the law here. Didn't Mrs. Sleight say if you had any more vandalism not to bother calling that sheriff of ours—it took him several days to get here after the windows were shot out, and when he did arrive his deputy pulled a gun on Mr. Odell, who was up on a ladder painting the ceiling. "Next time, don't bother with the sheriff, call a trooper right off.'' Swell, if my friends decide to put me away, I'll just call a trooper and, when he arrives, explain that they're all drunk; we've had a tremendous bash here and it's probably time they went home. Wonder how that would go down against the ascription of insanity. The trooper in his big hat trying to decide who's crazy versus who owns the place, versus who called him, versus some psychiatric jargon—without a doctor there the trooper can only shake his head in his big hat.

But do troopers nowadays have a list of the names of psychiatrists, radio contact with Hudson River Psychiatric? That would be the loony bin in these parts; it's not even far from here. Having made a wrong turn, I came across it once by accident, the grand big grounds—you think this is an estate or something out of the nineteenth century and then you see the squat buildings, the barred windows, the forlorn shapes within. God, how I hated the sight of it. Never mind, you now have a friend at Hudson River Psychiatric, your civil liberties lawyer.

"Who were you calling?" "Hi, Sophie, I've been getting the dope on insane asylums. Sheila gave me a contact at Hudson River Psychiatric. American Civil Liberties person. Seems the rule in New York is no forced hospitalization. The other side of it is you gotta keep your temper, not be a danger to yourself or others. Keep your cool and you're okay." "Well, are you okay?" "I feel fine, honest." "I think you're strange lately. Everyone does—they're talking about it."

Who's everyone and what is strange? But already I feel encircled. As if the telephone conversation with Sally had introduced her into the house. I should have shut up about it. My paranoia has provoked theirs; they are now somehow threatened here by a party they don't even know. "Her elder sister, her family might come . . ."—one hears the train of thought. For I can almost hear their thoughts.

I am now about to hear some of them to my face. Sophie announces, "We think you should go back on lithium." "Sophie," I protest, "why 'we'? It's you and I who were making the experiment." "Because it's interfering. Apprentices are getting fed up; they might not stay." "I lost my temper while trying to write a check." "You're acting funny." Suddenly I feel funny, I feel hot and frightened—are they right, should I take the stuff again, am I going over the edge? Cornered, I feel the way you do when many people are at odds with you, have discussed you.

If only it could be quiet and easy and just between the two of us, Sophie and myself, this matter so close to our lives; without other people dragged in, strangers to me till this summer, youngsters making judgments in that awful pseudodemocracy where we are all supposed to be peers in some commune of orthodoxy, further complicated with American popular psychiatry wherein each of them can make a judgment about normality, the group thereby legislating a norm and enforcing it.

"Sophie, I really don't feel different. I'm sorry if I've been short-tempered. You know there are always a few times in the summer when it gets to be too much, having so many people around; you know what

I mean—we both have bouts of it.'' "But you wanted it. Having apprentices is your idea." "Yeah, the old teacher hunger, it's a vice."

Her voice is increasingly harsh; I am offended, insulted by it, each sentence and phrase as she goes on a blow, an accusation. I watch her, feeling demolished. "Look," she says, "I'm going to have to tell you; you are alienating everyone here, you may even ruin the entire summer for all of us. This business of going off lithium is a mistake. I went along with you because I could understand your not wanting to spend your entire life on a drug, but you better make up your mind to go back on it." "Well, can't we at least discuss it gently, Sophie, in private?" I can hear Marge, the cook, in the kitchen. If we talked out in our room in the big barn—the evening coming in through the big windows—there we could make sense, I tell her, we could be good to each other. "Okay, I'll bring you a drink out there." With her own scotch in hand, she begins on me again. It is that icy British contempt. Where does it come from; since when have I become despicable in her eyes? She hands me my martini and I sit trying to make it a cocktail hour for two, trying to push back the hostility, the terrible hatred I suddenly feel coming from her—has she any idea how condescending her manner has become? It is worse than the bullying in the morning over coffee.

"Look, I don't want to go back on lithium, because I am so glad to be off, to feel so healthy and alert, to have lost weight—no more diarrhea, no more hand tremor. I'm swimming a lot every day, even getting my stroke back. I feel ten years younger." My voice, which was enthusiastic over its subject, the total recovery of my health, trails off, wilts before the way she listens, the annoyance and impatience. I find myself becoming speechless. I wonder if she knows her effect, means to be as devastating as she is. "Nonsense, this is all nonsense, you are being stubborn, you are endangering everything, everything in your life for the past years and everything here for us. Do you realize what will happen if you get hauled off?" "Who would haul me off?" "You could just go into a store and flip and get hauled off." "I don't ever go anywhere, except to H. G. Page's lumberyard. They think I've been crazy for years." "It's not funny. Listen, you go back on that stuff or else."

I look at the martini, trying to get the taste of it, the effect of its little elation after a long day. Suddenly, irrelevantly, I remember the martini Sheila made for me last summer. It did look rather big, but I was grouchy and sitting out my dudgeon in the barn, and so I drank it without noticing the size, not finishing it before dinner, never finishing it in fact. I didn't need to—by dessert I had slid off my chair and then managed to get to the bathroom and be sick, stricken with embarrassment lest the apprentices know the old lady was soused. Indeed they did, were dancing about the door in glee when I finally came to and struggled out of the place. The next day I had an official hangover and was excused from work; while they shingled the barn room with cedar shakes I made fourteen drawings of Sophie from sketches, adding poems on the spot, and one big funny picture to celebrate the roofers. Fifteen silk screen editions were made from them, most of the summer's output.

How nice it would be to spend the time drawing. Sophie said earlier that I must draw to record my new experiences off the lithium. But it is so like an order. And the fact is, I am not aware of having any wonderful new experiences anyway. Besides, there's so much work to do just running the farm that I don't dare take the time off. It's moronic to be spending all your time over insurance and stuff like that, she said to me yesterday. "You're an artist; draw." "But I only draw when I want to, Sophie; it's my happiness." "You are missing this chance to record what you experience now." "I don't experience anything different, just that my head is a little clearer; lithium makes you feel a little fuzzy around the edges by comparison."

That was the last time we discussed it. Now it is a command to return to lithium: the drug, the life of barely concealed insecurity. The psychiatric command as conveyed by lay opinion. Backed by the observations of this or that apprentice, or perhaps outside opinion solicited somewhere, someone she's called on the phone and whose name she won't divulge. My God, this is making me dizzy. And the rage in Sophie. I look at her, seeing a changed manner, almost a stranger. How much of this comes of her own history? When she was twenty or so, she was picked up in Toronto for raving in the streets. Just raving, not very loud, a youngster in pain over a love affair, one with a woman in the days when you didn't do that. She never explained to them, she never even divulged her parents' names. They quickly let her go. It is something she will not talk of, this experience, it is absolutely off limits. And today she is sanity's paragon, ordering me back on the drug.

"If you flip, what do you want me to do?" The question, like "What are you doing about that tractor?" has the tone of directive rather than inquiry. Right now I am to decide what she will do if I flip. "Whatever you like." "Shall I stay here or leave?" "I don't know." "Fumio said you should be left alone.'' My God, they have already consulted Fumio. ''Leaving me alone is not such a bad idea, but really I'd like you to be with me; we're doing the colony this summer, let's just do it. We've put a lot of work into this and have so much still to finish . . . Sophie . . .'' She is in my arms, sobbing, both of us sobbing. ''Look,'' I say, ''we can be all right, I think so, really. We thought we could beat this thing and survive; let's try—hang in with me, go along with me. If it doesn't work, if I freak out, the lithium's there; we even have a new bottle, a fresh prescription.'' ''You'd need blood tests,'' she laughs, wiping her nose. ''So I get blood tests,'' I say, sniffing. While we hold each other in the dusk, I wonder if it is too much to take on, just to prove you're not crazy, the victim of a bewildering invisible disease that may still strike and destroy us. Hubris, is it hubris? I wonder.

6

Out the window I see a swimmer breasting her way up the pond. Libby probably, but I am not quite sure yet, until I catch the signal in her rather amazingly blue eyes. Now I see Kim too in the water below. Swimming before breakfast, a good idea. Kim and Libby are my coaches—the two have decided to resuscitate me and restore my wind. Kim swam for Stanford. They are both, in their swimming coach-trainer capacity, very sweet to me; we have formed our friendship around it, around laps in the evening; the wordless conversation of bodies crossing a stretch of water over and over again at the most beautiful time of day, the loosestrife around the pond like a crown, unreal at times when you look at it, the eyes also needing the uneasy reality of the old blue barn as it leans toward the water, the top of it always a bit drunk-looking, the mind always trying to straighten it out and find time and money for a new coat of paint. Not this summer. But it doesn't matter, their urgent young presence tells me, nothing matters but this delicious moment, this hour, this summer—this second.

Kim and Libby have come closest to me this summer, the other apprentices more distant. Yesterday we were in the field together, in the full hot sensual brush of grass and sun and wildflowers, mowing between the rows of white spruce down in the huge meadow at the back of our land. These trees will be our first crop; the success, even the continuance, of the colony depends on them. It is of the utmost importance that we mow them well, cutting out the brush, the weed trees that stunt their growth and take all their sunlight, the dogwood bushes three times the size of the little conifer that is trying to be a Christmas tree with all its limbs intact, its frame not stunted—that archetypical scaffolding which can never be replaced and must be perfect and symmetrical. Here from the beginning we must protect the young seedling, even getting the wildflowers out of the way of its roots, the heavy grasses. We have the Gravely mower and the snap cuts, gloves and shears, the thermos, and new Cutter Insect Repellent, our vade mecum out here. The Gravely drones on ahead, the power of its engine backing and destroying as it goes over the rough earth, strong young arms controlling its erratic energy, loving its power, the wonderful force of the thing, all those horses between your two arms.

A field day—no wonder it's called that. The secret beyond the heat and the labor is the mesmerizing sensual energy of it, the wildflowers all around when you look up, surprised to find you are in heaven, sweating like a farmhand, completely gone out of yourself, your supposed real life vanished into this moment of heat and the soil, the rub and tickle of the vegetation. If you had a lover along, you would lie among the flowers here and probably get poison ivy; so hypnotic the heat, so strong the sun, so sexual the entire landscape. Even the work, the repetition of it, the shears, the exertion—you think you can't do another row and then you can, the gang of us cheering each other on, speeding it up telling jokes or singing songs, making lame witticisms; funny at the moment because they are us and ours, they are the lines we save the farm with, that make the colony possible. They are our inner circle talk, our private language; time here staying with us always, a circle in the tree of our lives. And this heat which is July—next year we must finish the mowing in June—held over us like a truncheon, the sun annihilating, making us silly or sleepy or just so full of its soporific influence that we are like creatures drugged. And happy. Miserably hot and thirsty, tired as hell, and, still, in some high unlike any other, a stupor of sensual stimulation which makes the room dark when you enter the farmhouse, which makes you head for bed or a couch instead of the shower, which makes you sleepy even the next afternoon—this orgiastic exposure to weather and landscape, sun and sweat and grasses, the thousand kinds of wildflowers, the daisies that are yellow with black centers, the daisies that are white with golden centers, the Queen Anne's lace, the violets, the wild strawberries, which the tractor gang (Lauren and Libby and Kim) spend a good deal of time eating since the tractor will never start, the clover blossoms, the loosestrife, the wild dogwood—all so beautiful—

let me throw myself among them. Standing up after stoop labor, how good it feels, how good the water in the canteen. . . . Time for a break.

This is regarded as an excellent idea. Since I'm with them in this field today, I must show them the best place to laze; we'll go into the woods at the back of the Great West Field. The water keen in your throat, the shade of the woods marvelous at first and then hot, not the direct and fierce heat of the sun but something deceptive, sneaky; humidity. I demonstrate first how to wade in the stream. Lauren demonstrates how to lie down in it: like a monkey, spreading the mud on her undershirt (undershirts are a gesture to the neighbors usually discarded when we go to the far end of the pond and are away from the road), then without undershirt, the ooze on her jeans, on her feet, laughing in pure elation, the sensation of wet and cool—in no time everyone's trying it. Lighting a cigarette, how I love watching them, becoming one with them, some strange unidentified relationship forming among us.

The swimmers together now below the window, a steady stroke, forward, the breaststroke, quiet because Sophie is sleeping. Sophie is no morning person; there have been times she refused to get up for breakfast. An awkward situation in view of the fact that the apprentices and I are required to, a necessary discipline without which we cannot operate. "I am not your apprentice," she says tartly. "No one says you are, but if you don't come to breakfast, it's awkward for me, for all of us. If you don't bother, why should anyone else?" "I am not your apprentice." "I know it," I reply, hardly knowing what to say. Since she is not an apprentice, what is she—director, assistant director, what? I am just Kate; it's Kate's farm and she's trying to make a women's art colony here. That explains me. What explains Sophie except that we live together? She is a writer and photographer, and beginning to chafe at life on the farm. "Please, Sophie, there's so much to do here, if you take off we'll fail at the things we're trying to finish this summer. I can't show them how to build and stay on top of the field work and order all the materials, get prices, design the floor—I can't do all of it alone. Please stay."

And she stays, but more and more the fabric between us unravels. We quarrel about everything now. Even money. She could go to town and do some work, she says. "But whatever you earned would be consumed in just living; here you live without needing any money." "I want to be paid for work.'' ''I can't pay you, you know that.'' ''What I'm doing would be pretty highly paid.'' ''You have just bought a plumbing book; that does not yet make you a plumber.'' ''It will.'' ''I expect so. I expect that you'll learn that stuff like a shot. It's well paid—better paid than carpentry, which is a lot harder.''

She ignores this to pick away again at the lithium issue; she insists I should go back on it. ''But I feel perfectly all right.'' ''You're acting differently.'' ''Since when?'' ''Fourth of July.'' ''What makes you think so?'' ''You lose your temper a lot.'' ''It's Irish, and there is sometimes a little stress here in paradise.'' ''No, you've changed.'' I would like to say that she has changed, but the tone of her voice appears to forbid it, and the emphasis is upon my faults not hers. I am to be the crazy person going off her crazy medicine; if there are any untoward results they are in my corner. ''Listen Kate, you are making a mess out of everything. I mean everything.'' How her voice stings. ''In a little while you will have no one left here. Every single apprentice will leave.''

There have been warnings of this before. Last summer Sophie approached me and my martini at the pond, end of a very good day, to inform me that the apprentices were in mutiny up at the farmhouse. ''Why?'' ''The vegetarians are starving to death, that's why.'' ''Why not discuss it with Gail? She's cooking, she does the shopping. I have no say whatsoever about what she gets from the store. Let's just get more vegetables.'' ''They're starving and they're going to leave.'' ''Jesus.'' When I ran up to the farmhouse kitchen there was an earnest discussion between Gail and three vegetarians about Brussels sprouts and yogurt—all was peace. Maybe this is just the same kind of panic now; apprentices always find Sophie easier to tell their grievances to, and so they do. She calls this getting stuck in the middle between me and the apprentices and thoroughly hates it. I sympathize and wish she could direct them to me; it is silly that I should be unapproachable if I am the one they wish to complain of or whatever. If there were only something specific . . . If there is someone I offended, I can apologize. If there is something I should do and have neglected to, then I'll do it. I listen, in a cold fear. What if, indeed, I had without knowing it alienated people here? What if my experiment of living without lithium really did upset, obstruct, bring danger to what we're doing?

I watch Sophie sleeping and wish she were awake to reassure me. But lately she is so hard against me, so deeply angry with me, I already know it is pointless. And it would be unkind to wake her; she loves her sleep so, and there is only another hour before the horn calls us. But for me the morning is so ecstatic, the early time so full of promise, I love being up at this hour. I adore the first cup of coffee by the pond, the virtue—both smug and hedonistic—of being up before breakfast, the unselfish joy in having that one hour to relish before you must bow your head to the group around the breakfast table: Work, the collective, the discipline and the chores, the assignments to barns or fields or silk-screening. All very well once you start, the thing to be done after all, but this hour or part of an hour before the horn, an early swim or a cup of coffee looking at the pond, this is pure freedom; gratuitous—you are there only because you loved the day and the scene so much you surrendered sleep for it.

And it's not too hot yet, the air soft and bright by the water's edge, at the wrought-iron table, seat of my philosophy over martinis of an evening, coffee in the morning; the air is balmy and perfect and golden. Two figures trudge toward me, dripping and grinning in the skins of their nakedness. "You're going in, too," "Well, I must just have some coffee first." "No, you're going in or we throw you." "Nice offer." "Take your choice." "You persuaded me." "You'll love it—it's not cold, we promise." And it isn't. Yet with all the satisfactions of swimming—once you are in—there is that problem, even when it isn't cold; the body rejects the indecent idea of putting itself at the mercy of a foreign element. Even getting wet has a radical aspect, particularly the stomach, the pubis, the breasts, and the chest, with its little thrills of cardiac reaction to chill.

I float, watching the loosestrife above me, the great purple flowers coming ripe now, not high yet—that is August—still more magenta than lavender. The giant elm at the head of the pond, a guardian spirit here, an elm so huge and old you pray for its preservation from Dutch elm disease and lightning; our landmark. It stands like a mast at the head of the pond; you see it from everywhere in this part of the farm; a signal, all lines converge upon it; tree of the goddess, magical and powerful construct of earth, thrown up to heaven like a titanic blossom.

The two mermaids join me, swimming in unison the three of us. Sophie waves to us from her bed—how nice if she has plugged in the coffeepot. I'm still having trouble with my timing in the breaststroke; we practice it together, Libby's judicial eye cocked for how that arm is breaking. On the home lap Kim does the butterfly, the water showering in so many lights around her tan skin, her black hair shining when she breaks the water—even then one notices the serious line of her brows. The morning air is around us like a rapture, drying us, the sun warm after the towel and even more effective. I have a gauzy nightshirt; my companions have nothing, are developing their tans. Libby throws herself down on a towel, Kim sits with me at the table.

"What's this lithium stuff you were taking?" she says.

The way she asks, there is probably something in the wind and no airy comment of mine is going to settle the matter. Let's treat it as if it were just something you talked about rationally; the scientific information at hand, what there is of it. Perhaps in explaining to her you will understand something yourself. What is it? is a perfectly good question; so far no one has asked it, they have only smirked or suggested in an intrusive way. Or it has been something secret that is not to be talked about, private in an odious way.

"Never heard of it?"

"Nope."

"It's in the table of elements. It's a natural substance, present in nature. Still never heard of it?"

"Nope."

It was Kim who brought her essays along with her, an English major with the usual failings.

"Well, anyway the periodic table of elements is a nice little chart about the size of a piece of paper. Everything in heaven and earth is listed. With its atomic weight. That's quite an achievement. Fellow named Mendeleev drew it all up in the nineteenth century. Classify, they thought, you know; if you can classify everything, you've made some progress. There's one in every dictionary. Do you know where the dictionary is in the farmhouse?"

She's up and running.

"I'll get you some coffee," I call to her back. Then we look it up, sitting together, student and teacher, because for once I am permitted to teach. "The symbol for lithium is L-i. You see on the chart here, over there on the left. Atomic number, three. A small number and a lighter atomic weight than just about anything except air; only helium and hydrogen have smaller numbers, but not oxygen. For all its lightness, it is not found in the pure state in nature but combined with other substances; you can find it in rock formations that have been heaved out of the ground. As a metal that does not really exist in the pure state, it combines with other things to make a salt. The lithium they give out as medicine is synthetic, and it is combined with salts as well, so it's lithium carbonate or lithium citrate. Even then it's so easy to make, so uncomplicated, that it's as cheap as ten cents a pill. In its natural form even the Greeks used it. It's in Perrier water, too, though not enough to have much effect on you.''

"What's it do?'' Her face is serious, interested, without humor, let alone ridicule or embarrassment or even irony, which might be expected in the others.

"The Greeks used it as a tonic, perhaps in the lithium springs they would visit, like a spa. They may also have understood its purpose as a cooler, a balancing agent between moods of elation and dejection that keeps you on an even keel. The psychiatrists don't seem to know, or profess not quite to understand, just how the lithium ion, once in the bloodstream, affects the brain. They say that in mania, the synapse—the exchange of energy across the neuron transmitters of the brain—goes too fast; in depression it goes too slowly. Nobody knows why, but when that happens the doctors say it means you are chemically, maybe even genetically, prone to mania and depression, because something triggers this little response too fast or too slow. What they say controls it is some stuff called amines, a substance in the cells of the brain about which I can't find out much either, but there are a couple of these amines that could be the agent of this fast or slow thing. It's all up in the air right now.''

"So, what's lithium do?''

"That's just it, they don't know. Or they only know that 'it works,' they say it evens out the fast or slow business to a steadier rate and therefore levels out the two extreme states of mania and depression. But they don't know why.''

She listens and cradles her foot.

"Not that I can get them to tell me, anyway. When you take lithium into your body, the lithium ion combines, enters right into tissues throughout the body—it's not very good for the kidneys sometimes— and the brain. It also has some interchange with two other minerals in the body, sodium and potassium—I'm trying to figure out if it has any harmful effects on them. A grad student in chemistry once told me that lithium destroyed the potassium ion, and the stuff might be lethal over a number of years. I took that to be radical opinion, like her health food opinions. But it did startle me.

"And if lithium is synthetically made now, it's not the same thing as if it were in the natural state, and if it's prescribed, as it is increasingly now, not only for manic depression but for the blues, ordinary depression, and alcoholism, even for schoolchildren who are hyperactive, then whatever synthetic they are all eating so obediently has become a form of social control, don't you see, because this psychiatrist thing is in itself a form of social control and very much directed by institutions. Not just schools and companies and hospitals but ultimately the state. And in the processing of synthesizing it, what if they've added some stuff or monkeyed around with it, even natural products can get weird then. Especially if the substance's whole long-range effect on health in such large doses is something they really don't know yet—'cause though ever so many people are taking it, it hasn't been around any longer than maybe just ten years in its present prescribed form. The 'side effects,' for example, diarrhea and hand tremor, are coincidentally the classic symptoms of fright and insecurity; or take the danger to the kidneys—are these inherent in natural lithium itself or due to the size of the dosage, the product of additives, or the physical effects of psychiatric diagnoses on one's self-esteem?

"So everybody is dutifully swallowing an unknown. Not just an experimental bunch now but tens, maybe hundreds of thousands. And they are swallowing on the say-so of a profession that cannot understand the workings of this stuff on the brain and admits it but still goes ahead and swears to its efficacy. And insists you take it. I didn't take lithium because the folks who busted me into the crazy house made me; I got away from them without taking anything except what they forced down my throat. Once out, I was clean. I started taking lithium for a great depression which occurred months after I was out. And I took it as a preventive measure not against mania but against depression."

"Okay, I'm following you."

"I'm trying to see if I can live without either one of these states and without lithium either. It's a gamble, but it would be worth it if I won and lived in my own mind again without chemical assistance."

"What happens if you freak?" This from Libby on her towel. After we stop laughing I say to them seriously: "We deal with it. I deal with it. No forced hospitalization—that's the law. Involuntary hospitalization, busting someone, depriving them of their liberty maybe forever, delivering them over to things like electroshock, which is really torture—all that is simply fascist. So no white coats around here, for starters. I've been through that trip, remember; I told you about it once after dinner.'' One of those early talks, almost like consciousness-raising, intimacy created among us by learning a good deal about each other's lives. Sandy's mother's alcoholism, which she sees as the burden of her life. Meg's agony over her upper-class British accent. The first nights, nights we stayed up late getting to know each other—a drop in the bucket to the number of confidences exchanged among the apprentices themselves now.

I have from the beginning been honest with them about being busted, but now that my psychiatric history is no mere colorful tale of the past but something of a recurrent possibility, they waver and then right themselves and will waver again. They are young and fine in the morning air; I am forty-five and an unknown quantity to them. They are twenty-two, intelligent and mature, but still, how awkward and disorienting for them to have to deal with the magic of madness, its power to confuse and transform. How can they decide what is madness, what is sanity, what is stress or anger or annoyance or confusion?

7

We are dining on the grass before the farmhouse. It is night already; one sees by the light of the kerosene lanterns, looking down the table, the main course over, a milling about as plates are changed before the coffee is brought out. Having done my kitchen bit earlier, I go on talking with the person next to me, enjoying myself, the beauty of the scene, the feeling of a feast. Because we have a guest tonight: Sheila has driven up from her house in the woods, which is halfway between here and the city.

Off to my left up on the porch there is something going on, someone by the phone. I wonder about it. At first it is just a nervous instinct over the cost of long distance, because that's the farm phone, I pay its bill. In earlier summers I have been left at the apprentices' departure with ruinous debts for their romantic whisperings to California or New York—even calls to New York are very expensive from here. So I am "neurotic," if you like, about long distance. But whoever it was has gone away, or perhaps it was just Sheila calling home. I turn back to my companion.

Suddenly I am interrupted by Sheila, probably a bit in her gin. Grinning, yet somehow very ill at ease. There's something up, her manner is so peculiar. "Now I want you to take this, Kate." "What is it?" "Just something you ought to eat. Swallow it up." Nervous giggling. "Sure, but what is it?" "You just swallow it down—pretend it's the Host or something." Bent over with laughter at her own lapsed Catholic camp. "No harm but no help either, Sheila," I say, spying the pink of a pill in her hand. "Just be a good girl and throw it down with some water." "Sheila, come off it."

I look up to see the others are watching. There is someone again in the hallway by the phone, but I cannot see who it is. What in God's name are they up to? That combination, the "medication" and the telephone, makes me cold all over, the muscles of my gut contract: they can't be doing this. Keep your cool, raising hell will get you nowhere. The temper of all this is still tentative. The climate around the table being still covert, making a fuss works against you. Raising an alarm—who would be on your side? Wait it out and someone may be. Sheila recommences her urging, more disturbed now, the giggle grown hard; she is pushing the thing at me aggressively. "Sheila dear, really, this is silly. I can make these decisions myself. This is something I've decided on after talking with Sophie." "But Sophie wants you to, too," she says, the triumph, the elated, irritating child in her almost bouncing off the ground. "Take it, take it, we want you to, you have to." "No deal, Sheila, you don't force people to take medicine. That's just lithium in your hand—I've eaten thousands of them, millions probably, over six years on the stuff. Just one wouldn't have any effect at all." "You have to take 'em from now on and this is your first." "Sheila, you can't make those kinds of decisions for people." Her hand approaches my mouth so fast I hardly see it; she is forcing the pill between my lips, her other hand reaching to hold my chin, as one forces a child to take pills, even a dog. Sheila's a paid-up member of the American Civil Liberties Union. "No way, Sheila." Keeping my temper, my voice deliberate and even—the others will feel that she has gone too far. But we don't need contention over methods; I must save her face too, since she has just forgotten her own values.

I pull my head back and smile at her. "Sheila, come on, you're a civil libertarian. And it was so kind of you to give me the name of that woman lawyer up at Hudson River—she was very helpful." The others have stood up by now and are disputing with her, with each other; there is still the shadow of a figure by the phone. "Did you know, Sheila, the lawyer told me that Civil Liberties' position is no forced hospitalization? I expect that covers forced medication, too, wouldn't you think?" Sitting down again next to her, turning it to pleasantry, quiet, restoring the table again, the meal, the mood.

And then without warning there is a scuffle, on the lawn between the table and the porch, more figures now running that way, but beyond the range of the kerosene lantern light it is too difficult to see just who it is. Kim, maybe Libby. Meg, even Sophie perhaps. My God, they are fighting at the farm. You better stop that. Reason, hospitality, what the farm is meant to be. This is like a desecration—the brute immediacy of its violence is more terrible than the threat of a moment ago. And there is actually someone on the phone; are they really capable of calling Hudson River Psychiatric, a psychiatrist lined up already? Busting me. Here. Now. In my own home? They sure as hell are having what looks like a real fight in your own home and you better stop it—that's the first responsibility.

Real fighting. The sound of blows and shoving. Damn, what luck. Now, just at the very moment I should be sitting still, preparing to look perfectly sane when the white coats appear (the rest of them can be mad as hatters and jump up and down on each other, I am required to be sane). There is so much to compose yourself against, but compose yourself.

In fact, you ought to sit tight. Their attention is away from you for a while; let them wear each other out.

But I can't, not here, I can't see women fighting with each other anywhere, but for God's sake not here. The smell of the fight, the very smell of fights, this surely is deranged. Whatever madness means, this is the madness of anger grown mean. It hurts to hear the sound of them struggling, the sound of body against body, the panting, the distortion of the voice, the cruelty of it, the place beyond reason which would cancel friendship, happiness itself. What I watch is misery not even knowing its wretchedness. Later will be too late. Someone could get hurt. Finally, all this is my responsibility; even under these nitwit conditions, where the object of the mad quarrel is how to deal with my craziness.

"Ladies, ladies, pacifism at all costs—come now, we're friends," I say, seeing whom I can pry loose in the tussle. More serious every moment. I wonder if each of them even knows with whom they are grappling by now; I cannot understand the sides, only this chaos unleashed in the dark of the lawn before the lighted house. The mass of them stumbles toward it; there is no speaking to any individual, so entwined they are, wrapped in their very real anger. Though it cools when I keep talking to them soothingly, reminding them this won't do. They end up as a heap against one pillar of the porch, a slender old-fashioned column, fragile even against the force of hands and arms. One figure preventing another from going farther. About that phone, I suppose, about using it or not. Though there was someone on it before; gone now, disappeared back into the house. There is the apprentice phone in the cottage—they could be using it as well. What have they set up against me? This straining mass against the column, the ancient support.

I make my move, grabbing the other column, figuring, checking behind me to see if I can be taken that way; the wall of the house, the clapboard, and a window, and Phyllis Chesler's stained glass Star of David which we've always hung in the front window, almost a provocation in these parts. I had a black civil rights worker living here once and asked him if he would find it a burden, since it was hard enough living up here, just being black. "Hell, no, keep it there. I'll go for the whole thing," he said. That recollection and the sanity of the sight of the kitchen beyond the dining room, the old wooden shutters near at hand, a vine, the peaceful ease of a summer evening in the country. But the clapboard is in shadow now and there are five or six feet of porch flooring behind me. Where I could be taken. For I expect it now, facing them, facing the yard before me; the wall and the dangerous darkness of the porch behind me.

I remember Joan and her trial, the witch trials, the takings of witches, the captures. If I had brothers now, would they stand behind me or sell me out? I wonder, looking at a group of women but a moment ago fighting like men, as stupidly, as passionately, as dangerously and purposelessly. I have taken my stand. For a moment history flooding over me: the Middle Ages, kinship wars, sagas, and the heat of an hour blasting and burning and bleeding. This here is terror. And I a witch. Joan must have felt this before the Inquisition, or the night they sold her to the English. This is how it was. It was like this. This is how it felt. The dark, and you didn't know whom to trust. It is a memory, a recollection becoming real. I do not have to reach for the comparison, it settles over me as a tunic slides over the head and onto the shoulders; all of a clap and I become her, look as she did to find my allies, back to the wall. Though not really—a good warrior would line herself up against that clapboard. But I am playing another game, at a column the equivalent of their column, and when my heart stops pounding I will start my palaver again about peace, less necessary now because they are merely shouting at each other; the fight is over. Next I'll progress to reason and ask, What are we doing here? Is it time for dessert yet? Wouldn't you love some more coffee?

I relax enough almost to smile and consider the significance of what I have just felt, this merging with Joan—again, for I was Joan or the Joan figure every day when I went off to court in a long dress for my sanity hearing escorted in his squad car by the sheriff of Hennepin County, where I was being held in Protestant Minneapolis, over to Catholic St. Paul. St. Paul, which is in Ramsey County, where I was born and which my lawyers chose as venue. St. Paul, where Joan— Jeanne d'Arc—was an intimate of most residents, certainly part of my life since childhood, for I grew up in communion with her crouching statue at the entrance to our convent school auditorium. But it was still a statue. Now in those moments she lived in me as entirely and fittingly as do the suffragists on a feminist march. For all the horror of being nearly taken, the danger and the betrayal, still consider the wonder of reconnecting with the figure and the circumstance, experiencing the sense of being filled and joined, fused for those electric seconds with the heroic ordeal that the witch hunt became for the hunted.

Now only the banality of recriminations. The apprentices hot after Sheila: "You tried to call and we aren't gonna let you." Was she telephoning the white coats or were they? They are calling her an intruder here; she has no business and so forth. "She's a guest, though," I say, "so let's smooth it over. Please don't call her names." The danger is over now, the impulse has passed; better not to know, just to be sure it never happens again. And how do you do that? Concentrate on the moment, bring them all back together again. Somehow I'm going to have to get this matter of civil liberties across here, appeal to Sheila as a practitioner, a member, a thoroughly political being, a constant demonstrator for radical causes. With the kids, it's their fairness I must appeal to, the trauma of what forced hospitalization does to one, the arbitrary and absolute deprivation of liberty. With Sophie—what there? Of all of them she is the most ambiguous. While each person here has let her madness out—or if madness is a myth, her unreasoning self— escaping like a gas, enveloping them all until the explosion of the fight, Sophie remains the most crucial quotient of all. They accord her as my lover nearly absolute authority over me, all power to decide whether I am sick or well, wrong or right (since that is the issue behind the first pair of opposites), and her mystery, the unknown factor, is buried in her own fear in the world of the mad, the bins, the electroconvulsions. Is it far enough away to affect her little or not at all? Or does it lurk in some corner of her mind and memory she has not and will not explore, so that its power is still there to subject her, frighten her, in short, into turning me in? So much depends on Sophie, on her slender strength—which because of her gracious and persuasive manner is likely to be overestimated here. Even her voice, her British accent, slight as compared with Meg's exaggerated patrician yet most effective over American kids just because it is not that self-satire but subtle and full of authority. Even that changes as things degenerate and her voice becomes toward me a hard Tudor knife—to others it is still the very sound of common sense.

8

I am in the coop. Night now, an empty darkness around me—not the resonance of evening sun through the bamboo blinds as the last time here, only a few days but centuries ago. It was bright early evening when the apprentices came to bring us to dinner. Sophie and I on the bed and the pack of them after us, laughing. Coming in sight of the feast, where they were standing to toast like musketeers, I'd said to Sophie that this was the best summer of my life. The revels now are over. Around me the farm goes on, but I am no longer in authority, its author. There was the war at dinner last night, another tonight; though not violent, merely conspiratorial, dour. Sheila stayed over a day, things approach a crisis. And now the council proceeds over and around the washing of dishes. I am not invited to join, even excluded. Sophie comes and goes between me and the kitchen, handing me medicines, her voice sharp and reluctant.

"Here, take this. Come on, I haven't got all day." The voice mean, directed toward a wayward adolescent or a thing. I have not been talked to this way for years; one of the blessings of adulthood is that one is no longer addressed as a thing. This is the voice used toward the truant, the ungovernable, the mind in decay. When respect is no longer necessary. But later, the kindness of a nurse in a sickroom, or a lover to a convalescent—"Here, darling, have some orange juice." They used to put Thorazine in orange juice, and for an instant I am overcome with the memory. But no, it is nothing but kindness.

Truly it is night now and feels late, but the talk, the conference or the meeting or whatever is going on in the farmhouse, pulls her away again. "I'll be out in a little while and we'll sleep," she says. Here in her coop? Rather than in the big painting studio in the barn, where we usually sleep, where I love to wake up to see our favorite willow tree and the water of the pond in the freshness of morning? For one night then, the coop. A novelty. To please her. Though it feels so small and dark, so lonely the moment she is gone. No New Orleans whorehouse tonight, a corncrib, a little holding cell, the room where they stash you till you hear the verdict.

The offense of going too far. In fact, did we all go too far? The colony itself, utopia? So that there is a general drawing back now, a nervous return to convention, a reflexive withdrawal from freedom when suppression has been so long the rule. I have often observed this. It may not last forever but it can disrupt, undermine, destroy. Waiting it out in the coop. Anxiety in the dark. The hours going by, seeming forever, waiting for Sophie to return. Her displeasure, the curt dismissive phrases. I am in her view no longer valid. Invalid. Incompetent. Canceled by what I have become to her, a crazy. It is there in her scolding "Take this," "Take that"; little pills, pink, yellow. "What is it?" "Lithium, of course. That's the pink one." "What's the yellow one?" "Sandy thinks it would be good for you, calm you down." "Fine, what is it?" "Why not just take it?" "Why not just tell me what the hell it is?" "It's Valium." "So we give away Valium here now? Sandy isn't even a nurse—she helped out at some feminist health clinic. Did you read that piece in the *Voice* about Valium? It's awful stuff. When you're addicted—" "One little Valium isn't going to hurt you and it might help you sleep." "And if I don't want it?" "That's your own affair. We are only trying to help."

And still I wait in the coop, in the dark and the uncertainty, staying because she will come back and I am in love with her, trust her beyond anyone else, even now when I begin not to trust her yet still must. I wait while at the farmhouse they are deciding my case, arranging my life perhaps. And then the cold chill—they could be calling the cops, the ambulance, the state, and force could be brought into this absurd domestic misunderstanding, this impressionistic bumbling around the issue of my sanity or supposed insanity, which could at any moment become the very real issue of my freedom. In actuality, in locks and bars and keys—and it could be months or years before the mess was sorted out, and I could emerge a broken and condemned being if I emerged at all. Patients with my opinions on psychiatry are treated as hard cases. People with my attitude toward electroshock could easily get it as punishment; disbelief makes those in charge hostile; the battery of doctors and nurses, the very nice person who'd like to hear your history—all those authoritarian elements, whose tone and fabric contract when defied, grow rigid, and the jail reveals itself. Then it's no visitors, no telephone, no exit. And force, the tying up, the stretcher they bound me to going from Highlands into Herrick in California, pinioned facedown.

But that was years ago. You must trust these people, your friends, Sophie, after all. Having glimpsed it herself; she will understand. Unless it has made her afraid way inside. Like anyone who has been a prisoner, you must, after you are free, decide whether you will risk another brush with that or whether you will capitulate. In quietly going back to your life you can usually avoid the danger, and they are through with you; usually you are not likely to strike their eye again. But if you do, then it is time all over again to decide where your allegiance will fall.

Sophie is least likely to call the cops on me, but there are other solid citizens at that farmhouse who'd probably love to do it, for the thrill, for the self-importance, for the tragic dramatic possibilities. That is my house and my phone you are betraying me with, I think, furious even at the thought. But it's always like that; last time I even had to pay the long distance and a number of the airline tickets for those who conspired against my freedom. Tonight, as always, everyone is merely trying to "help," because they were so "worried" about me.

How I loathe that word. How worried it makes me, now hearing Sophie take it up; the harshness of its use in these situations; how it comes to be blame without coherent accusation, a reproach without point or reason. It is the refrain of her visits back and forth to me here at the coop. She arrives to announce this worry, the word aimed at me like a weapon, settling in like a fait accompli, a sentence without either evidence or trial, the same worry hurrying her away again to the others, leaving me on tenterhooks, waiting; one who waits, who is parked and waits. While the others decide her fate. One is not even permitted to hear the discussion.

I maintain that they are in over their heads, that the issue is my own freedom: to take lithium or not to as I choose. It's a voluntary program I was in. Even my shrink doesn't capture people and put them away; he has given me his word on this a number of times. I am free to go off lithium, then, if I so choose, though the results of doing so are in his opinion dire. And the experience of my friend Martha Ravich dire too: she ended up holding a sit-down strike at Rutherford's, one of those huge photography stores full of security guards, because they wouldn't take her check. One understands her chagrin, an old customer and a professional photographer—but they had her busted. Into Rikers Island. No mere loony bin but the jug itself. Took her a week to swing a transfer into Payne Whitney. And months of recuperation. She was manic as a monkey, they say. I'd like to know what she says. But I know she's back on lithium. Humiliation, capitulation, cure? That was her attempt to throw the drug; the shaky hands (lithium's side effect), which she hated just as I do, needing steady hands for the camera as I do for the brush. The fear in the trembling hands that hold a 16mm movie camera. I always thought her hands were unsteady because they had scared her, broken her confidence. Thereafter you are afraid, unsound; they have said so, proved it with incarceration with the parole of medication, the continual and eternal doses of lithium—without which you will always be crazy, will lapse into it again in weeks. Look at me—it is six weeks, and I do not feel crazy even though now they say I am. Because I stopped lithium? Or because I told them I did? If I had never told, would they know? Is it even possible that the fear in Martha's hands was not only lithium's tremor but also a fear put there? When she stopped being scared, she got angry; at Rutherford's she told a rude clerk she wouldn't leave until her check was honored. A peaceful little protest—we spent the sixties sitting down about this or that—and the son of a bitch called the police.

Martha, let me try the experiment, see if I can pull it off. Of course I could show up at the farmhouse, but the moment I enter the room the council ends, as when a child intrudes upon adults. Because that's it, I am no longer an adult—one of the more irritating aspects of this situation. And now a solicitude I cannot but regard as hypocritical takes over. Sheila inquires about my health in a most cloying manner. Kim and Libby will do the same a few moments later but with the smirking condescension of young persons addressing the professor in dotage: part titter, part a fraudulent high seriousness whose vacuity they cannot hear in their righteousness. I think I have had enough of all that for the evening, but the part I cannot see—the mystery, the calls to psychiatry, the invocation of authority, the final quick mean signal to the troopers or Hudson River Psychiatric—that is what I want to know about. Not that knowing can help me. There is nowhere to run; even a car gets you nowhere against this system. My only hope is "good behavior." So I take the lithium, even the Valium, who knows what. Swallowing as I am watched: two tablets—600 mg of lithium never hurt anyone. Even one Valium won't do much against a healthy body and a sound mind. Nor can it make me sleepy. I am in too much danger and far too afraid to sleep. Without the conspiracy I might have been asleep hours ago.

Odd how they manage to keep me awake. Each time I reach calm and have collected my thoughts, Sophie intrudes again. The bitchy denunciation in her tone—how it infuriates me to be addressed this way after two years of living together, loving each other, our voices invariably kind. No one in the world deserves this scorn, no one. Over and over I swallow my rage at that sound and try to answer sweetly, to replace what has come to be—her transformation—with our old way. How dare you, I want to shout, how dare you use that tone to me—to anyone? Who the hell do you imagine you are? Sometimes I even do say it as the last resort. But it makes no impression. When it comes to that, she moves to attack: Who do you think *you* are, ruining this entire summer, ruining the time these women have had here, wrecking everything with your crazy behavior, your irresponsible theories, lording it around here? I fall for it completely: When have I lorded it, over whom? I am sure that I am in the clear. "You were rude to Sandy at dinner." "I would appreciate it if she'd stop leaving her junk all over the living room." "You could have asked her nicely." "I thought I did." "You did not, you hurt her feelings—she's a very sensitive person." I burn to observe that we are all sensitive persons but I desist and go on for an hour grieving over Sandy. Will she leave now?

Sophie has begun to threaten me again with apprentices leaving, a mass defection or one by one. They are all "sick to death" of me, she says; the colony will be lost. All because of my own foolishness, my headstrong behavior. I have caused this disaster, the general failure of confidence. Because I am mad.

Mystical state, madness, how it frightens people. How utterly crazy *they* become, remote, rude, peculiar, cruel, taunting, farouche as wild beasts who have smelled danger, the unthinkable. One must maintain one's reason now in this, yet how difficult not to give way to rage. And after hours of patience I blow up, full Irish steam, a stream of words, abuse matching theirs. Mine counts against me, theirs does not. I know this. Better be cool, then; you have a lot to lose, may even have lost it—for all you know, they're on the phone right now getting the dogs on you. If that happens you haven't a chance. But if you are cool, calm, the soul of reason—you have to be—you could make it through. Till the accusation passes. How crazy craziness makes everyone, how irrationally afraid. The madness hidden in each of us, called to, identified, aroused like a lust. And against that the jaw sets. The more I fear my own insanity the more I must punish yours: the madman at the crossroad, the senile old woman, the wild-eyed girl, the agitated man talking to himself on the subway. But they are at a distance; we are close. If I am mad the farm itself is suspect, the colony, even the barns and studios become somehow insubstantial, the Christmas trees in their rows are suspicious, a con game or pointless. The whole utopian scheme is folderol, an illusion; they have been deceived. That is how they must see it.

And as for my work, the books that brought them here, the drawings, the silk screens, the mind behind the place and the plan—all ashes now, vanished. Figure their disappointment. Sophie's too; figure that into her nasty manner, her arrogance, her insufferable contempt and impatience with even my slightest expression of opinion or preference. Be patient, then, and don't get operatic about your ego or bellow your importance. Ah, but I don't. Right up to the fiftieth put-down I can still swallow my anger. I admire how grandly Sophie has become the lady of the manor even as I am furious at being bossed around and relegated to a bundle. That I can do without, but the sight of her queening it is still lovely.

When we were first lovers—that first time we slept together at the farm, July two years ago, when the Fourth of July guests had gone back down to town and we were alone—I watched them leaving, knowing we would be alone here then, knowing it might happen but still not sure of anything except that this new person had been there, all through Sita's death and then even on into the toil of scraping whitewash to convert the barns into studios, which was how the colony began—all through this she had been the kindest and most generous and sympathetic of friends. A new friend. And a perfect one. Why risk more than that? She may be appalled by any other notion; do you love her enough, would she love you at all—what will happen now that it is only the two of us here?

That night we became lovers, but the next day at evening she came and knelt by me and said that I could cancel it all if I pleased, if it was awkward for me, if I had thought it all over and regarded what had happened as a mistake. Part of me admired this as sublime; how generous to offer one an outlet it had never occurred to me to take. But for a second, part of me also thought it too much meekness. That side of her has vanished now forever. Very well, I had always thought Sophie coddled me too much, spoiled me. "How she adores you," a friend congratulated me back in town. "That is the charming part." The words gave me a start. No one should be adored, it's fundamentally immoral. And the other part of it is that no one is adored for very long. I wanted to be loved, and for a very long time. Living together was as happy as music, made solid in Iran by her courage and loyalty when we were arrested as feminists and held under machine guns; shoulder to shoulder when life was at stake, my trust became absolute.

The promise of it creeping over me these two years until this summer I felt the full force of marriage, even wanted to celebrate it with a will, the sort of thing she snorts at now. After all I'm a very shaky number now, unstable, unbalanced; being endowed with this farm is the last thing she'd think of, she'd be lucky if she can keep me from ruining the place in the next few weeks. And she's by no means sure she wants to stay that long. Several times a day references to the future become provisional. She'd like to run. To continue with me is to take on an invalid, a monster no longer my former self whom she loved. I can see the dead lover in her eyes. But not quite dead, only mangled and disfigured beyond hope. And then there is hope: medicine, shrinks, friends, the collective support to see her through the disaster, the comfort of all those goddamned long-distance phone calls in which my disease is spread and my reputation canceled from New York to California, eager conversants ready to report the news: Kate Millett's flipped again. Solicitude, the wagging of heads. What a pity. It happened once before; they kept it pretty quiet. Then she was okay for years. "She's up at her farm now and Sophie doesn't know what to do." "Has she got a doctor?" "Dakota's friend Marcy has a brother who is finishing an internship in psychiatry." "Really, you better give him a call, try anything, good grief." All the outside helping and the apprentices too, whom Sophie must frequently see as schoolgirls far less able than herself, capable of hysterics and intrigue with which she hardly needs to complicate things further; but then at times they must overpower her with their physical presence, their youth and energy, their blooming health, their humor and good looks, even their sensuality. Libby's succulent bosom to lean on, to weep on, for there is weeping late at night. Away from me, the culprit.

But the tragedy of my madness is not played out with me—in my company, there is simply annoyance at the headstrong sinner. The real tragedy, where the love and the home Sophie had have now perished, the woman she loved transformed into a lunatic, all that is played out with visitors and apprentices, with the voices at the other end of long distance who commiserate and reiterate how awful it is, what should be done. Finally, comforters admit they don't know what to advise; she must keep in touch. I have overheard bits of this, conversations ending when I appear: "There are moments, even days, when she's okay and then all of a sudden she flips again and all she does is talk and talk like a maniac." A pause. "Well, it's mania, what else can I tell you?" There is almost laughter at this, a little relaxation in the voice and then the tenseness as Sophie understands all over again that she has to cope with it all, she alone. And the responsibility, either of leaving me at liberty or locking me up—the responsibility is overwhelming. She knows how I would hate it; she must remember some of how she hated it. There is also the issue of how she would be judged if she did it. Most assure her she is in the right, even that she has no alternative. But she holds off; if it gets worse, if it doesn't get better, if it goes on longer, if it won't go away.

9

Here in the coop kenneled this long night of the soul, a black chamber, a tunnel into a lens. The result not an image but an apparition. I become not what I am but what I am said to be, as the self flails on, skewered by a pushpin, squirming for credibility even in its own eyes by the end. Is this the turning point, the breaking place, the ordeal, the descent into the underworld?

How easy it would have been to try this experiment of going off lithium if I alone were involved. If I had kept the secret. But now it is a circus of other people, a controversy, a conflagration. Some of this is my fault; I have not been discreet. In my first joy at being on my own, recovering the pure free use of my senses, I crowed over it, kicked my heels. I was healthy and sound, had been all along, my mind was whole without disease—they had deceived me into believing that I was a cripple held together with four pink tablets a day, that 1200 mg of lithium separated me from hopeless insanity, that only the drug kept me among the living, the free beings outside the mental jails. But instead, look at me; I have never felt so well, lithe, strong, young. I am swimming like a swimmer again; not a competitor, not even distance—not in that little pond—but a strong swimmer. I have lost weight, have my breathing back again. Even my vision is better, I am less myopic; it may even correct itself and I could see out of my own eyes perfectly again. For that is how the mind and body feel, rejuvenated, healed.

And now the joy has disappeared altogether in arguments and quarrels between Sophie and me. At the end of it I feel my back against the wall and the circle forming around me, the accusations of madness. That I am not quite right, that something has come over me in the last two weeks, some terrible change. "People would hardly know you," the solemn approach. "You're a little freaked out," the hip diagnosis. And the ones behind my back whispering that this is an attack she's having, she's flipped.

How little weight my own perceptions seem to have. I am the discussed; what do I know, experience, discover? For it was all discovery—so much so that I would postpone drawing only to relish the activity of my own mind, experience my senses undiluted by chemicals after six years of drugs. Lithium slows thought, clouds the synapses, holds it back, quiets it, represses the brain activity in order to prevent manic overexcitement and hyperstimulation—the great bugaboos. Depression is the victim's dread, not mania. For we could enjoy mania if we were permitted to by the others around us so distressed by it, if the thing were so arranged that manics were safe to be manic awhile without reproach or contradiction, the thwarting and harassment on every side that finally exasperates them so they lose their tempers and are cross, offensive, defensive, antagonistic—all they are accused of being. A manic permitted to think ten thousand miles a minute is happy and harmless and could, if encouraged and given time, perhaps be productive as well. Ah, but depression—that is what we all hate. We the afflicted. Whereas the relatives and shrinks, the tribal ring, they rather welcome it: you are quiet and you suffer. Two perfect circumstances. You should shut up because you talked too much before, you should close down all your capacities because you were boastful and extravagant about them before. And you should endure the torments of the damned because you have embarrassed them: remember the time you told your best friend to shut the hell up? For that, for those transgressions (ones they commit themselves all the time but never under the onus of madness), you should wither and die inside.

How like vengeance it all is, how like all terrible ideologies. And perhaps it's all fraud, if not in every case—I had seen the crazy and found them crazed as well—then at least in mine. I was never insane. I am not a manic depressive at all. That is the diagnosis of a shrink my elder sister delivered me over to one day when, acting in righteous spite, she made one of the sadder misjudgments of her life. Misinformed, promised a woman doctor, she deceived me into a hospital where she herself was surprised to find a man she had never met even on the telephone; her shrink was busy or gone or something and this man would do the job. After that she had no more control over the situation than I did.

Once out, I repudiated the whole thing, flushed the Thorazine down the toilet and attended my first Madness Network meeting in a San Francisco art gallery where NAPA (Network Against Psychiatric Assault) was formed. Months went by before the depression set in: Fumio left me; the city decided to tear down my loft, to destroy my studio, the home of my art for fifteen years, the place where I had grown up as an artist. At one blow and in one week I lost husband and home, marriage and studio, never really knowing which loss was worse but suspecting that studio cut harder into the self and its security; the roof over my head was also my identity as an artist. Ah, but Fumio, he was my life too, my anchor in the chaotic years of politics and fame, my anchor in everything; my sanity I used to call him, that love superseding all other loves, the women I loved as well—a suffering he had finally freed himself from ever knowing again. Now I was to begin it in earnest, for I could never disconnect the heart, pull it out like a plug as he was able to do at the last. So as he ceased to mourn me I began to mourn him. Seven years ago and again tonight.

My Bobby McGee, the hideous mornings waking in the sunny bedroom at the farm to realize it all over again, floating into consciousness only to remember that he was gone, that it was over, that I had blown it, the one great love, the one marriage, ten years together. I shiver and hear my mother's voice, St. Paul respectability; divorce, the word "divorce." But it is so much worse than that—in this room we made love, in this bed, with the same sunlight from the windows across the floor and the red coverlet. Jesus, I can remember the day we bought it, giggling at Bloomingdale's because we had a house to furnish up in the country. And the polar bear rug would be for making love on—his chuckle, "put in front of the fireplace—like baby picture"—and we bent over in the aisles of sheets and towels in our secret laughter, our magnificent and special happiness, as if no one had ever stood in that aisle by the escalator and known such ecstasy. The sun on the blue barn across the circle drive from that window, the barn always bright and filling the window; we liked that, that was the studio. It was perfect that one should see the studio the first thing on waking—perfect. It stands there blue now; it was gray then, when we bought it. It must be painted in his honor because it is his studio. I have even painted the damn thing, or rather Mr. Odell has at my expense, that monstrous big barn, no less than thirty gallons of bright blue paint and gleaming white trim, an object of respect to the entire neighborhood, the color and the courage of saving the old structure outweighing my faults as a city girl or a lady writer, even a woman of scandal—I have painted the whole damn thing for you and you will never come back to use it.

Finally I tried using it. Not for sculpture but painting there, coming upon bits of Fumio's woodwork, discarded carvings for the wooden typewriter he sculpted the summer before, bamboo for a painted kite, almost like fossils, each wonderful object the reproachful miracle of him, Fumio the better artist. After I'd done hundreds of drawings he even came up to see them once and nod his head in equivocal encouragement. Mornings I lay in bed missing him, all ten years of him, the way he would bound down the stairs at the Bowery as I got out of a cab with the infernal suitcase after the University of Nebraska or Colorado or Salt Lake or France. Both his arms waving, yelling his delight—this memory murders me. To lose so much. Remembering him at that temple in Nara, photographed by the pagoda, the boy with the tweed jacket and the weird haircut, the grin and the shining eyes. The boy the man the artist the husband, if you can call your best buddy husband, the one who cooks with you, figures out how to get together five dollars for two movie tickets; the naked imp who used to take long steaming baths in the downstairs tub which no one else has ever used, stoking the fireplace to fervent heat and then running about naked and naughty as an eight-year-old—God, I cannot endure to think anymore.

Then get up, it's already eleven-thirty—you have cried for three hours, nearly four, not even sitting up in bed, not even smoking and drinking coffee, only a coma of tears that would like to scream out in an empty farmhouse, dust gathering in the corners. There is no food here; you are too screwed up even to build a fire in the evening. By two I may get as far as the barn. There is no longer any point in writing; both the Sita thing and the thing about my father refuse to yield another word: eight pages and then a wall. For the first time in my life I can no longer write—so draw. It too wearies me, bores me, I'm no good. But do it. Doing it all day and till after dark through the cold of November in the unheated barn until my hands cannot hold the brush and the ink won't run properly; the only tears now are for the cold, or the despair of still working when there is no point to it but it is all there is to stave off further despair. A despair still waiting in the farmhouse in the form of dinner: wine, memories, Fumio's ghost. And again in the morning.

So when this became suicide I found a doctor and gave myself up for a certified manic depressive rather than just a suicide. I soft-pedaled my suicide attempts, applied them only for persuasion, was vague to avoid actual capture, mumbled rumors of gas, rumors of Seconal. After all, I had a record and I was down at the bottom, they could see that. For the doctors the remedy was lithium; it would prevent my becoming manic again, since it was for that I was busted. For me, on the other hand, I hoped lithium might alleviate the exquisite tortures of this depression, and I was rather disappointed to find that Elavil was prescribed for it instead. I made a face; I hate drugs; chemical stuff really does play with your mind, you're a zombie, even seeing and hearing are affected, it is like an unpleasant and unplanned-for drunk. But the pain began to lift, slowly slowly—because I now had care and hope, had thrown myself on this institutional mercy and found more solace there than I did in friends or lovers or work or my own life. Someone was saving my life from suicide where it had so nearly ended. And the lithium would gradually prevent me from going down into depression, they said, just as it prevented me from flying away into mania as I had that time in California, that shameful occasion of my arrest whose records they now had and which was always held over me as proof of mania.

I had my side of it, of course. I was not manic, but I was depressed. The loss of Fumio and the studio on the Bowery constituted a blow that had made me want my life to end, feeling that it was in all important respects already over. The life I wanted—Fumio, the dear old Bowery—had disappeared and I could conceive of no life after that, let alone one that could bear comparison. If not this, then nothing. Janis and Plath and Sexton beckoned; it seemed the time to bow out as a writer too; the residual effects of suicide on artistic reputation might cover over the fact that I had nothing else to write—*Flying* had done it all, said it all. Too much so in fact; it would be appropriate (here one doesn't think aloud) if the author of such a book atoned by snuffing herself out. Only this could forgive. Fumio's defection was in itself a judgment—what everyone had said all along about what that poor guy had to put up with, her infidelities. So you could say she wrecked that marriage, which was the loveliest companionship our circle had known. For we were a prize couple, the Irish woman and the samurai, the scholar and the sculptor, the two sculptors, peers, one vying with the other but never the running down and competition one saw everywhere: all the beaten wives who "used to paint." And when you are such a pair, there is the extra humiliation of being winners who lose in the end, losing the twinship, the two-in-one unit in which you shone resplendent. He will go his own way now.

Let him go, then. He's off for Sweden with one of my own students, my favorite student. Let him be happy—we had always wished each other that, even if it included other lovers. We were a little far out that way. I never loved anyone to the exclusion of Fumio; loving others only made me love him more. But he is past that sort of thing now, wants something conventional, monogamous. He was always a monogamist; it was I who tried to change him, something against his nature. How would I have felt with the shoe on the other foot, waiting alone at the studio while he dallied with men? The feminist would sure have resented this. So you imposed all your feminist women-loving women as a form of solidarity, etc., on him. He called it phony; probably it was. "The day I discovered my wife was a lesbian": the famous first line of Fumio's diaries begun two years ago, diaries in Japanese and appropriately closed to me. Perhaps that's how it seems to him; that I was a lesbian who married him and then revealed herself. Of course, he knew about the women I loved before I loved him, but he must have seen that as something of the past. Until it resurrected itself in casual horror in the present; that must now dominate his view of my future.

This is not how I wanted my life to end, not with the publication of *Flying* and the loss of Fumio; we stayed together all through the four years I wrote it, all through the publicity rocket of *Sexual Politics*. Now I am left alone as a lesbian, without the buffer of his protection against the world and what the reviewers and public opinion will do to me. A woman alone. A lesbian, only that. Are you scared of that? Is that why you are distant to Sita when she calls from California, saving you from late-night experiments with the gas pipe—at least the first one? Uncanny she could call that exact moment and catch you in the act, wrench you back to life. Or is it only that you want to be left alone to die? You are dying to her, too; but you only notice you are dying to Fumio, who probably doesn't give a damn or at least has steeled himself completely.

Janis whizzing through my mind, "freedom's just another word for nothing left to lose,'' and nothing's what my baby left me, for months now and this cold December night most of all. It would have to be Christmas or just before Christmas that the City Marshal would appoint for the end. I have played it out, the success and now the failure, the first book and the second. There is nothing left. There is no longer anything to write now, nothing suggests itself. *Flying* was the whole discovery of writing and it is over now, rejected and then accepted elsewhere and now revised and handed in; there are just the page proofs to do, and maybe they can manage that by themselves.

Let it be now—it's over and there is nothing more to come. From writing to live I have come to live to write, but the well is now dry as a vacuum. A terrible silence those days at the farm trying to start another and then still another book, and neither came; this would be a good time to go. Horrible to live on, straining for something that came once or twice and is never to come again. You had to wait till thirty-five to write at all, all those required courses and mandatory semesters of Eng. Lit.; your whole life a required course just to produce a thesis. Next came *Flying,* a first book really, one book of your own. Before the bubble burst and you lost your guts, sat at the dining room table at the farm and in two speedy afternoons discovered you were not a writer at all. You were scared when you started *Flying,* but now the scare is past all measure, a panic huge and unconquerable. Now is the obvious time. And you know it. Hating the knowledge, sure as taxes or gravity. But death, the foreignness of it, the possible stink, the mutilation—what if they don't find you, or not before deterioration? The aftereffects, the pain of the body after death—don't be stupid, you'll be dead; but disfigured by rats, birds—superstition. Found in the barn by Mr. Odell— how many weeks after? Then make better arrangements, do it at the Bowery where they will find you when they come to move you, when the truck comes tomorrow.

And the farm, property, a will, making plans, arrangements; there are responsibilities. I no longer give a damn how it turns out. Once I am in death, have turned my face that way and against life, I could give a hoot what happens even to the farm. My suicide note, a scandal of the banal and the speechless; here, where one really ought to make a gesture toward style, I say something prosaic about not being able to go on. I wince, looking at the phrase, the note is only a sentence. Wishing them all well, love, and feeling nothing whatsoever. A little unexpressed contrition for the shock they will have—suicide is painful to the survivors—but that is nothing to the desperation I feel, the nausea, the vertigo of leaving life for death, driven there, the "solution" every day more apparent, beckoning harder, commanding me. And I let go of everything—why sort your correspondence and pack your belongings when you are not only being evicted and abandoned, you are actually going to die, are really mortally ill?

A grotesque who never speaks. My friends see me mute and miserable and have a tact that does not comment. So absent that when they arrive to dismantle the bookshelves I must be reminded even to give them a drink. The hour of alcohol comes every day like recess. I can hardly wait for it; the first sip will bring a little respite; in thirty minutes' time near forgetfulness. Food and drink. When they begin, the day is over. Because the days are the problem now—there is nothing to do with the days. I no longer do anything at all, by which I mean I have no work. Not that there isn't plenty to move and pack, piles of mail to answer. But I no longer do anything at all. The anguish of knowing I should lingers on, but all impetus is gone now. I am dying, why bother? And, of course, this is still further incentive to die—if you don't die, you're really in trouble. Having let everything slide, you can never dig yourself out now; something like the income tax is going to come along and put you in jail. Sloth and disorganization like yours are dangerous, even criminal. Moreover, someone's suing you about that stupid little movie you made years ago, so there's another reason to check out—in dying you will miss the lawsuit. Because you are terrified of it, terrified they'll win and clean you out and even take your farm. So die and it's Fumio's farm. Who doesn't want it at all. What should he do with it? Sell it and keep the money? Sell it and give the money to your mother and sisters? He needs some too; you ought to make some formula about this. But I don't.

It turns out I don't care. Even the farm—which I love most, hate most, fear most, and treasure most—is too much for me. Alone I could never keep it. I am a sculptor, and what the place needs is a carpenter, plumber, electrician, gardener, architect. I am a woman alone; small, incompetent after all, too poor and too naive to hire people. I don't even want to bother. Any more than I want to bother finding another studio. Although every day my friends call with another lead, Fumio hears of places, will even go and look at them with me, strict in his insistence that this is for me alone, not us. It is only for us I would want a place, so I am bored and unwilling to look at these lofts. And they are terrible. Ruth calls and suggests the old Houston Hotel farther down the Bowery.

"Since they've condemned your building you could make the city relocate you there—they don't want it and it's good space." "It's a bums' hotel." "So what? Your old place was too, probably, at one time." "Okay, show it to me." And she shows it to me with a flashlight in its absolute cold. Boarded up, the electricity and water off, a real derelict. Like my own place is becoming day by day. "You could fix it up, you see that, don't you, that it could be fixed up? Look at the windows, the space, there's terrazzo on the floor. The second floor could be restored too." But on the second floor the rows of urine-soaked mattresses, the cages, the lines of naked light bulbs. "It's despair," I say. All other possibilities have been eliminated.

Wanting death versus getting there. The success of suicide—harder than anything I have ever had to do. I have always had enough courage; no matter how scared I was, I could shut my eyes and bumble through it: coming out, speeches, exams, hassles with the cops in demonstrations, mean guys on the Bowery streets—always there was just enough guts despite the terror. But here I fail over and over again. Last night, Sita stopped me by calling from California and caught me the very moment I had opened the pipe. Afterward I closed it, shamefaced. And tonight I begged Fumio to sleep here, to come up with me if only to rest, since his back hurt him cruelly; I could help him—not even yet understanding myself that if he were here I would be saved from what I must do. And tonight, because it is the last night here—tomorrow morning is the truck and then we are forbidden to return. If I did it after that I would not be found, and I want to be found; it frightens me to think of the bulldozer, the wrecking ball, the fall of bricks even on my corpse. Claustrophobia even past death, the abuse of this body, its disfigurement, my arms and legs broken, my spinal cord.

How death is an obsession of the mind with the body, wishing the body out of existence. And yet it was only last summer, six months ago, that I enjoyed life as if I had just discovered it. Free, free at last. From the booby hatch. The third nail in my coffin, because when you come right down to it, whether you were even crazy or not, guilty or innocent, manic or sane as a bedbug—you've been jailed for madness and that doesn't go away. It hangs around in everybody's eyes; it's in the talk you don't hear and in the tones you do. And the shame doesn't go away. You think you'll live it down, and that's okay out in the country. But when you're in town you are jerked back to your official self, now so wonderfully humbled that you are homeless in this freezing, filthy, dislocated studio, its beauty and comfort all gone, iron cables tearing through its windows supposedly holding it together for ten more minutes while you are evacuated. Yet here you are endlessly addressed by phone and mail as the woman who wrote that landmark book, and you alone know that since doing that she has been declared to be without her marbles.

And maybe they *are* gone. I can no longer think or remember in the manner of an intellectual, facts at fingertips. My entire memory is a land mine of other detail: Like this Mexican cummerbund that I bought for Fumio, and he looked a young god or a courtier with it around his slender waist. He has forgotten to take it with him. Like these gas stoves my pal Jacky Witten installed in return for the money to get to his brother's funeral. They are totally ineffective in this weather; there are about three weeks every year when the place is completely uninhabitable, we used to laugh. This house, 1806, Dutch architrave, one of the five oldest residences in the city; Landmarks couldn't save it nor could we. I loved every board and beam in this structure, want to die with it. I lived my youth here, alone and with others: we named the place Bohème. Sitting up here nights is sitting with a corpse or an animal shot in the leg that refuses to die. Callous and unnecessary death—it was still sound. Even the black paint on the old broad floorboards. The way Fumio and I used to paint the floors before we went on vacation each year. Arriving at the bottom of the stairs filthy, but the turpentine was already down, and our suitcases—off to Cape Cod—it had two weeks to dry. The sight of this funny little orange bureau in the dressing room, painted orange because we thought it was terribly smart. Like the blue wall in the kitchen. Reporters used to gape at this place, unable to believe people lived like this, a good deal past quaint or bohemian. Long before I wrote *Sexual Politics* our loft used to make the papers as an archetype of loft living, although the more primitive aspects like the toilet and the homemade shower were signs of ingenuity rather than the new trend in home decoration. But all the books climbing to the ceiling and Fumio's painted kites floating in space were romantic enough. All gone now. The place is stripped to its ancient barrenness, the terrible cold challenge I had rented fifteen years ago as a gutsy kid, growing as I grew. And now we are cut off together.

You had everything going for you; you had come to town with nothing, worked hard, exhibited, studied, written, been boosted even to fame, and it is all gone now—you blew it all away. That is what the madness was. Janis's phrase—blew it all away—didn't even know you were doing it. And you can grind your teeth with remorse and fury at your own folly, but that is what it is: you had the loveliest and best marriage, Fumio himself, and you blew it. Women, you had to love women too. And they're gone now. Where's Celia now? Sita so far away and with someone else maybe but good enough to keep track of you. You've lost everything, blown everything, you haven't got enough energy to tell the phone company to disconnect you. Acedia, the sin of stasis. That's now. But when you were blowing it, it was the big talk, the big love affair, the big living, the big boasting, you and your high *Flying,* as if every breath were some fucking miracle. The egotism of that book. Thank God you won't live to see it. 'Cause they are going to squash you like a bug; the reviews for that will be first-rate invective.

You have lost everything—now if you could just unburden yourself of your life. Aquavit. Let's see what it can do. Fumio says it's the best, the most powerful stuff in the whole family of booze. Now that he's going to Sweden he affects this stuff, which tastes like shit. But it's the power I want, not the taste. And then the amazing sound of the gas. A two-inch pipe, a major source, but the sound was still alarming, amazing, falling asleep hearing it, no longer listening, sure I would not change my mind and turn it off; just as sure I wasn't going to light a cigarette and demolish the neighborhood. I read a little of someone's life of Albert Schweitzer, ironically aware of how inadequate this particular piece of writing was to the occasion but quietly grateful that there was anything around to divert me into sleep, unconsciousness. Coming conscious again a few hours later—you could turn that roaring gas off or you could leave it on—this is your last chance to change your mind. I didn't change it.

As proud of that as I was ashamed to wake up in the morning. The loft was too big, too drafty. The stench was terrible, but a headache was the only effect of the gas in this space. I could have slept right by the pipe, I should have blocked all the drafts in the windows—idiot. Opening them now, airing the whole house now, both floors—the odor must be gone before they come with the truck. I have failed. For this time anyway. There would be others.

And there were. Enough and insistent enough, more and more of a crisis to die. So that at the last I could turn away; having failed, unable to die or live in death any longer, and give living a try. Find those doctors, that wonder drug, whatever the hell it was; leak my secret to my friend Janey Washburn, let her suspect and then go along with her suggestion the next morning. Plan B she called it, medicine. Try lithium, try anything. I could not die. And I could no longer endure despair.

10

Out in the coop, the dark, waiting for her, then lying together, quarreling, exasperation, and then unforeseen, unimagined—I got up and left. Something I had never done before, leaving a quarrel. But that was not all—remember—you left her bed. The first time. "If you leave here it will never be the same again," she said. And I knew it. I shivered. But I could not stay; I needed sleep too badly, rest, peace.

And here it is. The big barn, the painting studio. Alone in the middle of the night. The barn is high above me, the hand-hewn oak beams, white plasterboard around and between them, that conjunction of white painted plaster and old, dark, worn woods like a Japanese rice warehouse. We made this when we saved the barn from collapse and had a whole new roof built, Fumio and I, when we first got the farm. Lovely it is now as it is always lovely, soaring twenty feet high—what a place to paint. In the morning I will paint, I think, lying here waiting for sleep. I look up and there is even that beam over the painting table—that was the one. Suicide days. Over now: I have never wanted more to live than just now. The eye like a camera scans the beams overhead, the leap and play of them, these vast weights suspended so surely in air.

If I can sleep I can draw tomorrow. If I can sleep I will not go crazy, lose my grip, for it is slipping now; I can feel the sleeplessness undo me. The mind cannot bear that much wakefulness, and it is two nights now that I haven't slept. Arguments, dissension, quarreling. Why does she go on goading me if she knows I must sleep? As if she is unaware of what she's doing, ordering me to sleep and then harassing me so that I cannot. I fall into the same pattern, responding to her reproach, sarcasm, petty details such as where the weekend guests should sleep, new nagging problems with the mower. Lovers having our troubles. But they consume too much, not only ourselves but the farm, the others living here.

Troubles politicized as my craziness and Sophie's patient sorrow. I can no longer distinguish between the two, and I am the only one interested in trying except perhaps Linnea. Probably because she is older and has several children, Linnea is less likely to fall into the attitude of lesbian drama and marital convention in which the others are frozen. Have I so absented myself or been so long incompetent merely in order that Sophie would have to take charge? Or is it the other way; having refused the half of it, she is declaring me null and void to have all of it, with the added advantage of having it alone, since I dwindle so now in prestige I may soon be shut away out of sight?

There is talk of sending all the apprentices away so that we may spend the rest of the summer peacefully, out of the glare of gossip. This is to abandon farming, the fields we're clearing, the little trees already in the ground, to abandon all the silk screens we're printing and the work on the lavender barn, its conversion into a house for the apprentices, our biggest job this summer. Without the apprentices we could accomplish nothing, finish nothing; the summer would be wasted. "It is already, and you need quiet," she says.

I have found quiet here. Alone in this high room for once. My solitude is so new it has the excitement of sacrilege; for two years we have never spent a night apart. Yet I have come here just to be alone, to be away from her.

I had asked her to caress me, to make love to me a few moments so I could sleep, so the terror would go away, so the fury would stay put, so that my spine could unclench itself—because I needed so desperately to sleep. I begged her, and she would not, was not in the mood and couldn't put herself there. "Only so that I can sleep, please touch me." "No." I lie there and am afraid for my sanity if I cannot find sleep soon; there is a sound in my mind already like some electric charge. Suddenly it seemed as if my mind would split open if I could not feel the touch of another on my skin, be healed by that, find sleep possible at last in that consolation, the act of a friend. That she would refuse this out of pique or cussedness—that I had put myself in the control of someone who could refuse me—after persuading me of my infirmity to the point where I now feared some dreadful injury could come over my brain if it didn't have the rest she prescribed and enjoined and I now believed, too, was absolute necessity; another twenty-four hours without sleep and I would have, through abusing its tired cells, done some damage to the psyche which is permanent—I had made it possible to be thrown away.

But instead you get up and leave. That is what I am learning finally: to go to sleep somewhere else, not to need. Even the thought of it dangerous, risky as going without the drug. Stubborn maybe, stupid probably. Yet to belong to myself at last. And can you hold on long enough, last through the strange exhaustion in your mind, find your own peace, be well, drifting off to sleep, the mind unbending its daytime logic, permitting fantasy? Two big red balls jumping through conscious-ness up through the open window, summertime, childhood, my aunt appears, my elder sister, all the favorite characters of childhood, the pillow is so soft, the tree and the pond outside so pure, so barely visible in the dark, and the dim white of the ceiling overhead, the peace of it, my hand hugs my arm in delight, finally going to sleep, finally it is happening. I can even perceive it happening, watch the secret event; the mystery takes place, another second and I descend . . . Like a hornet sting, it is so sudden, torn out of sleep, jerked awake. I had been there, just at the edge of sleep, when it bit me, this terrible warning, as if my physical self were in mortal danger. A robber, a thief, a weapon—that level of danger. A danger like death so urgent one had to wake up to resist it. But it was nothing. The warning was false—the room is quiet and peaceful as before—the warning then was a lie, a deception, a trap. Where is sleep now? Miles away; I have missed it. Startled and afraid as I am now, it will be hours before I can sleep; another night will pass.

And what did happen? Just before sleep an eruption, a storm in the mind, jerking me awake. Like a little explosion in the brain cells, a short circuit. If the brain is full of electrical impulses, do they become over-loaded like any other type of circuit, do they wear thin with use and abuse, tension, too many patterns going at once? Has something hap-pened inside my skull which will unfold quickly or even slowly but which will be my downfall? My God, if anything should happen to my mind—realizing only too late how precious it is, and now how fragile. You can hurt it by not sleeping; you have been playing some champi-onship game with your opponents, day after day without rest, all to

show you are made of iron and saner than God. And now you have
blown your own fuses. I tremble for what will come next, the breaking
apart which this awful current of fear has prefaced. Maybe I will go mad
this time and watch it happen, trip out like drugs and bizarre states of
mind, the altered consciousness Sophie predicted I should draw or write
about. Humbug, I thought.

But be honest. You've had some moments. The loony-bin trip, the
Thorazine, even just the terror. Everything becomes symbol and significance, echo and gesture, doubles and representatives. Did you tell
yourself that last time it didn't happen or you didn't see it, disbelieved
it, remembered it only blurringly in fleeting recollections as irrationality, embarrassing grandiose illusions? Like your cavalier comparisons
with Joan on the way to the insanity trial—that must have been it, that
was craziness, I'd say to myself. Or confusing the cleaning woman in
the hospital lavatory with Sita; their age, their darkness and humility—
that was crazy. And I would wince that here, surely, was confusion as
to persons and places. The way the black man in solitary at Napa was
Michael X, as all blacks in imprisonment were counters, doubles.
Knowing I could justify these displacements in my own mind as poetic
logic, but still finding them corny or overdone or just plain delusionary.
That was crazy. And I have no interest in any more of this, loathe and
dread it.

But what if there were something on the other side of crazy, what if
across that line there were a certain understanding, a special knowledge?
Don't you remember so many times during it, telling yourself, swearing, that you would never forget what you saw and learned, precious
enough to justify what you suffered? And didn't I then repudiate every
vision—didn't I even disparage the knowledge I had last time, trample
it underfoot in my haste to rejoin the sane and the sane-makers, the
shrinks and the family? The betrayal of forgetting, of shame, of denial.

But what if what I saw had value: the shadow of the dark woman in
the baths, the screams of the man in the locked room, figures of humility
and anguish, even the wit and riposte of Joan under the interrogation of
a lady psychiatrist who wanted me to repeat the multiplication tables?
All your scattered learning came back; you were a scholar again and able
to remember, given the ocean of dead time, everything you had ever
learned: not only literary but church history, myth, linguistics. The roots

of language back to phonemes. The nature of numbers—how they fascinated you. The nine times table, how each sum composed is composed of itself and equals nine: one and eight, two and seven, three and six, four and five; then five and four, six and three, seven and two, eight and one. Like a paddle wheel. And the conjunction of six and nine, the tricky one, my father used to say, teaching me math, an engineer with a curious child. Six and nine, the numbers for which the witches were accursed, remembered only but perhaps best as a sexual picture and act forbidden. As if an entire history lay submerged in me which only the loony bin could uncover: the persecutions of the past, their passwords, their jokes, their terrors, were all at hand. As if a Catholic girlhood and then feminism and finally the grave of the bin placed over the top of them could cause an entire memory to open up, race memory, mother wit, the memory of women betrayed. Therefore it is most painful to be betrayed into these keeps by a mother; lovers one might suspect, but the very woman who gave your body birth, that is too much to bear in these coffins.

However, not all I learned in madness before was madness, but the mind reacting to imprisonment: the madness of the sane. And how am I to know finally if the blurs in my perception were not Thorazine, after all, a visionary drug to put it mildly, under whose influence it takes a miracle of concentration even to stay awake? To appear coherent requires genius. But you had Thorazine only in California; in Minnesota they gave you no drugs at all and you still imagined you were some little Gandhi sitting on your bed practicing nonviolence.

Is it mad to play at being someone else, to fancy yourself? You answer your own question; of course it is, in the sense of being an ass. Madness, then, is merely making a fool of oneself? Surely enough, isn't it, when you remember and are embarrassed? It was how you were conquered afterward—oblique references to some dotty thing you'd said, which could quell you if you started getting hot under the collar at having been locked up. What silenced me, finally, was coming to understand how absolutely those who locked me up had to believe in the correctitude of what they had done; nothing in the world could let them doubt it. They would never give in, never see a middle ground of being a little crazy (flipped out, upset, frazzled), or see crazy as a mixed state, an ambivalent affair, or that crazy was not a crime but rather a point of

view and need not be locked up, that locking up is an invasion of every
human right, an invasion essentially insane—no, no, they stood against
all that, they had to. Sanity itself demanded that of them, and sanity is
a religion to them, an ideology.

Don't we all, at some level or another, terribly need the staff of logic,
of order and coherence? You merely permitted metaphor and simile to
have the aspect of reality and fact: the old woman, shadowy in the
underworld of the marble bath, represents Sita, her Indio side, her
frequent poverty, her coming age. So it's all right, given these details in
symmetry, this figure becomes literary counterpart for a real person.
Whom your mother, for example, induced into bringing you back to
visit her in St. Paul so that she could commit you as our elder sister had
done two weeks before in California. And Sita was there, too. How
many times attendant on your betrayal into the force and riot of places
like Napa? Of course, it was necessary to see Sita in the pathetic figure
in the bath; how else could I go on believing in my love for her? For
them all?—because that is the hardest thing, that one must so perfect
one's love for those who brought one to this.

Examine it, madness. What did you learn there? What does it all mean
that once in a crazy house, the Mayo Clinic in Minneapolis, I saw a
figure in the baths, fleetingly, just as she scurried across the floor and out
of sight? Abject as a rag, dark, foreign, Egyptian in her darkness and her
antiquity, the wretched of the earth and of centuries, biblical as the
woman at the well, evanescent this presence as if a shade, her age, her
poverty. For she was lower even than we the inmates. She was a servant
in the place. I loved her and I named her Sita, the presence of Sita in this
godforsaken spot, the memory of her, the reminder sent to me in the
pathos of a bondswoman, some messenger of mercy and therefore Sita.
In her very appearance to me she had done me a service, as if she had
washed my feet, my hair, loaded me with crisp white towels, this dark
stranger flitting away at my entrance like a moth. But still the signal was
given, I had been touched, warmed, given secret intelligence of hope,
a password of love sent through a representative; a double.

"Opposite numbers." I saw them everywhere in the madhouse. Sent
by their originals. As a middle-aged black woman, encountered at Herrick somewhere amid cups of Thorazine and other wonder drugs the
mind resisted in vain, was Sita as well as Désiré, the wife of Michael X,

the man whose life it had been my job to save until I was derailed into the madhouse. Counterparts. And this woman's presence by lamplight and the soft kindness of her voice could assure me that the others did not see me as malingering; here in hell I only explored prison further, a different circle of the Inferno, another ring, further plains of drought, more barred doors. And Michael himself was represented by the man who shouted all night in his cell: the ultimate sacrifice in solitary and under restraint, his deep-throated cries were Michael's transported from Trinidad and the Royal Gaol, a representation but real as well. In the perspective of this charnel house the spectacle is analogous; the man in these chains is the man in those. Both are black and both protest with a nobility that will not surrender; one must stand by and watch and be helpless. I had wanted to help, to right the old wrongs of black and white, to bridge that distance of crime and error. And the woman who was Désiré could absolve me, a prisoner like herself; we were both prisoners. Just as Désiré had wished me well in England where they would not give her entry to plead for Michael's life.

Parallels and similarities, the merging of figures, the fatigue of those evenings, the light of a table lamp, a "lounge" area, coffee cups (coffee fights off Thorazine), sitting near this Désiré and scarcely speaking, embarrassed because only platitudes came to mind, too moved even to open my mouth, yet the transformation works on me. Crazy or not crazy? Rediscovering charity, compassion. The pious in all ages have been comforted in the pits and dark places, jails and dungeons, by the specters of saints and ministrants. I had only used the movies, the double-identity trick of spy pictures. Madness of poetry or sanity holding on to healing and what heals against despair.

After the Egyptian flitted like Sita out of the room, I held her presence through a long, wonderful, even exquisite bath, magnificence in warm water in the marble tub, for the tubs were so old they were even marble and you could look at the grain of the stone and see in it the hundred thousand years of the earth, its age and composition there between your legs, the vein of blue and green at the foot of the tub. It was nearly like sex, could almost rouse one to caress oneself, to that energy and optimism. But quiet, cool still, even with the heat of the water, cool as the ages, as the names of stone, as the etymology of stone: "litho," lithium, lithograph.

That bath restored me, was worth hours of sleep, refreshed me again for the long hours in court the next day, the hours I would need to prepare my case. Even keeping silent, never permitted to speak in my own behalf, I still had to prepare my case, to go over what had been said against me and ready my defenses for what would next be said. To read the information for the little notes I would pass to my lawyers. For the notes I would make in my own mind, the rebuttals, the objections, the ready facts and contradictions—so that I would not speak out, shout, bellow, and ruin it all. The perfect surface I was congratulated upon each day by the outlaws, the social workers and feminists who came to sit behind me, also silent.

Say, say what you know, what you knew and denied in order to become sane again, to be one of them again; six years lying and hiding. No one could mention the other time to me and no one ever did. With the family it merely started a quarrel, so we dropped it and I became one of them again, almost. The good daughter or a facsimile, every conversation with them still beginning with their question: "Are you taking your medicine?" They must know now; Sally must know—how long before she has me bagged again? Or they use the long arm of Mother? Even here in New York, where I have a better chance, particularly if my behavior is faultless, here in the country where I own land; odd Tory reasoning, Republican reactionary ethos, which ironically may help me now.

But I never forgot the knowledge, the things I saw, the strange vision of those places, their characters. The labor organizer whose arm was broken on the ambulance ride; wearing a cast, he used to whisper the rules of the joint to me over and over like the good tough guy he was—"If you can't get this straight you're never gonna get outta here"—while I tried to concentrate through Thorazine. Afternoons in Napa, the green of four o'clock, the whole big room to myself, tired of drawing, not yet ready to kill time in the bath, despair settling in with the end of another day. And I rolled the wheel of Buddha, the *Namya-horingeiki,* turning the chant like the handle of a grinder, like a great round drum on its side, moving, moving, then the water pattern, the waves against a wall in that wonderful vine-filled green light, then the canoer's chant from home, the steady optimistic rhythm which brings vitality again, like the life force in the dip and swing of it. Nam ya horin geiki. Until I moved the world, it seemed, sitting tight on the top of a table and leaning against a wall practicing my magic, my patience, my

final card. A nurse came in and rebuked me for sitting perfectly still—
had she felt me rock the wards?

The wheel saved my life and made it possible to endure solitary the first
night in Herrick, when they gave me Thorazine and locked me in a
padded cell. Sally had carefully explained to the day staff that I was a
claustrophobic; the night staff managed to overlook this information and
put me to the ultimate test. I passed it. Perfectly sure I wouldn't. With
a devilish Three Musketeers swagger drinking off the Thorazine they
gave me as I was put in the cell; toasting these two nitwits, the boy and
girl night guards, probably students with part-time jobs, and I the full
professor from Sacramento am throwing down their poison. Having first
inquired politely what it was, the civil rights formula. Medicine, they
parrot. Of course, but what kind? Just medicine—take it. I have to take
it. Voice quavering and legs going weak because I know this is the end
and I will not survive what they are about to do—for how long? How
long can the mind endure solitary confinement? Days like months, years
once they have you here—it could be the rest of your life; you are now
totally in their power. I drink. If it were hemlock I'd drink it—there is
no alternative; now all is fate, having no idea what it is. Useless to ask
them what it is; you are in their hands. I have never heard of Thorazine—
the name would be meaningless. This stuff could be poison; I have never
been forced to swallow something unexplained under malign conditions, the two of them fierce, perhaps frightened themselves but terrifying to me. I drink, having no idea what it is, hoping only that it is
strong enough to quell my fear this first night in the ultimate trap.
Bringing it off with a little panache, in my fright even trying to amuse,
propitiate: "For Athos and Porthos." I raise the cup to each of them—I
being D'Artagnan, of course, holding for that even against their youth
and athletic aspect. Then it strikes me that they don't know what I'm
talking about, have never heard of the musketeers except perhaps on a
candy bar, and my gay little toast means nothing at all, fails to register—
I am really only a nut to them.

And then the door slams. Forever. So the wheel, prayer, was all that
was left, the last resort. And I amused myself with it all night long,
entertained myself with my mind, with pictures, covering the walls with
pictures, the wave pattern, the light of a swimming pool. When you
discover that this room has not only no natural light but no natural air

either, you begin to grow particularly anxious: blackouts, power fail-ures. You are kept alive by air-conditioning only. And if there were a power failure would the fools in charge realize you have no air in these cells? Of course, you would never be able to tell them—the thick door, the long passage with you at the end of it, built so that you can scream your head off and they never hear you. I was never even spied on through a judas eye, to my knowledge, all night long. Nor did I sleep. A fear so great that it resisted even that massive dose of drugs. Instead I rolled the wheel for the first time in my life, needing it, inventing and reinventing the power and magic of that force.

Toward morning I saw terrible things, my mother who had borne me, even the American flag and apple pie, childhood, the folk images dis-figured with blight, saved from cynicism only by a leap of faith that was conscious myth, a truth created against fact. But I had gotten through the night, could get through anything. It wasn't long; if it was only one night and not forever, waiting for them to come for me in the morning, release me back into the "regular population," breakfast and a visit by my sister so I could give her very particular hell over this. Or maybe, by this time, maybe just so I could see her face again, Sita's, Fumio's. She arrived with my checkbook and instructions to write a check for six hundred dollars for staying at Herrick Hospital and the privilege of being put in solitary confinement. I look at her: "If I write this check, do I get out, do I get to see Sita?" "You get to see Sita."

Again and again, just as I had set myself up here or there and talked to my lady banker, got permission for a few amenities, and could soon expect paper and brushes—really, this is the least they can do for me, having my car and my money—figured out the conveniences of the place, begun to relish its institutional food, acquired a few companions, matched wits with the authorities and resident psychiatrists, and learned the rules and how to enjoy the place tolerably well—there is a flurry. I am to be moved. Naturally I hope I am to be released. Or if moved, then to a better joint with more freedoms, greater chances of visitation, more Sita. And it is Sita they send to move me, to talk me into it, to reconcile me, to make it seem an improvement, another romantic adventure. But it is only more of the phony wheelchair (wheelchair or stretcher: you get your choice) and a long drive into the countryside, realizing with every mile I shall only be farther away from her, from Berkeley, where she lives, or San Francisco, even from Sacramento, where I am still prob-ably a professor, this broken thing in a wheelchair. Hardly able to see the green of day in the wine country as it speeds by out the back window just below eye level in a wheelchair. I am going to Napa but it's not the Napa I know with Sita, the Napa of our visits to the vineyards: those wonderful afternoons have degenerated to a rotten state institution. Sally has decided Herrick is too expensive: three days there consumed my whole month's salary. Napa is for the indigent. I will now be among the poor and crazed; their terms are longer. Even in the duplicity of what she does, leading me, Sita gives me comfort, courage. Helpless herself now; she is not even family. Sally and Fumio have authority, blood kin and husband; Sita has no rights even to visit. It is by a ruse she is sent in to accompany me from Herrick, a ruse on her as well as on me. The decoy, they have made her the decoy. And she will do it, to see me, to help me, whatever the hell she imagines she is doing—but it is such heaven to see her.

By Napa I was bitter with Sally in the induction area, the visitors' lounge, a big dirty room where I begged her for dimes, for cigarettes, for more Coca-Cola money than she doled out—my own money, and I have to haggle for a soft drink and not mention wanting to use the telephone. No, more than that, Sal, the damn Thorazine makes you thirsty all the time, goddamnit, I drink Coke after Coke, I need more. Yes, I use the water fountain but I still need more. And some candy bars—the food here will be awful. Look at the place—what on earth do you mean locking me up in a place like this? And somewhere in her poor hurt eyes I can see she is sorry and ashamed. We who are sisters and rivals always as well; look where your better wisdom has brought me, your asinine theories, your big deal knowledge of psychology, look how it has run away from you. Because again she'll think she knows the doctor, the friend-of-a-friend business, and it will turn out he isn't here. Just do what they tell you and keep cool, she is lecturing me. I am so angry with her, hate her so entirely for this folly, this new humiliation from which it will take me years to recover if I ever do.

Sitting on the floor next to a Coke machine and squabbling over change; nickels, dimes, quarters—I want a five at least. And the sight of her eyes; the eyes of her childhood still make my heart turn over with love. She is the most powerful person in the world to me now, my purse string. She arbitrarily bestows on me Viceroy cigarettes, although I smoke Marlboros; the family, our aunts in childhood and Sally too in emulation, smoke Viceroys—so will the ward now. All the checks for cash are made out to her; they buy her team gas and groceries. I may be funding a whole base of support here in California—so be it—but why no dimes for the telephone, why no telephone book? They have removed mine from my bag, my own battered address book of friends everywhere in the world. Start a call with a dime, get help. Just what is to be avoided, of course. Lest it leak to the media: "Do you want this all over the papers?" "Hardly." "Then stay off the phone."

Sisters. Like twins. Like our own opposite numbers; though in agreement as feminists, still opposed in how we have lived our lives as women. For political direction she has her lieutenant colonel husband in the Strategic Air Command, I have my black rabble-rouser about to die on a rope. The line of our sisterhood long as our lives, spent in passionate contest and emulation, marbles to mumblety-peg to wrestling, and she had always won. Then one day I grew up, turned twenty-one, and outmuscled her, arm to riveted arm, as she tried to throw me off a back porch in Massachusetts twenty feet above a cement driveway. I have never had to truckle since. Until now. And even then, when I realized her goddamned crazy mean temper might really throw me off that structure to get smashed on the concrete below, even then I loved her. But God, was I mad. And I am again now. This moment in this particularly grubby hellhole she's saving money on today. Because, baby, I've worked in these joints and I know: "Look, this place is just St. Peter's Asylum all over again, same smell even—I know people get parked here a long damn time. Now tell me what plans have you got for getting me out?" The blink of her impatience and that infinitely slow voice used in forbearance with the desperately stupid: "I have just finished telling you; you will get out when the doctor here thinks you're ready and not one moment before." The punitive extra flick of the whip—not one moment before. "Goddamn you, do you realize I'm now in the hands of another mystery—you have no idea when I get out, if ever. He decides. You have turned me over to somebody you can't even control." "Damn right—the man's a doctor." "A fart, an entire industry of farts." "I'm not going to sit here and listen to this . . ." Cantankerous, self-righteous, she gathers herself to move away.

And even then I love her, seeing her about to go, already terrified of her absence; alone with all this noise and confusion, the mad walking abroad and muttering to themselves. I know they are harmless but it is years since I have seen this flagrant display of the alien, the drugged, the

desperate, the ragged ward of despairing refugees. I do not want that
smell again, that noise, that futility—it means I am in the real joint at
last and may be here forever. How long is forever? Two weeks, two
years, or more? How long can they go on holding me in a state whose
laws call for only seventy-two hours of detention for purposes of observation? Using two hospitals (the days begin over again in each new
venue, and weekends, holidays, any days court is not in session, do not
count), they have already milked a week out of me. There must be fifty
mental jails in California of various types and kinds. Remember, they
don't count weekends and holidays—it could be months. And they will
find cause for commitment. Then it could be the rest of your life. As
Sally rises to stand I feel the night coming on here, so little money, how
long till the next visit—damn her—and then just a rush of affection like
an embrace, for all the things she ever was to me; being nothing to me
now, a corpse of herself, a buffoon thinking she's won. Yet the very fact
that she is wrong would make me defend her to the world. And in her
eyes, when leaving, what a mixture of feelings: pity, tenderness, shame,
all that forgiveness requires.

But not only will you forgive everything and renounce your own claims
as a precondition of getting out of those joints—they wouldn't let you on
the streets without that—you must conceal your opinions and keep it
under your hat about how you were wronged. It won't matter. Once out,
they will beat you on the final draw—you will abandon your own
convictions. Outside, you will no longer be right; far less will they be
wrong. Outside, you will have a record, be a declared lunatic. Inside,
this hardly bothers you; if you could just get outside: freedom, sunlight,
air, your car, money, the sight of the sea, sex, music, the coastline.
Once outside, there's a lot more than the coastline and it begins to wear
you down—snarling quarrels with your little circle of intimates about
whether or not you were crazy, whether they should have put you away.
A total stranger can destroy you by asking how you are—she heard
you'd had a breakdown—and then it is all there about your ears again.
   So then shut them out and forget it all. But the prison begins to take
over inside your head, your body; you are branded. It is in you, impla-
cably growing like a cancer, the more sure and strong because the few
persons you try to describe it to fail completely to understand or even to
be interested beyond their shock and disapproval at your attitude toward

a place of healing. Their embarrassment becomes your shame. And your deliverance from the hell you lived through so heroically is not cause for rejoicing and congratulations but a stigma you will carry all your life. Spoken or silent.

And that is what stopping the lithium did; it stopped the shame, the compliance. It brought me back to that time again—the six lost years fall out and hang aside and I am knitted up, a being murdered and buried and back again. Hypothetically, I could still be taking lithium and come to this conclusion, validate the past. But lithium represented collusion; when I stopped I was no longer cooperating in some social and emotional way.

The barn's white ceiling floats above, the strange pale blue light of dawn. I had thought it would be a lightning strike, the big revelation Sophie spoke of, piles of drawings, manuscript; but it was only this, this quietness. Then I had feared the electrical short circuitry, the terrible reflex that tore me awake and made me fear sleep and dread the future, fear my mind would snap: like crossed eyes in the old wives' tale, snap, and I would be forever on the other side of madness, trapped as behind a mirror so that I could never come back. And instead it is only the quiet dawn at the farm, the new light coming into the painting studio through the big windows onto the pond, the blessing of it—and the little willow tree, our favorite. I must find Sophie, I must make peace, love her—we should all be at peace here; anything else is silly. How I love her. Then go and find her.

The blue of her shirt is like the blue of the air just now. Go find her, make up. I can hear them swimming this morning in the pond, Libby, Kim, the muffled sound of their strokes through the distance. Tired as I am and strangely happy, I can see the flesh of Libby's arm and back, the sparkle of the water, the chug-chug of her flutter kick, her face turned in a crawl. There is safety in the morning after the watches of the night. This was a long one. Like Joan's nights in the field. I grin to myself, remembering the tradition, the long cultural habit of a vigil. Crucial but safely past.

11

Kim and Libby are my companions now in the division of camps between me and Sophie, between my proclaimed sanity and my conjectured madness. Kim and Libby form a sort of comrade bodyguard whose purpose is to test me, to keep track of me, to kid me along yet to restrain as well, to supervise but also perhaps to provoke. We have taken to seeing the sun rise once or twice already, the three of us rocking on the porch in the hour before dawn, talking softly in the dark like a set of pirates. The talk a kind of rebellion like the hour itself, like my notorious inexhaustible energy these days: the proof of my manic state for some, for me only an index of my insecurity, my need to avoid capture. I have difficulty sleeping when Sophie, with whom I sleep, embroils me in argument and quarrel after which I am both too angry and too sad to sleep. So I stay up with the kids, who enjoy me and delight me, despite the thin thread of their patronage, their watchfulness, the possible condescension of their camaraderie. Being with me, they must—probably for her sake, since they adore her and have great doe-eyed crushes on her—they must keep guard over me because she has conveyed to them the whole force of my folly, the brunt of my derangement. Which they might call being off my rocker, if they have any need to discuss it. It is all done with loving kindness. And a smugness quite beyond their recognition.

This does not prevent their being good company, clever and funny. It can be very lonely here, the other apprentices are more distant or asleep, Sophie and I are at odds. But Kim and Libby are natural buddies, pals to hang out with, favorite undergraduates, prize students. So bright, so serious, so whimsical—you really can rock on in the heat of the night on the front porch with them, chuckling about how to get another Coke without waking anyone or how to filch a whole bottle of wine and three glasses, between forays into novels and plays and politics or what might really be wrong with the tractor, how psychology has failed to distinguish between guilt and shame, or even what might be the sexual practices of the Trobriand Islanders as remembered from a book or an article. And when the sun comes over the field before the farmhouse, inch by glorious inch, we have generated a collective ecstasy which has little to do with their assignment of slowing down a madwoman; they are as crazy as I am.

I go down and sit with them. The sun, the fragrance of the morning—it is too fresh and early to hassle with life. I reach out for comfort: "We're not getting along so well, Sophie and I. I'm sure you've noticed; it would be hard not to." I smile at them. "Lovers' quarrels," Kim says, smiling back. "You'll be all right," Libby turns to assure me. "You two love each other very much." I have done the impossible, committed an indiscretion—for though Sophie consults everybody in her trials with me, I have consulted no one, out of loyalty to her. Also because I have no one to confide in: everyone is younger or an apprentice or someone Sophie would particularly resent my discussing her with. So I am isolated in my supposed madness and isolated, too, in my quarrels with Sophie, the authority on my madness, who reports on me to all and sundry, from New York City to California, the telephone report. Maybe the whole mad business is a by-product of a lover's quarrel, a love war, madness being a kind of blitzkrieg, the final firepower conveniently made possible by my stupid revelation that I had gone off lithium.

The apprentices will go soon, they will leave at the end of the summer. They will go out of your life, you will go back to the city, travel in Europe, meet new people, but the scar will remain, ugly and liable to itch; a knowledge that forms the way a drop of water coagulates, that it is already too late with these two—it will always be that. You had them and you lost them. Slippery as fishes, like losing one's footing coming out of the pond, that instant when the slime on a rock betrays you and you fall back into the water.

Enjoy the moment with them then, the golden beginning of the day, "mellow out" as they would put it; there is only the sanity of here and now and whatever presence of mind you can make felt. Then they will say that you were pretty good this morning, or even "better" today.

12

Lauren brings in the tractor, the great hulk of it zooming up the drive and onto the gravel in the triangle behind the farmhouse and the lavender barn. I shout a greeting; it's the custom here to welcome the tractor and the driver on safe returns, since so often they haven't returned but remain stuck in the mud in some far corner of the land—still-unknown bits like that tongue of land by the runoff—capable of grabbing the wheels and burying them up to the hub, while we sweat and scratch ourselves and conclude we're going to have to ask Ed again. For Lauren the tractor has been a cause, a personal quest. And it has responded, lethargically, but incontestably, to her dedication. Libby's too of course. Lauren's passionate intelligence, a bit like my own passionate need to get that damn thing running again, might slave and lather, go nuts trying to follow the instructions and understand the diagrams, but might lack the medical finesse of clear reason I saw in Libby.

Lauren's seen this all along and found me unfair. At any rate, she has persisted against my misgivings and proved herself. There is still some-thing of a chip on her shoulder, a resentment in the set of her bare shoulders in those absurd overalls she wears now; with her cropped hair she could easily be mistaken for some farm boy. Agricultural affectation has gone pretty far here, I think, watching her turn off the engine and haul her work boots over the side. That and a very decided butch manner which a few apprentices have taken on as the right tone for dealing with machinery, the out-of-doors. I have seen this come over Lauren all summer, watched it with a certain dismay. Butch makes me queasy—it is not what I had in mind for us, for the place. There is an ongoing tension even over the Amazon style of going without shirts where we will be seen from the road and provoke storms of Yankee dislike and the vague ominous possibilities of vandalism. Beer bottles are still thrown on our lawn at night from passing cars full of male voices that yell "dyke" as they bravely speed by. The studio barns were badly vandalized a few years ago and I fear further attacks, even fire. We need diplomacy.

So we will hold an open house this year, arrange wine bottles on the old white oak boards of the trestle tables before the farmhouse, heap up sandwiches and snacks and pretty dishes, squadrons of shining glasses, and propose ourselves to all and sundry. The kids in the neighborhood are already running the invitations Petra and I have handwritten, and marshaled their delivery by a fleet of bicycles. We will build our credit in the community not just the old way, by paying bills right on the nail (with the usual exception of H. G. Page, to whom, like Visa, it seems I will always owe money), but we'll do better, by being friendly rather than closed to the life around us. We are inviting people from both the roads nearby to studios open for inspection, pictures hung, the silk-screening explained, the work we do there like a little art show. Petra and I occasionally get giddy late-night notions we could sell prints up here one day, a little gallery by the side of the road and other la-di-da, but this is down-to-earth; we will demystify ourselves as a colony of women and the art process, too. "Everyone will have a good time and go swimming," I say. Petra looks up. "Bathing suits": that lovely understated irony of hers. Everyone knows we swim naked, the whole neighborhood is aware of it through its children. Better forget the swimming, make it down-home and ladylike at the same time: the sun through the trees, people strolling about, that sort of picture. The lawn must be mowed—we'll all put on our best manner.

A Sunday kind of thing. But this is a mean Tuesday on a real working farm, and in her overalls Lauren resembles a very resentful younger son sick to death of working on the place. Nevertheless, she ought to get that mud off before it dries, hose the tractor. Do it now and it won't be so hard to get off as it was the last time we let it go. "Lauren, the radiator could use the hose, too—it's overheated. Ed told us those little bits of hayseed make the engine overheat." "Later." She hardly even turns to say it to me; the word is dismissal itself. A little bad temper here. Maybe it's better to shut up and let her go get washed up. But it's only four—

quitting time is not for another hour. "Let's get the hose," I say. "No way." I look over at her; she is on the other side of the tractor, toward the house and the hose. "Nope, I'm finished." "Listen, Lauren," I begin, then stop. Cut it out, I would love to say, who the hell do you think you are, you surly brat? A moment when we simply look at each other. Then, ignoring me, she turns toward the house. You can't use someone's machine like this, I want to shout but don't, knowing she is ready to tell me that if it's my tractor I can clean it.

One of Sophie's pet peeves is people's bringing in the tractor early and not servicing it, which is part of the job, but Sophie is in New York today—all the more reason to keep my temper. Last thing I need here is an insurrection or for apprentices to leave. Sophie warns me every day now that they might. If Lauren or the other lavender house builders left we would not be able to finish the thing and the summer would be a failure, would be merely the summer I went crazy and ruined it all and we didn't come through despite that and get the house for the apprentices finished as planned. It would mean that all Sophie's judgmental predictions, all her damning indictments of my deranged state, were true and I had blown it. Of course, confidence in me is, sadly, much eroded by the presumption of madness but my tactic has been to ignore it, keep calm, and find confirmation where I can: in Petra, in Linnea—whose parting statement that she thought I made perfect sense was delivered as she left for Wisconsin, where her father is very ill—her portly matron's body, her good common sense: "Don't let it get you down." She squeezed me; what comfort.

But things have degenerated a long way since then. It is now possible for apprentices to disregard me completely. You cannot hear all that they have heard and fail to disregard one so touched. Lauren, of course, is also just plain angry, thinks she is being ordered around. Impudent kid, I think again, aware that our democratic style does not really grant me any literal authority over anyone; it is all to be a product of personality, and mine is in ruins. That leaves only Sophie in charge, and she isn't here today. For a second I feel like a lieutenant, negligible enough to be shrugged off. But there is something so hostile, so angry and full of hate in Lauren that it makes me curious. That and the insufferable, inexplicable contempt in her. It surpasses disrespect, it is an assault on one's standing as even the meanest excuse for a human being. How dare she,

I wonder—I have had students put me down, felt the cold of their dislike a few times, but this is annihilation—what is going on?

"Okay then, damn it, I'll do it," I say, going for the hose. Either this will shame her into helping or provoke some conciliatory remark about doing it later herself or maybe a word of thanks for doing her job. She quits at five, I get to work till midnight—but then I wanted to make an art colony more than she did, so there you are. Suddenly she is bellowing at me a stream of obscenities I do not hear so much as feel. Feeling it to be an act of war, but also some strange indictment of me, whereby I am unworthy of Sophie. Interesting new twist, but Sophie is an idol to them; remember the Sophie Fan Club dinner. Lauren will not do one more goddamn thing around here. Temper, I think. She'll cool off when she is finished.

Sometime tonight there will be an awkward, loaded, embarrassing apology, a grunt and eight words wrenched from her throat, and then you hug her and it's all over. Or it gets better each day with the clearing of the air. And there is ever after that a certain reserve, a certain closeness and a certain distance because you have quarreled. And on great occasions like feasts you toast, remembering it, or dance together and the younger ones wonder what it is between you. And late at night when you're asleep and they are talking the endless talk of their deeper intimacies before the fireplace in the farmhouse till nearly dawn—though the cook comes down or whoever is still trying to sleep in the big bedroom and shushes them or joins them two or even three times and there are complaints at breakfast about the noise at night—it's told of round the campfire. Someone had really told her off: " 'Fuck you,' yeah, I said it right to her face." "Did you really? Outta sight." "You should have seen her, her mouth dropped open to here—I was so mad I just went crazy and told her. But it was okay later."

So forbear. If this kid is yelling stuff, being younger she will get to take it back if she wants. And you won't, since you have to live by an entirely different standard. Privately, I would like to throw the whole tractor at her. She would also like to throw it at me. She could very easily punch me out, I perceive with a little surprise, realizing that she is a good deal stronger than I and really in a mood to fight. The tractor is between us, my head in a fever of anger. But pain too, a kind of anguish—what is happening is awful, a tragedy is taking place in this absurd yelling match across an aging International Harvester 300 between me and a musician in overalls who seems to have forgotten she is an artist or even a woman and has become a bullying malcontent youth—a mean tough boy—I remember boys in my childhood, Catholic childhood in St. Paul's snowy winter afternoons, who pushed you down on the ice deliberately as you made your way home from school. One of them I will remember forever was even named Butch. He would jump on the ice slide behind you, the way home being a succession of carefully nurtured ice slides and therefore swift and amusing but treacherous if anyone was cruel enough to take advantage of your quiet fearfulness, your trembling legs, your small girl's vulnerability, and jump on behind you. Having cultivated a greater momentum, he could slide right into your feet and knock you down, jumping out of the way with a laugh. Butch did that. It is what Butch means to me: meanness, cruelty.

And here, all these years later, is an irate young female ready to slug me as her oppressor or something. And I, the oppressor, am smitten with horror that she hates me and quite afraid she may slug me if she gets across that tractor and within range. I back off. This must certainly never come to blows. For one thing, I could get creamed. For another, I can't engage in fisticuffs without being thrown into the loony bin. "And get one thing through your head—I'm leaving and I'm not coming back, do you hear? I'm getting in my car and going."

It may be irremediable. Will she—after a shower and some satisfying griping in the kitchen to her favorite buddies, something to eat, a beer, the temptation to swim, a look at what's for dinner—will she just shelve that whole idea, or does she mean it? If so, if she's really going, my stomach turns. Sophie will come home to discover this. And it is my fault, simply that.

I go over to the cottage for an anxiety attack. Entering this lovely room, I can blank out for a second. I laid every one of these black and white tiles myself on my hands and knees; every time I see them they give me pleasure. My papers on the table, neat and orderly—the hell with these temperamental kids. She's just forgotten who she is; what is a composer doing brawling in the backyard like that? You too, I say to myself, pacing the tiles, regarding the stacks of papers on the desk and all other available surfaces: unpaid bills, unanswered letters. A great dissatisfaction comes over me, with the room, with myself, so buried in incompletion, branded with it. Idiot, you have driven one of them away. Right or wrong between you and her is irrelevant; that she is leaving is everything. Run, stop her, apologize, prostrate yourself, cry, talk her out of it—anything. You cannot let this happen.

No. I sit down at the desk. No, you have to let them go. There are times with students—I cannot help but think in those terms now, however covertly, since no one here has regarded me as a teacher for a very long time, if ever—there are times when they must launch themselves, even with a curse. Let her go back into the world and think about it. I write down just these words on a piece of paper: "Come back when your attitude has changed"—a cliché, a chestnut, almost a parody of grown-up teacher talk, the sort of thing I would have torn to pieces at her age. But it is exactly what I mean. Both verbal phrases with the time quotient in the middle. Let her open it after she's on the road, because through the window I see her car being loaded. She's going to do it.

I see the little orange car and the funny terrier, the two constants Lauren has in her life right now. That and the store detective job and the hopes of composition. Indeed she has been composing since graduation, played a tape of a setting for a poem by Carlos Williams to us one night in the living room of the farmhouse. Moody, sensitive, romantic and classical all at once, carefully crafted. I shushed people who didn't listen in real silence, who rustled and refused to concentrate. Caused some ruffled feathers by insisting the work had to be treated with respect—someone we knew had written this music. The admonition was regarded as embarrassing. I asked Lauren to play it twice. She was torn between this attention and the youth culture that felt I was being rather "heavy" that night. Lauren was ambivalent—why not just knock it off and if the guys don't turn on to this sort of stuff (their tastes then ran to Cris Williamson played over and over), then screw it; as a classical composer she was used to loneliness.

I wonder where she will go next. Further into the avant garde, which is even more isolated in music than in the other arts? But now she also has a rock band in mind. Lauren as a punk rocker, sequins on her cheek, a tougher haircut. That ferocity could be very hard rock, the ego screaming like a caged eagle. The classical and the popular are fighting it out now. That is part of what happened this summer, today even. This kid is an orphan, I remember, watching her load the terrier, who is always wet and nearly lives in the pond when he isn't tied up to dry so he can come in the house. The absurd little dog and the orange sports car, an MG convertible. So lively Lauren could be, so witty, so irreverent, such a bounce to her.

The busy little dog gets in and out of the car for the hundredth time and then sits down in the leather seat; the moment has come. There's a lurch in my stomach at losing a friend, an apprentice and companion here, one of the band that saves this place or lets it slide. An empty, exhausted feeling of abandonment and shame; the others, knowing and watching, have here an example both of how to quit and of my failure to persuade. Accused in the merry ring of their laughter, standing off to the side with my foolish envelope, which I hand to her in a swift gesture that does not really permit our eyes to meet.

I wonder how far down the road she'll get before she stops to read it or maybe throw it away or on the floor and not open it for months or forever. No, if she stops on the road it will be to remember everything and hurt for what she has lost. And in that moment I wish I could take away all the grief that floods the child in her who has lost its paradise, a Valhalla among its peers. For the farm was always that to her: the other apprentices. I was a convenience in that I bought and paid for everything and brought the place into being. Otherwise, I was an inconvenience, a nuisance with airs. Maybe that's all wrong, maybe affection was always there but forever unable to express itself. I had it too but didn't tell her, or not enough; the prickly element was too uppermost, critical. It goes through the chest like a trouble that will be there a long time. When the little orange car disappears from the spot across the road it is only the beginning of a grief that stretches on for years.

13

Petra has come to be my assistant, since she is free for a month. Yesterday we went over the color slides I've done, the series of nudes I shot down by the stream which, in honor of my former medical regimen, we call the Lithium Fairies, as there probably is lithium in the rock outcroppings along the water's edge. Petra herself was up that weekend and in a few pictures too, the only person dressed—apart from the others, the nudes sporting in the rock pools. Petra in a big flat straw hat, sitting quietly on a hill above the stream, dressed, dressed even in a hat, as discreet and silent and thoughtful as Cézanne himself, an observer always, the art historian. Calm and dark, her hair undone from its bun, her face shadowed and serene, the hat itself calm, calmness. She does not resemble the others, is foreign, European, Semitic or Iberian, something exotic, like a visiting spirit.

"Whatever you hear, Petra, the work goes on this summer—I'm photographing and printing hundreds of silk screen prints in the studio, farming, and building a lovely carriage house out of the lavender barn. Then there's Europe this fall 'cause of the show in Amsterdam, and now the Irish Labour Party has asked me to speak in Dublin. A lot's going on." A summer full of making and doing, planting and beginning. A creative summer, manic in the innocent popular sense of elated and exuberant activity. A sense that a rationalist like Petra would understand. Together we relish all this activity, happily disorganized at moments, euphoric, like kids planning a clubhouse at one level but concentrated and adult at another.

Because there is so much to do we've decided to turn the cottage into an office. After dinner we work there, setting it up, redoing the filing system, converting the cottage's kitchen cupboards into file cabinets. With Petra to help, to take interest, to encourage, I am busy every night going over the bills and figuring out how to pay them: which to pay, which to pay first, later, latest. How to keep going, how to find more money for the lavender's floor, for the plumbing, for the electricity. These are the next items. The second floor of the lavender barn is being divided into rooms, bedrooms, study, bath. The other two floors will be open. But it is necessary to enclose these rooms, frame them out with studs, then insulate and Sheetrock them, mud, paint and so forth. The wires are in already. At night I go over every bill, totaling receipts and invoices, listing prices to check out comparatively the next morning, soliciting more and more estimates. Studying more books on how to do more of the work ourselves. Feeling each day more like the harried young contractor my father was. But younger, more inexperienced, naive, a little too honest, eager to pay cash, undercapitalized and heading for the brink.

He is with me every night, that handsome young man who was my father before his disappearance in his forties, a bankrupt my mother exiled—the first of his deaths. And the old man on his way to die whom I met again after twenty-one years, that spring in 1970—another man, the man he lived to become. Very much a gentleman, calm, self-contained, serene, but not the father I had. Not the young man who finally had his own firm, his own company, his own adventure, after all those years of working for the state, building someone else's roads. Now on his own and trying frantically, heroically to make it, to survive until he could succeed. How much more he knew than I did—a builder, an engineer. And they could kill him, ruin him. I could see my fate in his every night I worked on the books; I too would build, not only barns into studios and houses but a whole company of women, a whole dream into actuality.

And I am only a few steps ahead of the sheriff. While the light burns in the cottage, Petra reads or makes us another pot of coffee. Petra, her hair svelte in its bun, the scholarly glasses. Without them she is a beauty. With them she is not so much a beauty in glasses as an oracle in academic values, feminine reason, pedantry punctuated with delightful humor; understatement that becomes outright funny. She is wonderful company. I've invited her to come to Europe with me this fall, to Amsterdam and Ireland—and she has already bought her ticket.

There is Sophie's step on the back porch. "Are you done?" "Not really, just taking a break." "How much longer will you be?" Sophie objects to my spending so much time with Petra, particularly at night. "I've just got to figure a few things out—I still haven't written my checks. Preparing my soul, you might say." Sophie is abrupt: "I'm going to be in the lavender barn tonight with Kim and Libby. The coop's too dark. I have to be where there are some people."

What does it mean—that I am to call for her there when I finish or that I am to leave her alone? With Kim and Libby. Is she lovers with them, one or both? I feel as though I have just been slapped—the feeling I have after most of our encounters lately. This morning she accused me of sleeping with Petra. I was astounded. "Petra is my friend, you are my lover—what on earth can you mean?" She persisted, yet something about it is phony; is this a smoke screen for some amour of her own? Nearly every apprentice is already in love with her, but has it become something more with one of these kids? With Kim, with Libby? Libby the antimonogamist. I remember with a shiver a speech Libby once made arguing against monogamy. Should I pursue Sophie now and try to recoup, prevent? I dislike preventing, am not the policing type. And I feel a bit foolish in front of Petra. Those checks really have to be written and sent off. And the lists made out for tomorrow, things to do, things to get. Better finish quickly and then find her.

It is late when I do. Standing before the lavender barn in the dark— there is something sinister about it. The place is by no means ready for its tenant who will arrive all too soon. The French windows are only temporarily installed and will let in the winter when it comes. The ground floor is planned but still undone, a dirt floor still—a height of achievement impossible to arrive at. But something worse now, the place has become a mystery to me at night. Nights here are I know not what, some club of three, Sophie, Kim, and Libby—what unholy alliance I do not know. Last night, while I slept in the cottage in one bed, Petra in another, the two of us having worked half the night, Sophie slept here. Under what arrangement I cannot imagine. What do they do at night, the three of them—who sleeps where? Or do they all sleep up in the loft like some commune of sisters? I look up at the darkened front of the building, my legs shaking in anxiety at the prospect of calling her. Or should I go in, not disturb whoever is sleeping? And surprise them— never. I call softly, feeling slightly ridiculous. From the third floor a white shirt appears and a figure gestures me in. Clothing is some relief— they seem always naked in the heat here. The apprentices' house, like a tribal lodge, the world of youth—I have never been here at night. It is now Sophie's world, too: she spends her evenings and some nights here; she has joined them. It is here she seeks relief, unburdens herself, finds comfort in Libby's famous massages, Kim's conversation, the company of whatever other apprentice wanders over from the farmhouse. A place alien to me, which I now enter through the absolute dark, feeling my way across the dirt floor and up the rickety stairs. Wondering how we will replace these steps; they will be too far out for any tenant, too wobbly and original. On up to the second floor, which has been Sheetrocked already. But the bathtub lies on its side still unplumbed. The next staircase is one we built ourselves and it already needs tightening. And into the loft, realizing that to Sheetrock its cathedral peak will require genius. The place assaults me with what is poorly done, what is unfinished, overwhelming. And then the three of them by the light of a lantern. Kim is sleeping at this end of the loft. Sophie and Libby are down at the other, mattresses everywhere like a college dorm or a high school sleep-over. All talk must be in whispers, perhaps on Kim's account, perhaps because by whispering Libby can command and give instructions, insist on a certain form of speech and behavior. Maternal, comradely, nurselike. I should have a massage. So tired, so much stress. It is clearly going to be some sort of therapy. Hydrotherapy, I grumble to myself inside, but her massages are splendid. I've had one; they begin with a very hot towel.

Part of me is an animal afraid that on this occasion I may be taken, sedated and silenced and then conveyed to who knows where according to some preordained plan. And part of me is an animal jealous that Sophie and Libby are lovers already and shall be again as soon as I am gone or asleep. Outside the back casement, the one I'm facing, is the great dark of the red pines and the white pines, trees I planted years ago, now a stand, a forest beyond a lawn I am shaping so that it just feathers out into the trees. I feel their presence though I cannot see them, will not for hours till the dawn, and they are a reference in this strange tableau of light and figures; the unknown, the gentle and possibly treacherous ones I have brought here. By the same token they are seductive, nude or nearly so, strong, beautiful. The great young nursing breasts of Libby bending over me with her cure. Sophie's slenderness. Kim's brown form prone on its mattress. They are a brave and possible new world of Amazons, or they may be the new liaison team for Hudson River Psychiatric or even a liaison to betray me with a sensuality I am only momentarily, as a favor, permitted to share as an intimate. Or I'm inventing the whole thing.

The hot towel descends but does not strangle or waylay me, it merely feels delicious. How tired it makes me; the fatigue of weeks oozes out. Sophie is nearby and reassuring, kind again, not only polite as she would be in front of the others but actually kind; the relief is enormous. Perhaps they have decided to cure me in their own counterculture way. If so, I'm delighted to cooperate with the hands on my back easing me, easing me. If this is Libby's medicine, it's impressive; if her seduction, it is good too. I remember again how she had always stirred me, an impulse I always sensed and never succumbed to. Why shouldn't Sophie have been tempted when I was? But I held out; here with the two of them I intuit that Sophie hasn't. Or if she has, she will not much longer, an understanding which has its own acceptance for further sorrow. I am older, different, have more to carry.

Through a fitful sleep waiting for the dawn to fill the windows, I have spent the night with them unharmed, treated with kindness and hospitality; comforted according to their way of comforting the disturbed. Yet ultimately it is neither safe nor home to me anymore; the early summer's camaraderie would have made this night ecstasy, but now it has a hypocritical face to it. The connection between Sophie and Libby has produced secrecy and discretion, a certain disingenuous ''sharing'' and alliance; my nomination to mental illness has upset all balance and created categories and disparagement. The wholeness is gone, honesty, respect. I watch the mist forming over the trees, glad they are still there: the fundament, the base, reality here. On mornings like this you can often see deer on the lawn before the white pines. I imagine the outline of deer in the mist, not even needing to stand to see them. It would disturb the others. I have made it through another night; another moment when I thought I might be taken, I have survived. The place is still there in the glory of the morning mist; even to see the loosestrife in the mist I need not rouse myself. It's there—sleep a little, it will be there when you get up.

14

The Nelson kids stop me on the road. "You're gonna go to the auction today, aren't you?" I look at them and can't resist them—for all the intermittent annoyance, their endless hanging around the place when we want to swim naked, their devastation of the icebox, the way a six-pack of Coke mysteriously disappears can by can on the afternoons they visit. Their eyes are full of horses today. Little John Nelson on his bike, a horse substitute. At thirteen he is beautiful and blond and said to be slow in school. I used to think they were all slow, until I got to know them. His mother paraded past the farmhouse with them in the old days, imposing her company on me through long embarrassed afternoons. Fumio would shake his head when they left, convinced they were morons of some sort.

Upon acquaintance Janet Nelson is only fat, lonely, beset with children and an equally fat and domineering husband, big John. Who can also be very funny and is good to drink beer with and talk irreverent talk about the government and gripe about what things cost and how shabby they are—until he drinks too much beer and begins to sing. He was a man who wanted to be a country-western singer until Janet got pregnant at eighteen and he fell into reality. Janet had probably always been there—thrashing about now, trying to feed four kids on six thousand dollars a year. Which is all the highway department pays big John as their dispatcher, his tenor voice transmitting calls about stalled cars and accidents, the unborn soul of an artist making him sometimes a very angry man.

And his children poor, so that at times need leaks out of them like greed even though it is merely hunger. We are all of us the pariahs of the neighborhood. And the pleading of these children before me on the road is complicated. Because they are tempting me to buy them a pony, and I am tempted to do it. Though I know that if I go to the auction I must be sure to buy nothing—absolutely nothing. This place cannot afford horses. There's no one here in the winter to take care of them, there's no money for hay or grooms—though two grooms stand in front of me begging for the job. And little Janet, their mascot and my favorite: a remarkable child of perfect instinctive intelligence whom I love to take with me on errands, her small body awash in the big front seat of the old convertible, her child's voice saying things rather past adult perception; she is exciting company. I sometimes feel the proprietary urges of an aunt with Janet, which her parents encourage when excited with loose talk of adoption. Not that they would ever be separated from this treasure for a moment—they still begrudge the months she was in the hospital after her birth being fitted with a pacemaker. My adoption would be more of the fairy godmother variety, which beckons with all of these children. They are so eager to play with me, visit me, tell me things, teach me about frogs and special plants or how to change a tire. They ride by my house some hundred times a day, hailing me each time as if I had just returned from India.

Sophie dislikes this sort of thing; it is an interruption to have these kids around all the time. She is suspicious of them at moments though very compassionate at others. But she has already glimpsed the pony business from the farmhouse porch and forewarns me. Of course, kids always say, if you let me get a dog I'll feed it; a horse, I'll break it and feed it and brush it every day—this is as old as the hills—don't we already have four farm cats because Sophie and the apprentices found them in the milk house, abandoned with much foresight by their mother just for us to discover and feed? Eight different people sneaking scraps to them every day, until all notion of wild cats making do on mice over the winter was thrown to the winds. We could ask a tenant to feed the cats over the winter—but with horses what do you do?

She reads my mind: "Winter is coming sooner than you think. It's August now but the grass in that pasture won't be enough for them even in the fall months. So, are you up for hiring kids to haul hay and water? You don't want to get into all this stuff, you don't need horses, you got enough problems—it's stupid even to go to the auction.''

She's right. I feel that small turmoil one feels when about to commit an indiscretion. Because I have wanted a horse all my life. Like the kids on the road—that excitement, that pure rush of worship for their beauty and their speed, their size and personality—even the high of highs, to ride one. Growing up, it was like that. Summer camps where you saved money from months of baby-sitting, since riding was an extra—you laid by a fortune of twenty-two dollars to ride twenty times. And it was never enough, you never learned well enough, you were still too scared and inexperienced and insecure from the heartbreaking rarity of it, so that each year you had to learn all over. In love with horses. And even with the horse counselors, grand strapping gals whose romantic character lay in their association and skill with the magic animals. Animals so big they make you feel little, so strong they terrify and excite—if one could be friends with a horse, hobbyhorse hacks who had endured thousands of child rides and would never know you, no matter how you yearned for this one's black nose and that one's roan coat or the great hips of a dappled gray. Especially the sorrels and chestnuts, and the more so if they had white feet, like pictures in a book. And all the horse books you studied to learn to draw them, having through this activity some possession, some contact with the wonders.

The hell with riding. In my old age I would be content just to look at the beasts. To sit by the pond and enjoy a martini and the sight of some splendid creature right across the narrow leg of the pond, the brown of its body, the grass going from green to blue in the evening light as this figure pondered and was beautiful—for they are more beautiful than anything in the world, kinetic sculptures, perfect form in motion.

As we climb out of the car, there is the feeling of an outing, a picnic in the country. To confront the sporting set, every one of us is dressed up, smartened with sunglasses or scarves, and we have taken the convertible to emphasize our holiday air. In fact I feel we are a little ridiculous in the eyes of the horsey people who are everywhere—trailers and horse trucks, horses being given their exercise, put through their paces. My own ignorance begins to crush me. I am not a holidaymaker really, only an ignoramus with a lurking intention to buy a horse; perhaps only a tendency, a predilection slithering up from below the surface. Here, however. are real horses. And people who know about them. My friends have come along to see a spectacle out of curiosity; I have come to be swallowed up in one. I feel like a mark. No wonder everyone told me to cool it today. Sheila particularly, stopping me by the side of the car just as we enter the horse kingdom and while we are still in our own rather conspicuous territory—this many women together—and beginning all over with her dire warnings and predictions: "This is going to be awful, you ought to know that. I went to a horse auction once and it made me want to heave. They are selling to the killers here." I can't believe that of this place—we're pretty near where Ralph Odell lives—Amenia is really deep in the country, an old-time village. They'd be too straight for that kind of thing. Ralph himself is here, has come to sit with us and give advice, bringing Frank along, his ancient sidekick. "We gonna get a horse," Frank whinnies. He and I have been waiting for this day for years; the strange, tiny little man reaches up and kisses me on the mouth. The straw hat, the long white hair: Frank is a folk painting that cavorts in the body of a small boy dressed in overalls.

"You gotta listen to me," Sheila persists, as if everything depended on her saving me from my fate. "It's gonna be awful—that's one point. The other is that you don't know one damn thing about buying a horse." Well, I would object, an artist should have a good eye for conformation, pleased to be able to remember the word on this occasion; there's some hope. Hadn't I loved and looked at horses all my young life, even though I realize that was a while ago and my knowledge was very limited, amateur? I don't see much about them that Sheila, who has owned a horse, notices—important things about their legs, for example. "You're likely to get one with bad pasterns—look at that one, the one there. Can you see what's wrong with its lower leg?" I can't, but it does suddenly come over me that horses must be like cars; you have to know engines to buy a used car. My God, of course I would make this kind of mistake, be carried off by a lovely chestnut color and never even worry about legs.

"Come on, let's go inside," Petra says. We troop behind her, Frank squeezing my arm and gleeful over the prospect of buying a horse. "Haha": the aged child delighted—our day has come at last. All that summer when we scraped whitewash in the barn Ralph would talk dairy farms but Frank would talk horses. His whole life was spent as a hired man in farms around here, managing horses with an Irishman's passion. The object of his life was to talk me into having them at the farm. I'd laugh, remind him it was impractical—maybe someday, Frank. And against that someday I have for five years kept an unpainted patch in the doorway of the farmhouse where Luther's Auction, address and phone number—this auction—was scrawled in pencil until the day we would finally come here.

We are in the auction barns now, huge warrens of pens and stalls; though it is day outside, it is twilight here. And misery. Sheila was right. "They know, don't they?" "Oh yeah, they know, yup, horses know everything," Frank says. And then he's gone.

Petra looks shaken, a little dizzy. "They understand what's happening to them—do you feel that, or is that just imagination?" I say. "Of course, look at this one." She's found a pony. An utterly miserable pony. He is crying. Actually crying in small little cries as he mouths your shirt cuff—carefully, so as not to hurt you, even so as not to damage it. "It's uncanny, Petra." She is nearly in tears. I've begun to realize these creatures are like slaves—bought and sold to whomever and wherever, without control over any part of their destiny: the trucking, the food, the owners who can beat or strike or neglect or underfeed or refuse to get vets. Given the conditions of its life, a horse might look forward to a change after the unsettling experience of auction. But it isn't just that. It's not the auction block and being sold to another master—it's being sold to death for the slaughterhouse. As if nearly every animal in here were going to die soon. And knew it. All but a few—because there are always a few in any crowd who don't want to know the truth, would be content to remain largely but not entirely wretched. But even taking the ones still composed into account, the atmosphere, the tangible climate of fear, is sickening. Horses are screaming; some over there in the darkest corners, where the auction hands are herding them into their pens, are ready to bolt. Everywhere else is resignation. This is too big a fight, so there is little temper or viciousness, only an occasional rumble and starting up. Neighing, but no bared teeth. It is not anger they feel, any more than deportees in boxcars or behind barbed wire—it's gone way past anger. Their situation is too desperate, too inferiorized for anger, that implies some peer relationship, a testing of forces that are matched. They are no match for Luther's Auction, not even the hundreds of them. No, they can only ask humans for pity, the few who drift through. The pony, of course, knew his mark in Petra. And he has hooked me, too, through her; how could you not take pity on this little creature with its sweet face? Though the last thing in the world I want to do is buy this pony, it does look as though we are morally obliged to bid on him. Petra has picked another for herself.

The barns are too much finally; the suffering of the creatures astonished me. Beasts this large and so massed together in their helplessness—one is reminded of descriptions of beef—the slaughterhouses, which as a meat-eater I deliberately evade knowing about, arguing for sensibility to reform conditions if the topic is raised. Reform could keep me a meat-eater.

I'm near the barn door, looking out to the run where the horses are being put through their paces, when I notice something out of the corner of my eye. In deep shadow. A stall with a huge chestnut gelding, though he looks darker in the gloom. The light from the door is very bright; away from it, his great face is in an umber Rembrandt darkness. It is startling because it is sorrowful, so much so that it makes me ashamed. We've just been told that horses are sold by the pound here, like horsemeat, currently around fifty cents a pound; if an animal weighs a thousand pounds, five hundred dollars. This is a big horse; he would go for a good deal more—six or seven hundred dollars. Maybe he's well paced, his conformation is beautiful, he's a spectacularly handsome animal—he could very well be bought for the saddle. There will be horsemen here tonight; he is just the kind that would be noticed.

I see his blanket, and then a green halter, vivid against the dark of his coat and the blanket. It is the green of the halter I see first, just a bright line of color floating in air, his coat so darkened by the gloom that it takes an instant to notice the animal himself. And then he is overpowering in his sorrow. Even before his beauty it is his anguish you feel, are shocked, mortified, accused by.

I lean toward him, he leans toward me, his soft nose a dignified inch away. You don't condescend to this animal. The pony is like a kid; this is an adult male; awesome, proud, powerful. And reduced to this. I swallow and know far below the level of admission that I have decided something; it is only a matter now of getting it done. Number 700 is his tag, degrading bloody figures; memorize it, someone is coming.

As they take charge of him I stroll the few feet out the door and attempt to look nonchalant, standing by some horsey people who are sitting on the loading platform. Many of these animals are camp horses, and now in August the camps are closing for the season. Avoiding the expenses of boarding a horse all winter, the owners put them up for sale.

Do they know what they do—do they know that in auctioning a horse here they are condemning it to death? They could shoot it themselves but then they couldn't get the money. No, they'd say—if they knew or cared—somebody could still buy it to ride, it could get lucky. So all the onus is on the dwindling number of those who come to buy to ride. Damn few, by the looks of it. And the killers must be here in force.

They have brought out my horse, 700. I have already renamed the big chestnut horse in my mind: Jim, my father's name, the name of every handsome black man, gambler, riverboat hero—Big Jim, in fact. Good racehorse name. He looks like one, too, even white feet. A dream horse.

Sheila watches as he is put through his paces, then insists on leaving. She presages that I will do something foolish like bid, and she will have no part of it. "You ought to stay and gag me," I say, "hold my hand down when I feel the inclination." "It's on your head—this is sheer craziness. Anyway, I just can't bear to see them brought in and sold to death like that. Listen, Kate, the way you can tell is, when they sell by the dollar, the animal is going to live. When they sell by the pound, it's for slaughter. And Kate—remember that story everybody had to read in high school? About the guy who had to pick a door—one door went to life, the other one went to death? Well, look, all the horses go into the auction theater through this door—they come out one by one. If the critter goes back through that door at the right he's gonna live, he's bought for saddle. But if he doesn't, if they take him out the back door at the left, he's been sold to the killers. Look over there—off on the left over on the other side. Okay, they got another door past that—you may not be able to see it from here, but it leads out to the trucks and they're right there waiting. Check it out—the trucks are huge."

Of course, logically, if I'm to sit on my hands there's no point in my knowing this secret. I look for that door and can't find it now that I am in the little arena, a tiny steep-banked theater with an open space in the center for the horses to show their paces. Hardly big enough to show anything at all—one would have had to watch in the yard out front if one wanted to buy a horse to ride; here you only glimpse the body of an animal ridden a few times around a tiny circle far down below, the tiers small and crowded and packed with sound. The endless unintelligible mumbling of the auctioneer barely audible. Old Mr. Luther should have lessons in elocution. If this is a public auction it is far too exclusive a procedure to qualify for the name. Moreover, all bids are by the pound—all. I'm stunned. And the weight of the animal is registered only once—

if you don't happen to hear it, tough luck, because you cannot do the arithmetic if you don't know whether a bid of forty-seven cents is to be multiplied by 1,100 or 1,275, 1,078 or 892. "My God, you need a calculator to figure this out." "Yup, they're running it pretty dark today," Ralph says. Frank refuses to pay attention; the proceedings offend him as a horse lover, so he takes refuge in making fun of it softly with *whooee*'s and *haha*'s. We are an interesting collection; Petra's smooth young lady self, Ralph a credible countryman, Frank an eccentric, I an obvious bidder about to plunge in over her head. "Remember the pony," Petra says. "He's two twelve. The other pony we saw is two fourteen. Either one would do for the neighborhood kids if you want to go for that. Either one—if we could save either one's life it would be great."

I'm getting a little pissed off at the way this auction is run. Buying by the pound is a scandal, and the exclusiveness of it all is unfair to the idea of an auction. I dare to ask Mr. Luther to repeat himself. Then I begin to ask him fairly often, very politely but firmly. There is a commotion. He answers me somewhat tartly but with a fatherly New England wit and I reply, very much the lady and good-humored, that it would be a good idea to post the weight of the animal in nice large numerals so it can be remembered throughout the bidding. There are little jokes about eyesight and attention and skill in mathematics. But to my surprise I win my point and the numbers are posted. Odell is amused. Petra is excited: her pony is coming up, it is time to bid. And we do, multiplying crazily in our heads cents per pound by the posted weight of this sad little animal who took our sleeves and begged, but bidding as hard as we can, we still lose him.

We watch as he is led off. It's to the left—where they have all been going. Petra puts down her head and I don't bother her; the other pony is coming up. Bid like hell, get it, save something from this deathhold. I hate the place, even the funny little miniature circus arena which I had thought so charming at first, the hard faces around us. That tough-jawed man ahead of us, whom we have picked as a killer and even commented upon to his annoyance. When he bids he scarcely moves, and the auctioneer's men always glance at him for a sign, so he's a known bidder. Much of it must be done this way, the only object being to acquire a certain poundage, an amount of weight in carcass without any regard to what sort; if after all the object is dog food, ponies would do. Please just let me have this pony, I think, bidding desperately against the man in

front of me and determined not to lose. Then, to my astonishment, I
have won. I now have a pony and owe Luther's Auction one hundred
and twenty-five dollars. "It's not extravagant, the creature's life," I
mumble to Petra. "Though you can be sure it will be regarded so at
home." She squeezes my arm.

Sophie and Kim have been sitting off in another section and come to
say goodbye; they must leave to meet Ellen's train in Poughkeepsie.
"Don't lose your head," Sophie warns me, "don't make a fool of
yourself." Bug off, I would like to say, so tired of that clinical manner.
We part on bad terms, which I immediately regret when she is gone.
Why didn't she stay, send someone else to meet the train? I would like
her with me to make these decisions. She has a favorite horse coming
up, a big dappled gelding, a very good riding horse, admirably gentle
for his size. I will buy it for her. As a way out of my anger with her a
moment ago, or perhaps to prove a different point: I will do this for love
of her, to please her, to persuade her I'm doing the right thing in buying
horses. Wait till she sees it. And then in quick succession I buy a little
palomino, because it's cheap and I want to save the little mare's life, and
then another pony, because they cost so little and this one would bring
such joy to the kids. Then I subside into silence and a spender's anxiety.
"Do you realize what you have spent?" a stranger asks me. "Yes,
about eleven hundred dollars," I say brazenly, as if I did things like this
often while of sound mind and sober. I am extremely embarrassed by his
question; it has the ring of parental authority, of psychiatric testing.
Does he think I can't add? I grumble to myself. He's probably never
seen anybody buy something just to save its life; perhaps from his point
of view he has just watched a woman throw away a good deal of money
on beat-up stock and two funny little ponies.

I stand in the little office before an old iron wicket, a plaid shirt next
to me, the loud friendly talk of country neighbors. The checkbook and
the check, a gambler paying a debt of honor. It only now occurs to me
I must find a way to transport these new creatures home. Part of me must
have felt that once I bid and paid and spared their lives they would then
disappear into freedom. Somewhere else. What I begin to see now is
what my friends were trying to explain all along, that you have to take
care of the beasts. I wanted to save them from dying; I am still not so
sure of their living with me, that's all new territory. It's embarrassing
how little I know about all this. I am trying to imitate a farmer while
dealing with Mrs. Luther's cheerful hardness. Gambling here is money

on the barrel: you pay right after you buy, and even before the auction ends it's expected you'll show up here and prove your credit. "And if your check ain't good, we'll come and get 'em," Mrs. Luther says. A smile—she's taken a shine to me. I'm flattered to have passed. Does she understand what I've done and approve?

Back in the hall it goes on, the slaughter. The killers are closer to the ring now and more indiscreet, bidding everything and taking it. Number 68 comes up. Mr. Luther wants this horse to go for saddle and makes it plain, stopping the proceedings while each gait is shown, praising the horse as a horse, not so many pounds of meat. One begins to understand his position: as auctioneer his responsibility is to the seller. If it's a farmer going out of business, it's Luther's job to get him the best price he can for a combine or a bailer because that's all the guy is getting. But if it's some breeder indifferent to the fate of his animals, then a horse will go for meat, may even be slated for that as a sure thing. Rather than depending on the handful of sixteen-year-old kids who cannot go over a few hundred dollars, or on the horse traders who will not bid as high as slaughterhouses unless a horse is remarkable. Because there are so many to save and the killers' buying price is higher than everyone else's. But even in this situation a few animals escape, and 68 goes to a college girl. Then it goes back and forth with the next few, but there is a drift toward the dollar. "Bid 'em on the dollar, damn it to hell," a voice calls out toward Luther from ringside. A horseman. We take up the chant, trying to spread it through the house. "The dollar." "The dollar." More voices from the ring, the horseman's side. Snarls and guffaws from the opposite side. Luther is furiously calling us to order. "Dollar, dollar," from the bottom and the top of the ring—a little insurrection, a small rebellion.

"An event, a performance piece," Petra says. We go on proselytizing, excited, astonished, victorious or sensing a turn of the tide. Something is happening to Luther's Auction. "Number seven hundred," Mr. Luther calls out. Big Jim. My horse. "Well, that's luck," I say. "Bid anyway," Petra says. "Impossible, but I'm going to watch the bidding, I'll tell you." He's a big animal, a great number of pounds, so that the price, if it goes that way, will be very high indeed. But the first bids are dollar bids from the horsemen's pit; the traders like his looks. Even the killers are forced to bid dollars—why couldn't they keep out of the bidding for once? They are only looking for a certain weight in carcass; they could get it by any combination of ponies and old horses and leave the fine stock alone. But that is just the point: it's just as cruel to kill the little guys and the old guys. Yet to see a magnificent animal like this one with all his fine form and learning, his gaits and handling, put down in his prime to make dog food is more than cruel, it's wasteful. "Hang on and watch what happens," Petra says. Frank jumps up and down in a fever of his own. Ralph stares through his glasses and says softly, "You gotta watch 'em now, that cowboy or whatever he is. See, that one down there, looks rough but he's got a sense of humor. He's the one that started them calling for the dollar—and he's gonna get this horse, too." I'm pinched between reassurance that the creature will live and a longing to have him myself. The horses and ponies I have just paid for are not creatures I wanted; I only wanted to save their lives. Except for that, I would never in the world have bought them. But this horse I would have bought, this horse I wanted. And the fellow down there is going to get him. "Well, the first thing is to keep them alive, isn't it?" Petra asks. "Right."

"Gone. Number seven hundred. Sold to . . ." but we cannot catch the name, and the horse is led away to the right and back into the barns, to live. "We could call Luther's tomorrow and get the guy's name." Petra has already figured it out, but her real interest in following up is to find her pony, the first one auctioned, the one we lost to another bidder. She will get right on top of that, and if she can locate him in time there is a possibility of staying the execution. I figure a big slaughter-house would relinquish a little pony, an inconsiderable mite in the maw of their carnage—if she can make a fuss. They might just decide that the animal was either in good health after all—it seems there's some disease each animal is declared to have so that it may be slaughtered—or that it could be released to her for private veterinary care. "I don't think there's much hope but I'll do anything to save him," Petra says. She takes Frank and Odell with her into the night and the dark of the yard to search among the trucks, where the slaughterhouses are loading their eighteen-wheelers, animals shoved up the tongues of ramps and into them; cries, halters, blows, shouts.

I am alone in the yard, toward the front, waiting for them to come back and for my own animals to appear; there are hardly any trucks on this side, only a pickup or two. I begin to get nervous: what if the killers and sellers were angry that the auction went from the pound to the dollar? I was conspicuous there, protected by the public process, the auctioneer, the rigid order of things. But if I were spotted alone after having challenged this business, criticized it even to exposing it, I could get in trouble here. There's money in all this, and anger. As a woman, an outsider, a city idiot and writer, I could attract some very real, possibly physical hostility. It's one thing to cheer along at the top of the gallery, rooting for the dollar, all of us grinning and telling each other it's animal lib—the scalawag tactic of zapping procedures that is part of the radical's way of life—but this is a back-country cattle auction in the heartland and you don't fool around with that sort of thing. You could get run down or beat up very nicely out here alone. It's an odd sensation to be far from home and without a car. Petra has my purse, so I don't even have money.

Just then a pickup starts to come down the track and past me, slams on its brakes as the driver sees me, and I stiffen. He rolls down the window. ''Are you the one who bought that big gray?'' This doesn't seem much to be accused of. ''Yes.'' ''Well, he was mine and I think I can get some papers for him if you want me to try.'' ''Sure.'' Sophie's horse. Papers are no great object with us—buying as rescue doesn't go into pedigree—but why not have them if they're to be gotten. ''Here's my card—I'm over in Connecticut and I'll be home tomorrow if you want to call.'' ''Gee, thanks.'' And he's off. The paranoia lifts. People are really nothing like as bad as you think, I mumble to myself, watching Petra and Ralph and Frank appear from the left, while to the right our horses and ponies are brought down out of the barns and into a little cinder-block room off to the side, where Mrs. Luther has said they can stay until we can get them trucked. And here, assembled together for the first time, meeting each other as it were, are the two ponies and the two horses, the little palomino and the big gray. We stand at the entrance to their grotto, for it has that feeling, and watch them bedded down in the straw in the soft yellow glow of a naked light bulb. There is such peacefulness in this room it seems like a crèche and the beasts a part of a Nativity scene.

When the horses and ponies were delivered the next day Sophie relented and loved her gray and delighted us all by her knowledge of horses, her lovely confidence leading him forth from the truck, as the apprentices and the neighborhood kids danced and squealed and petted the ponies and the palomino like oversized toys. But as their procurers, as auction hounds and notorious spendthrifts, Petra and I began the day feeling very unpopular. The farmhouse side was like a wake, but over in the cottage Petra and I were busy tracking down Number 700, Big

Jim. Mrs. Luther gives Petra a number in New Paltz to try for the guy who bought him; his name is Joe Something and he's a horse trader. When I get him on the phone he sounds as if he's still drinking beer and celebrating: "You gotta come right over. We're auctioning all the horses we bought last night, right in front of the schoolhouse in New Paltz—to kids. Can you believe it? We saved a hundred horses last night—thanks to you, we sure as hell got them to bid by the dollar. Wow, you should see it! This afternoon, it's gonna be beautiful, all those kids are gonna go crazy."

I slide to my purpose—is he going to auction Number 700 or keep him. "Good horse, that one—I figured I'd keep him." "How would you like to sell him to me?" Silence, a horse trader's maneuvering silence. I squirm and confess my love. Hardly a way to horse-trade, but I'm lucky because he relents. "But you gotta pay me something for trucking—you're a long ways from New Paltz. Give me fifty dollars extra, so I get something for myself." "You sure will, you're wonderful."

When Joe arrives the next day with his grand big truck he is indeed wonderful, leading the great horse carefully down the ramp, kindly. After all the frightened moments this creature has had in trucks, his long ordeal is over at last. As we lead him away from the truck it is not toward the field where the others wait but toward the pond where Petra is bringing champagne and a tray full of glasses; I want to thank Joe and to toast Big Jim on his arrival. Marveled at and admired by all of us, this beautiful horse stands by the table, so male, so magnificent. Several women take his picture. You hardly need to hold his halter or the lead rope; he is so glorified here he would not think of leaving this attention except perhaps to graze a mouthful or two, expressing independence. To think this creature is mine.

But then the other horses whinny from the field and he whinnies back. The calls are imperious, urgent, powerful. They obliterate people as they call from kind to kind. How eager they are to claim him and how entirely the need of them takes over the big horse. I bring him along behind the barn and toward the road; with each whinny he goes faster until I am running. Then I am only something impeding him. Take it easy, you're scaring me, I say to him, and he actually slows down a bit. But he cannot contain himself, cannot resist, and we take the road to the gate of the field in far too much of a hurry for me. I have discovered what I feared but already knew, that he is mysterious and of himself and will not always do what I want: thank me for keeping his life, hold me in gratitude. He is bigger and could hurt me, maybe kill me. So there will always be this distance of awe between us, the unknown across species. I want to understand this more, test my crazy theories of communication further, but this is hardly the moment—horse to horse now, they are blood relations at a holiday and their tearing need to meet is something I must serve. Getting the gate open as quickly as possible, I let them be, let him through it and leave them to themselves. It is a passion, what they have toward each other, the urgency of that neighing. It must be more than they feel for humans except in rare cases. And these refugees must have everything to tell each other, to heal each other of death, having nearly died in the auction barns and escaped here, which must seem heaven: five acres of grass and fifteen country children to fetch them water. The ones here already can describe the place since they have one more day's experience of it than this big horse. A top horse, bound to be a king among them. But the remarkable thing is their kindness toward each other, the courtesy, one almost wants to say, of their society. The way they have already paired off, pony with pony, and the gray horse with the palomino, and now Jim with big Molly, the mare who is boarding with us, a neurotic who chews on wood and is forced to wear a restraining band. Jim has gallantly taken on this difficult personality and they are from the first inseparable. Gentleman Jim, I think, going back to the pond, what a very nice fellow he is, this horse, and how charitable they are toward each other as beings.

15

I have come out to the horse field to be with these new creatures. Supper is over and the talk goes on in merriment and a good deal of wine tonight. But I wanted quiet and a chance to be with these horses beyond bringing water to them, watching them graze from a distance, showing them to the neighborhood kids. Tonight I can merely watch them, discover them, these still unknown shadows walking in pairs: the little palomino and the big gray, the ponies naturally together in their diminutive and constant young old age, Big Jim with Molly in her constrictive "cribbing strap." This device would make any creature neurotic and I long to take it off her to see what would happen. Big Jim consoles her in this as in all her many other troubles, a perfect escort and companion to this irascible overweight female. His good nature surprises me for, though a gelding, he is very much a stud in personality. A show-off, a champion, a hero and racehorse, a creature of enormous and superb beauty who lives to be admired and adores praise, as if it were the food and reason of his life. It is interesting to watch them all with each other, their grace and gentleness, now in their own utopia, they are contentment itself, all of its good intentions and sweet ways.

Whenever we enter the field to see them, they come running, like children, like friends being visited, the whole herd making their way from the top of the field down to the gate at the bottom, where we stand with sugar and apples, pears and words and hands to stroke them. How I love this—that coming in tonight by moonlight, I could see each shadow raise its head and hear me and make its way to me, gently, for

I am afraid of them still and they sense it. But given that disadvantage, our alien species, how close will he let me stand after greeting me? He leaves while I greet the others; then I make my way halfway up the hill to where he stands with Molly a bit off to his side.

I have taken all precautions: a flashlight, a blanket to sit on, the last of the wine, lots of Marlboro cigarettes, which should fit in nicely because I have come out here to know my horse, in this odd way I have chosen—being rather past riding him or not quite up to it; perhaps some weeks from now, when I know him better. Sophie has already ridden her big gray. In fact it ran away with her up the Con Edison road. I am not getting myself into that sort of scrape. But then suppose he decides to step on me as I sit here? What do you know, I wonder, brute, who are you, what mind have you? I stifle these thoughts for their lack of generosity, politesse. Do they read minds? Do they understand goodwill at once, perceive double-heartedness instinctively? Or are they stupid after all as people go on telling me? Censor that—what if this magnificent great creature heard you thinking?

I have forgotten even to bring you trifles, pears and sugar, bits of greenery. This is a serious visit and you hardly seem to miss them; that sort of stuff is for the kids, the ponies. This is to be me sitting at your feet, watching you as you graze or merely stand before me, wonderful, big, gorgeous in the moonlight that fills the whole field—one could nearly read by it. And what do we read in each other? What are you besides the strength of your shoulders, the perfect line of your back, the great fast hard hooves? Horse, animal, beast, other life, existence, intelligence, sensibility, sensuality. Your great cock, that surely is a fascination. When you first arrived and we toasted you in champagne next to the pond, you let it down for us, a show of force, your great black cock outlined against the blue of the barn, the gaiety of your white stockings on the green grass, and then this cock.

Looking on, one would love to laugh and clap one's hands, but alone at night with the mysterious force of creaturehood one is awed instead. And horny with lust past reasoning: this is pagan, the echoes of its long-forbidden paean ache with danger and the desire to recover what has been outlawed for thousands of years. Since the takeover. Since the witches were burned. Since Joan rode before an army. Since Amazons disappeared into legend. What schoolgirls remember only in riding lessons. It was once women and horses. Men, too, I suppose—everybody, pandemonium, pansexuality, everything possible went on in the mystery of sex, the great ritual and energy of life, the one and only true religion.

Who gave a damn?—do you hear me, horse?—the species were not enemies, did not slaughter, mated and married, whomever whenever however, all rife in the early agricultural dawn of the world. Until enslaved, property, in livestock, then children, then women. Next, castes and slaves, masses and kings, priests and laws; finally, armies. All chattel—most people; and every animal, called now merely beast, creatures not even separate or at odds but subject. That was our bond, the horse and the woman; we stood for the last freedoms, riding to Orléans, against Theseus, in Crete preserving the rites, in the Near East, in the new Indies of America making a last stand. Of course you are noble; consider the sculptures of you in the world, the Han horse on my aunt's mantelpiece in childhood. The Chinese worshiped that form in clay and in the strokes of a brush-made tail and back. You are everywhere admired, revered, remembered, if only in art. The cartoon and the Wild West and the corny sketches after Anderson of my own horse-stricken adolescence. And now at last I come to be with one of you. Not to "own" you, after the obscenity of an auction where another could have bought you for death—the entire thing a kind of sacrilege, a crime; the auction, the place of the crime, gone now. So there are only the two of us. With whatever remains of my responsibilities and your perfect freedom to kick me in the head.

But instead you drop your cock and remain all gentleness. Were I to take an interest in this, do I trespass upon you, invade? Is there a rape in this somewhere, exploitation? I wonder, lighting a cigarette and making a face at the radical catechism. But there's more to it—between our two species what communication exists, what possibilities, say, that you turn me on? The phrase is comical; say instead that the sight of your magnificent cock appended so long and invitingly below your magnificent body is aesthetic, but also erotic. What is the eroticism? Not only what if anything does one do about it but what does it even mean to be thus excited? Am I inspired then to jump a horse or another person? Or is this a show of sexual force itself, meaning only itself? I have forgotten the way if I ever knew it. And you calmly dangle this heroic dong and look on out of your noble face. Being what men never permit themselves to be: tantalizing, naked, uncovered, fetching.

This mere flesh, always with us, centuries of peasant wisdom and springtime could still carry on its work in the folk remembrance, and with those who dared. You stand there daring me. Calmly. Quietly. Without the trace of a threat—or even a brag, though it is surely something to brag of; it is natural to you. What might be a giggle among women at table on a farmhouse morning or a good laugh at dinner— things being unreal these days—pushed aside: the magnitude of a horse's cock is, after all, funny; cock is funny and must be made funny to be removed, neutralized in ex-husbands or college romances abandoned for the true lesbian path. If you said you love cock it would be heretical if not outright crazy—though I remember my redoubtable younger sister, Mallory, once proclaiming such a love just after a particularly euphoric luncheon. It was in the ladies' room, notwithstanding the fact that Mother was there, too—though nearly everything is permitted to Mallory since she demands it so convincingly—and listening to her rant while inside my cubicle, I thought what nerve. She can say this out loud three times in a public rest room, hardly even fazing Mother, and I have grown up in this family a lesbian and have never been permitted this sort of insistence, surely never such exuberance. "I mean it," Mallory goes on in stentorian tones, telling my mother and sister and the world at large, "I love it, I just love cock." And I thought what crap, because what does it mean to love cock? Fumio's surely, since I love Fumio and I also love his cock as if it were an extension of himself but with a life and personality of its own. But not cock in general, all cock, indiscriminately, any cock—they treat her like dirt, those damn young actors of hers.

But now I can see what she meant. For the object before me, Big Jim's grand dangling black cock, is cock in its quintessence. Suddenly the maleness, the majesty of its maleness, opens itself to me and I love it, revere it. Remember in a burst how I have always loved it, maleness, men themselves, all things masculine and other, grand, mysterious—as if this glorious overblown equine cock were a symbol of the male itself, the masculine principle. Not only had I forgotten the rockabilly fun of riding this penile rod, of reveling in its tickle and flush, but I had forgotten, too, its place in things, its half of the universe. As if in the years of feminism and the need to square imbalance it had seemed necessary to negate what claimed too much for itself: the power to defend a dry and desiccated privilege that had nothing to do with the real joy and juice of sex. Or even with living males, still less with their organs, "members"—what a charming word, I think, looking at Jim's. The system had appropriated the charm and feckless humor of a flaccid cock, or the silliness of its gentleness, naïvete. Or the pride and surprise of a stiff one, the quest of it, the small heroic fist of it—vulnerability made potent and actual, gleeful, obstreperous. And, of course, the delight of possessing such a thing, this organ different from the satisfactions of breasts, the hidden overture of cunt. All, there must be all.

And a horse to provoke this Lawrentian tirade—I grin to myself in the dark, looking up at the beast and his great hung-down velvety cock, remembering the years with Fumio. Even back to my father. As if in working for the mother and the sisters, I had neglected fathers and brothers. *Sexual Politics*. Are you here to remind me, wonderful obscene presence, to recall that modest man I lusted after in childhood? An adolescent dying of curiosity about the wonder between his legs, hidden by custom, gentlemanly and pointless custom, whose effect was only further curiosity, mystification. Having missed sight of my father's red genitals, an inch glimpsed between the folds of his shorts as he changed clothes before his bath, after a day building roads, have I found again in your grand black dangling cock something of the hero in that tired man?—that force, that aging grandeur, that prizefighter's fatigue, that exhausted athlete. Who had designed, tramped, surveyed, figured, endured all weathers in his jodhpurs and duck boots, so tired from the cold and the miles he can hardly remove his socks, stand up again, and march to his bath. But being a gentleman and something of a dandy, he must bathe. It is his office of an evening—and why not, because after all his enormous effort he must know some ease.

And he is going down in defeat anyway—they will kill him with money and credit, the two things he cannot control, though he can win over everything else with his mind and his math and his muscles and his guts, the courage and ingenuity they cannot kick out of him. So, in his final realization of defeat, a realization made every day for months now, it would be nice after all to have a bath and talk to his kids. The brown-eyed one who has such a crush and is spying on him now. My primal scene, sitting on the bunk bed in my room, watching him undress in his. A man seated on a low upholstered chair with a footstool before him, untying his boots. In his shorts, as I peered toward where the revelation would come, having heard the facts from neighborhood kids, even from Mother. Being a man you would have one, a penis—I have been waiting my whole lifetime to focus on the discovery of this moment. Not on your fancy clothes, which I adored—the cord trousers or the gabardine shirts from Canada with sixteen pearl buttons down each sleeve. Nor the white linen shirt of everyday dinners, the white flannels of a Sunday, the white buck shoes I polished as your page. No, it is a new creature who observes you and is chiefly curious about your white shorts.

Have I invented a horse thirty years later to represent you, Jim, to figure you forth, to be some spiritual link between a dead father and the male thread? Not, of course, that this is not a real horse with a very real cock. Blasphemy to name it after a dead parent, an Irish joke. But more: filial piety of a bizarre order. And I did it in reverence and affection actually, so that his magnificent animal's form and stamina would be your continuance, tired man from the dead. You were once as sleek as his chestnut hide. . . . Old photographs of you in whites, perched on the guide rails of roads you'd just built. Fresh as the paint on the marker, the black and white posts between the guide wires, your grin above the white shirt and flannel trousers, the white shoes of your twenty-sixth summer. A courting man. Then you had this power still unbroken that remains in the mature but young again aging horse saved from slaughter—the thud of Big Jim's hooves running his new five acres, pounding down the hill when he sees us coming, frisking with Molly, traversing the field. It is that courage and strength, that nobility of head and back, that animal satyr spirit, all centered in the cock hanging before me.

I would touch it. With respect as well as lust, awe even, not only for its size but for what it symbolizes. Touching it would be to connect with the last taboo, past bestiality to incest: utopian prehistorical world. The Amazon's perfect freedom within the pleasure principle. And if we lived so with horses here, would we be safe? Would the word spread and bring persecution?

Petra's figure in the dark, downhill, approaching me: "Another night in the fields?" "The first actually, but I forgot my armor." "How about a sleeping bag?" "I'm really not that earnest about it, I'll only stay till I'm cold. Have you ever noticed a horse's cock, Petra?" "Rather difficult not to, isn't it?" We glance in awe at Jim. "You ought to ask

Sheila about that—she's full of stories. It seems that owners of male horses are under obligation to clean them." "Interesting work." I blush in the dark. "Hmm, something called smegma or something like that builds up otherwise." "How do they manage in the wild?" "Got me. Try Sheila at breakfast—it will liven things up. I'll leave you to your adventure, but put on the jacket I brought."

I watch her figure depart. For all its primness she knows just what I'm up to, the sexual bent of my rumination, and is amused and sympathetic. What would the crazy squad think? I wonder, but of course Petra wouldn't tell them. How amazingly tolerant she is, more than anyone here; no adventure is too ribald or crazy or speculative or abstract or outrageous. Because her moral sense, like her honor, is so nearly perfect, so close to her mind's own reach. A slender shape in her neat coat and narrow trousers, her beautiful black hair bouncing a little, she goes down the hill and out of the moonlight past where the fence opens into the paddock. Then she is around the corner into the dark, and then onto the road by moonlight, back to the lights of the farmhouse or the cottage. Where is Sophie now, in the lavender house with her troops of admirers or with one admirer alone? The prospect of finding her is too dismal lately. Here is some better wisdom, something to be learned from these beasts, and the company of animals is suddenly interesting now that they are so large and gorgeous, so social in their behavior toward one another, an improvement on people in their friendship and courtesy. Like Gulliver in the fourth book I'll be, I laugh to myself.

And I have the spectacle of Jim's cock, a treat in itself. I must show this wonder to Sophie, I think; it will arouse the old randy in her, delight her. It will be a mystery, a secret I can introduce her to. Not that she probably doesn't know all about horse cocks—she used to show horses—but maybe she's forgotten. Tonight in this moonlight, though, it is for me alone Jim hangs down his cock, to let me touch its alien velvet, really quite afraid of him and his size, of the taboo and the forbidden, of my own adoring lust before this amazement. Can he sense it? Would it occur to him to lie down on top of me and squash me to death? I lie before the horse wondering if the musk of my cunt reaches his nostrils and then deciding that if it did the consequences would be more than I could manage.

And I must take care not to offend Molly, his mate; I sit up—she could walk all over me in a trice or kick me in the head. Though she seems disengaged and peaceful, much as he is. The hand is all that can know him, the hand he permits to reach out and touch, to lower his great cock. In its velvet blackness I am connected now not only with my father and Fumio but with Edward, the black convict out of Folsom with whom I corresponded for years. On being freed, he offered to come here to the farm—I have always wondered a bit if I should have taken him up on it. But there was Dakota then and later Sophie; always the women prevent the men, and a penniless con might have been a monumental error in judgment. So I was discreet and encouraged him from a distance and then lost contact after a few touches for money. But I had loved this beautiful young man as well, not only with the platonic love of prison letters but in the flesh on visits; he was beautiful, full of dignity and intelligence. Now he has gone on to work in prison reform, I hope, rather than to be lost again somewhere in the streets. I can remember him by moonlight holding the cock of a horse—which would make him grin that convict's patient, infinitely patient grin. The scar upon his cheek, the gray eyes of all his French blood so amused and worldly, yet still there is a boy in him much like Fumio who would laugh and slap his leg.

And what would my laughing, drinking Irish father say to this prank? I am past spanking now; you would have to surrender, man who was all manhood all those years, to the woman now, not the girl—beating children is a poor substitute for molesting them. And you were chaste. If you were living I could fuck you finally. But you are dead. Not even married to my mother anymore, dead. You are not even married to your second wife—how betrayed I felt to hear that you had begotten three more children, two of them boys. Yet when I saw you that last time, it certainly never entered my head to regard you in any sexual light at all. You were an old man, going, as Fumio said, toward death, already something of a ghost. But what remains of you, my father, here on this hill in the stark mad moonlight, what remains is my never-satisfied desire of you. Leaving me forever, leaving in my adolescence, in that moment yearning and bereft of you, the moment of sex discovered. Surely not why you left; you had plenty of reasons. In fact you were kicked out, dismissed as an adulterer, by Mother and not by me—I've been an outlaw, too.

I had only the memory of a father forever young, forever handsome, forever sexual and just out of reach. The man of men. Touching this beast, I can know all that, come home to know how much I wanted you then; not only then, but later. Back then, an adult male would have been an intrusion, as with all the girl children aggressed upon by loutish fathers keeping them in secret bondage, the rapist fathers of incest. No, I was willing, and if not able then, in all the years to come I could desire you still somewhere in my mind. The more so as I approach the age at which you left me—so that you are now forty-five when I am. A vigorous and beautiful prime you are, the moment before your bankruptcy and disgrace. The moment before you were driven out of your home and away from your children. Surely she had her reasons—they just weren't mine. If you drink, so do I. If you can be murdered by money, me too—try running this farm—ah, but you could run this farm with one hand. You are all the things I am now trying to be. Having finished the things Mother gave me to do, scholarship and books and speeches, now I aspire to your bridges and your roads, your land and surveying, your trees and growing and felling. The land—working the very land that was your medium, earth builder and heaper, sculptor on the grand scale, the ultimate scale. I sculpt still, only differently, and in being a sculptor first, I followed you first, and do again in the last crafts of building which I learn so poorly, so slowly. With you inside me like an engine turning, turning so that I move at all.

I would be both parents, and being already a woman, I would marry and fuck the father that is the male in me, too. How's that for irreverence, old man? Do you chuckle, or are you really scared to hear such heresy and raise your hand to strike me, siding with authority—are you with God the Father these days, or are you one of us, a man broken by this world who can sin by thinking and enjoy it? Past life now, past all thought crime: wise, free, amused, willing, of the earth and flesh and spirit again, animal; animal as this animal I hold by the cock. Are you dead or alive, Jim Millett? Dead, yes, but alive in the will, the spirit. I don't mean any afterlife optimism, but is your will still in the air about me and does it wish me well—would it finally permit me to love it?

The last time we met, saying goodbye on a bus platform at the Port Authority after twenty-one years of being dead to each other, you held a copy of *Sexual Politics,* the book I had just written and so proudly presented—and somehow you had read a bit of it, maybe all night in your hotel room during this charity-like visit to your daughters before you died: a trip laid on by your rich sister's generosity. You had said not to mind when another of the sisters sent her copy back unread, because she had not understood that the first passages were quotations and had taken the book for pornography. "Forget it, that's how she is," you chuckled. "But as for me, I think you got something there." Another of those divine chuckles. "Yup, you got something there." A whole book against patriarchy, and you who had been my patriarch were approving, detaching yourself from it and siding with me—a rebel, too. That you approved—how grand it was, that gift; there was no time to understand it and hold it as dear as I should before you were dead. And now dead, damn it, all these years, and on a little hillock in a field by moonlight I communicate with you through a horse. Irony and absurdity. But what else is left? Call the horse a spirit, a personification—no, nothing that elaborate. Call the horse an animal, a male animal of splendid proportions, see its wonderful head and back—this is a beast not a man. But something in it, and not only its cock, can invoke you, my dead and adored father, so that I remember my love for you and the horror of your loss all over again, past weeping and into another set of tears that are gratitude—for knowing in this creature the memory of you again, the consummation of my lust for you unconsummated because impossible in him as in you. But only to touch this great wonderful cock is to touch all maleness, beloved and tender, heroic and other and still the same, because joined in the very meat we are all made of, the coursing life in the blood that engorges the veins or the breath in my breast. Which will never touch yours, will never lie with you, will never even embrace you again. You are indeed dead. Great powerful permanent word.

But he, the animal wondering and restive whom I let go of and can see again tomorrow, will be some Zen representative alive and with your name. This animal presence is some connection with you and with all I have missed of you, the male other side of life, its devil-may-care and courage, its potency and power, its laughing hell-bent fun, and that will help me in this place. Like you, it will help me to run it, to dare, to change it and restore it, to mow and dress it again, to take on the tools and the confounded machines, contraptions I am half afraid of. We need male patrons, sources, energy; if not male gods, then satyrs.

Go, Big Jim, in the moonlight and off into the dark and again in the light, be all you are and can be. And stay, aura around my head, bless and surround me, Father, protect and comfort me, laugh and beguile me. Stay close in my mind so that we can drink together and tell each other everything. The dream I had always when you were still alive, of getting drunk and talking our heads off—damn, when I saw you the last time you were teetotal. So, of course, you were dying; it made you a ghost. Somewhere I hear a chuckle: "Life after death is full of Canadian Club."

16

I am worried about Kim. She seems sick of everything: the warfare here, the doubt, the difficulties and setbacks of rebuilding the barn. There seems little hope of finishing it, the project that was to be the heart of the summer. The tenant we had engaged to spend the winter in it has refused the place, convinced it would never be done in time. It all looks hopeless and the women here are drifting away one by one. Lauren. Libby, leaving soon for college. The achievement of the barn was to be our all; now we have failed. The youngster in Kim cannot bear this failure and cannot bear to go on trying either. She is tired and afraid. So am I. So is Sophie. Summer is ending. Every day it's harder to go on. We have only two weeks left to finish the building.

Lately Kim refuses to do much of anything at all; living in the loft at the top of the lavender house, she even neglected to get up yesterday morning. Later I was told she was ill. A whole day of this. The next day, only an hour or so of effort before lunch. At lunch she is unwell again. Can I even put up Sheetrock in the same building without disturbing her? I wonder, annoyed at the kid for her surly dereliction, for her spoiled behavior, for her taking over and creating a drama of her disaffection. I remember when we were buddies watching the sun rise together on the front porch. "If you bug Kim, she goes too," Sophie warns, "so for God's sake don't get on her back."

The work has to go on; if she stays she ought to help. If she goes—but I can't bear the thought of another defection, abandonment, judgment upon myself. So put up with Kim till she comes around. She's just lonely without the others, and badly disappointed about the barn. It was my fault it wasn't finished and we lost the tenant, not hers. From her point of view the lavender house is apprentice land, built for her and hers, the women's colony. How I manage to pay my taxes or recoup what I spend is not her problem. It is really not her affair if you face the winter broke because you put your grocery money into floorboards. They're yours now—figure it out; you build the damn house. And so Petra and I and Sophie labor on at insulation, Sheetrock, and plumbing. By the end of the afternoon the last pipe in the vent system emerges into the fresh air through the cedar-shake roof. Waste and vent systems are done; only the water is left to do. We pore over the books illustrating this miracle. We are ready for the big fancy torch at last, the hundred-dollar professional rig we bought at N & S plumbing supplies, the biggest and best in these parts. We made the twenty-mile drive a month ago, every apprentice coming along for the experience—we were all "going to learn plumbing." There are fewer of us now; in fact Sophie fits the water pipes alone while Petra and I soldier on finishing the walls.

It is a hot August lunch, and still no Kim. Then an afternoon without her, only the sight of her taking a walk. Tomorrow she'll be better; you must be patient. Sophie is terrified she'll leave. And we need Kim so now to keep going. Maybe she needs it, too, to go back to work, not to let it beat her, to keep trying. Remember, she has never tried to do anything this hard in her life. Only Sophie keeps her here; Kim is angry with me, and only her loyalty to Sophie's cause in saving me from destroying myself and the place with me—only that keeps her with us.

But the tie is slipping. It must occur to her by now that perhaps Sophie is wrong to stay with someone so unstable as I am, wrong to go on slogging away at her pipes. Working for a mere house when the place is too empty to be amusing anymore, alive as it was before with all the others. Now there are not enough to swim with, to play with, to gossip with in the grass on long towel-strewn Sunday afternoons, with drinks tinkling in cold glasses as the tray is brought down from the farmhouse, and the shout goes up for iced tea or beer or bring down a bottle of wine, too, and some more glasses, it's late enough to open one now, and bring suntan lotion, better bring the Cutter's 'cause the mosquitoes are out, who has the book section, are you done with the theater section? It's all gone. Only this dogged attempt to finish something, to end up having something, even if it's not fully habitable. Even if one might just as well let it go until spring. Surely it is academic to try to get any further now. Why not silk-screen or mow or just relax? It's the end of summer, nearly everyone's gone—why keep hammering away at the thing? Yes, I know that siren call and hear it in my mind all day, observing Kim's nature hikes, wondering if she'll hold a hammer tomorrow morning.

Kim did leave. What follows is the text of a tape she left for me, which she had made quite a few days earlier, while still deciding whether to stay or go:

This is perhaps my last present to you. It's a tape of everything that I wanted to say to you in the last few days, the last couple of weeks. That you haven't been able to hear. Partly it's because you think that I don't care enough about you, that I don't respect you enough. And that what I say isn't worthwhile, or that I'm too young to really know anything. But I think I do know something. And I've experienced some very important things here that I wanted to share with you. Because I don't feel that right now . . . you're really the Kate Millett that I knew in the beginning. And that a whole lot of other people must know.

I wanted to share with you some of my journal selections, my reactions to you and to the farm and the other women here while I've been here. And to try to give you some perspective on what the apprentices are really like, and what we really think. Because right now you are really wrapped up in how you perceive us, how you've been hurt, what we came here for in your eyes. And they are not the same thing.

Tuesday June seventeenth: The greens of pine trees, oaks, wild grasses and fields of woods gather themselves before me through this open window of a barn. I sit at a small table of dusty unpolished wood and a window with no pane, shutters bent off, not meeting, open to the sun. This used to be a chicken coop, I hear, but the bare walls and ceiling have been scrubbed clean. The foam mattress lies on the floor and besides this desk and chair and a huge long weathered table, there are only empty picture frames on the wall and a rocker without a seat. The sun shines down on me through the window and still it's after six. An evening of birds—I must learn their names—singing choruses from the trees. The pond lies down to my left. . . . We can come and go as we like here, passing from work into talk into art into silence. We all await Kate and Sophie's return from a trip to the city. Someone just now calls out—hey, here they are—and we go. An hour later a new set of people sit by the pond, the sun now just a yellow globe behind the trees on the hill. Kate

Millett becomes Kate, a funny older woman trying to sell her art and make life interesting for herself and her friends. We become the "kids" with Mom—Sophie. We become artists sharing what we have learned and are learning, lesbians and feminists. . . .

We launch into dinner from the kitchen, talk again about the afternoon and yesterday in the streets of the city. An interesting conversation. We sit at the table arguing and talking around the point of violence and women. Sophie is kind in coming to the point, wanting to hear Lauren's and Sandy's militant positions as they are felt individually. I go on about women needing to express their anger in ways that are neither self-destructive nor externally destructive—my thesis. And I am heard. And Kate goes on in wonderful melodic discussion of our history, how to accept changes slowly and gracefully and yet not compromise our values. To confront the anonymous but autonomous man on the street who is hassling us, trying to buy or beg power. And we try not to kill but to reason, make sense of all these unintelligent senses. . . .

The next Thursday night—I'll remember that always—Punk Night. And you were the whore from Forty-second Street with your pimp. Hilarious. We thought we'd scare the girl from the Laundromat to death with our antics. You were familiar with us and so we were familiar with you. You were Ma. No, you weren't the university professor—we didn't come to be with a university professor. I left my life back at Stanford for that. I came because you are an artist, because you are a scholar, because you are a feminist. And certainly not because you are a celebrity. I came because I could learn carpentry, I could learn mechanics, I could learn the silk screen method, learn to write. I could learn to be strong. And I've learned all those things.

A sigh.

And what has happened to you? Well, I found out . . . one of the problems we had seen over the last week was that you were coming off lithium. Because you and Sophie had begun to argue late at night and we heard. Sometimes in the morning, we heard the shouts. . . . It had been the night of Lauren's music performance, when we all argued together and you were so bitter about how musicians were treated and went on and on. And that became an argument about how the apprentices were treating your house. That night, I remember trying to tell you that it was only because we came here and didn't understand some of the rules of the house, things that you take for granted: how to treat a Persian rug, where we leave our shoes, how to do the dishes, when to get up in the morning, when to arrive at a meal. We all came from different backgrounds. If there are certain things you want to have happen in your house, you need to make your apprentices sure of that from the beginning. That's easy, easy enough for us to do. You're an anarchist or something and wanted us to figure out all those things by ourselves, and then got impatient when we didn't know already.

So Friday the eleventh: I had my driving lesson. And that weekend your sister Mallory came and your friends Petra and Dakota. And you gave them all prints. I wasn't around much. But Sunday night you gave us prints and you started in on your lecture about being a university professor, and how we didn't give you enough respect and how we treated the house badly. You were giving us these presents, these beautiful prints, and scaring us with your anger. And we thought, what have we done so wrong? We came here to be with you, to learn from you. And we've become these children—nasty, negligent, ignorant. And we're not that.

And then the grand arguments over dinner began. And by Tuesday night, Sophie was trying to get you to take the lithium again. Because you had spent all of Monday night up sleepless, talking. You had begun laughing to yourself. Talking, talking. Brilliant talk, everything connected—from the way a ceramic pot looks to Japanese philosophy to American politics to your childhood. Everything connects, yes—but I suppose there's a time and a place for everything. And if you wanted to give us lectures, and if we wanted to hear them, then there would have to be a better time and place . . . than when we're trying to hammer a nail into a board or something. I'm afraid as I say this that you'll misunderstand, but it's not practical.

Before Lauren left this weekend, I was trying to get all of us together to talk into a tape. I wanted to be together with the remaining apprentices—we think of ourselves as the stalwarts of this family—and prepare for ourselves and for you a memorial of our experiences here. Memory is so important—or have you forgotten? I can come to cynicism very easily, too. You are so unreachable these days. You say that we do not respect you, that we have insulted you all the time, that we are ignorant because of our youth. And in these accusations and in others, there is some truth. We have been negligent and silly. So perhaps have you. But we have never been disrespectful or malicious. . . .

I'd like to read you a story I wrote, I think a week ago.

". . . We sit down to eat and the phone rings. Kate makes some comment about the salt and pepper not being on the table. Charging us with not taking care of things, the melon rotten for not being in the refrigerator—'You're either a melon head or a spoiled rich kid,' she said to me this afternoon, wanting to throw the melon out. 'Choose!' I could laugh that off. The butter thrown away because left out too long. Never mind how well she copes with and cares for the chores to be done here—how blind she is to herself. And should we provide the least complaint she would fire back with intimidation, call us disrespectful, something.

"So a few moments later, over silence, the phone rings again. This is too much. Kate charges out of her chair screaming, and answers with some control: 'Hello—she's not here. No, I don't know where she went.' Slams it down. Comes ranting back to the table complaining about this stupid bitch, Gretchen's little friend, who calls her on Kate's phone. . . . The words sear me. The hypocrisy: Kate, who knows how to love and give, has shown us this side of her and instead wants us to hate her through her own anger. Hate her? This madness. For what? We can't be sure. Oh, please come back. I take my plate and hurry off to eat alone. Yes, it's sad to eat alone, no one to talk to, slow down the hurried pace that is mine after years of jumping up from the family table. Do you not remember my story about my mother, her anger that has consumed her . . . consumed most of me until I could get free, struggle for my own sense of self? Remember and let it free you. And us. My friend, the farm awaits us. Our work and love.''

And you said tonight, something about our having minds of our own— as if we shouldn't—if we dare to spend a few hours with ourselves: writing, reading, being with each other, being the artists that we came here to share with you. The reading that I gave here was the first one I've ever given. And I loved basking in people's praise. I loved speaking the words of my poetry and perhaps seeing them move people . . . you gave me that opportunity, of course I'm grateful—and I'll hold on to it, the happy memories. Tonight you were so tired. You called yourself an old woman at forty-five. Nothing we said could be quite right enough; you had already decided we had done you wrong, and that was that. It's also strange for me to see somebody behaving this way.

Laughter, then a sigh.

It does seem self-indulgent, but it's also balanced with Kate the civil rights activist, Kate the New York artist, Kate the feminist at large; it must be confusing. I think I have a lot more to say—but I think you will be angry at what I'm saying anyhow—and so I'll finish soon. . . .

Here someone seems to enter the room and the pronoun changes from the second to the third person, the tape beginning midsentence:

—is that she acts like she's being really persecuted by all of us, while she's persecuting us and getting down on us for being twenty and what . . .

The other person in the room turns out to be Libby. And the conversation drifts into one between them, unintelligible until Kim asks Libby to speak louder and her voice booms into the tape, Libby seeming to address me through the tape recorder:

You don't even have to ask permission, all you have to do is talk, all you have to do is hear, all you have to do is love. It's not the sob that takes the breath out of you because you've been crying so hard and you can't breathe and cry so hard at the same time. Sophie, your lover, is just as unhappy.
Why? 'Cause of you, your affliction.

Libby's voice loud in the tape. Kim bursts in.

I don't understand the morbidity of it, the enjoyment of being hurt and hurting others. I mean, everything Kate's inflicted on us, hurting others, is really just being hurt by others.

Then Libby:

You know, it was like being out in the storm, like when Kate screamed at us that the windows were open in the barn. She would come up here and then she'd rest. Once she came up here tired and she said, "Hello, you ladies, hello you high ladies." Even in the craziest fits she came up and into the lavender and I gave her a massage and I put all the love I could into my hands and she cried and she cried. I just looked at her with as much love as I could put into my eyes and then she cried and she said, "You don't know how you have pleased me." I touched her more gently than I have ever touched anyone. Don't ask what quibble can justify our actions—how are we to understand what we do?

Kim interrupts:

Don't you understand that Kate is crazy?

Libby says:

Not crazy, not Kate. She's not crazy.

Kim says:

That twistedness, that's the thing. I think with the type of mind-set that she had—like tonight, sitting there being so bummed out on the world and on herself. To me that's only crazy 'cause that's not natural. I don't know the other Kate well enough to know if this is a regular part of her evening's entertainment, self-entertainment. But it's not natural to be so full of despair—

Libby interrupts:

I've got to go now. Okay?

The tape is shut off and begins again. Kim's voice:

It's next morning, I don't even know what time it is. Many of us think that the problem has largely been that Sheila has been around all the time, giving you a pair of ears. And the adoration that you so desperately feel you need to keep you talking. And to divide you from us. Yes, this is very complicated; there are many levels of conspiracy going on here. There were a couple of days during the last week here when you were euphoric about being here, about being an artist, about the work we were doing. You were bursting with plans; you almost drove me crazy: here's a project, and here's a project, and you can do that, and you're capable of this. And I enjoyed knowing I could do so many things, that I could put so much energy into this farm and build it with you.

And then Sheila came back and the division started again. I don't know if she's whispering to you that we're doing this against you and also that Sophie's pulling us away from you. And none of that is true. We came here to be with you and it's only under the circumstances of your chang-ing behavior that we pull away and wonder why you are so angry. One morning you said we are disrespectful and that you wish you had more respect from us. Libby tried to explain why she is leaving. Sophie asks me to explain. But I can't, I have no words anymore. I don't wish to put forth any words for you to talk down and to interpret however you want to. You will look into your cup of coffee and mumble something. And I just don't need that anymore. . . .

I said to you last night, "My mother is happier than you and she's not even a liberated woman." And I remember thinking that in the beginning—that for a liberated woman you sure need a lot of liberation. Because you seem so attached to all of your fears and hatreds that you had, growing up, against one parent or against another. Against the art world, against the feminist world—you've attached yourself to those things and you seem to suck life from them and death from them at the same time. And now you're so big on us being disrespectful, that this is a paradise and we're ruining it because we're too self-indulgent, and we're too self-important. . . .

Well, it is a paradise. Remember my first journal selection—I was in paradise! I couldn't imagine anywhere else in the world that I'd rather be. And I still feel that way, this moment of my departure. God, I would love to get up in the morning, sip my cup of coffee, and sit at the breakfast table and listen to that chat, whether it's about love or the interests of sick people, hear the list that you can read so brightly—our little addendums of the day's chores—and come into the purple barn and put Sheetrock on the ceiling or fix a window frame. There's so much to do here: sanding down the floors, the mudding and taping we've never even started, fixing up the first floor, the kitchen, turning it into a real room. There's more mowing on the tractor to do, and the Gravely. There's days I wanted to spend taking pictures of this farm, taking them back to my women's center friends and showing them what a community of women can do. And someday I will. Because someday we will.

I don't know, if we leave—if you're going to change. But something that's always bothered me about this is that it's not, to me, as feminist an endeavor as it sounded like in the letter we got when we agreed to come here. And I don't know if it's just because you're on this little trip now about how we hurt you and we're doing this to you—and this is your place. But that whole possessiveness is never going to work out with any artist who comes here, if it's continually your place. We can share in your place; you can make it part of us. And we can have no less respect for this silk screen studio, for the barn, for the property. We can take care of things if you'll trust us that much.

I don't want this to end—the letters I wrote home, so full of praise, love, excitement—not only about you and the farm and the other women here but about the changes I was making in myself . . . I was so excited about the work I was doing, working hard every day out there, mowing and feeling the muscles in my back pulling, moving the tractors, learning how to drive them. Learning to use my hands in ways that I never thought possible. Walking around without a shirt, to me a sign of shucking off the society that says I can't do this, that says my breasts are indecent, that says I must be constrained. I'm trembling from thinking about it. So many joys from being here and living here. You were such an integral part of it. And now when you turn against me, and I am nothing but a twenty-year-old who has no respect, I'm hurt again and again and can't stay either. I didn't want to lose respect for you, respect I still have. As Libby said, "I'll respect you to your face." But not when you're mumbling about how much I hate you and don't care about your presents—all of them—from the softball bats to the farm to the books, to the prints, to the philosophy, and the years of scholarship and artwork. I respect it all. The only thing that's crazy—it is that you don't see that. That's all.

An afterthought. Shit—how you go off with that *your* farm and *your* barn and *your* being the artist here! I write. We paint, we draw, we sculpt. We create. How can you say that? That's against your own principle, my dear. And I sit here and I think: I put this little bureau together out of two milk crates. And I fixed that chair. I pulled those prints. I mowed that field, put up that Sheetrock. And none of that matters.

We only have a few moments left—the car is ready to go. I'll be back tomorrow night, Monday. And I guess I'll decide then whether I want to stay, whether you want me to stay or not. This morning you were talking about preparing a document. You read it at breakfast, the petition; it's wonderful hard language, strong, angry. You are the Kate that I love, that I care for, that I want to work for. See you tomorrow.

A youngster's truth—how deftly it accuses me. But the colony, devastated hope. My being crazy has just blitzed the colony, done in the dream. If only no one had told them I was mad. Then I wouldn't be. They wouldn't imagine it and act accordingly, nor I take exception to their manner, alienating them further. Nor would I have been so vexed and irritated that I probably was crazed. Interesting how they dislike Sheila and Petra, who "encourage" me by treating me as sane. In their company I am calm, rational, at ease. But the moment I am approached with that hesitant, vaguely patronizing, coaxing firmness reserved for children and for maniacs, I become terse, short-tempered, cynical, sarcastic, impatient, annoyed—all sane responses perhaps, but in the context they are seen as positive and irrefutable evidence. Stuck with this label, picked to be "it," anyone could be manipulated into position, squirming for credibility, looking in all directions at once for safety, for escape from the approaching net. One could make a scenario of it—it is like a game, a malicious game.

But this confounded game—which is not a game but a nightmare and real—has lost me my colony, my beloved youngsters. For I have loved them far more than they loved me, in the moments they did. And the moments I didn't love them—only moments—tripping over their shoes or something—they spent days disliking me for. I had hoped to be loved in return, to have a whole circle about me; for years, this bunch, other bunches, as they grew older and closer to me in age, closer friends as well. Instead I am left with the humiliation of their leaving early, walking out. Not only on me but on the job, which will fail now, which was too much to do alone, to build a whole colony for women without other women to help—and all because of this craziness shit. It would be easy to trace it back to Sophie, mastermind of the insanity plot, or its chief believer; but she too is aghast as they leave. Though she predicted it, warned me about my behavior, how inevitable it was that they "wouldn't stand for my temper." The temper being provoked and the apprentices, of course, refusing to stand for it—how many private conversations with them went into that? But the way is prepared through her dismal prognosis, through the enormity of this illness, the folly of refusing treatment, the classically self-destructive character of all my doings, which follow the doctor's blueprints to the letter.

But there is still something about Sophie that I refuse to stop protecting —the brutality she herself endured in the belly of the beast, and the fact that the beast is behind all that has happened. Hers is a role already laid out: the hand-wringing spouse trying desperately to understand what the doctors say, follow their guidance, obey instructions, while torn between their orders, their way of seeing, and the culprit, myself, or any appointed crazy who is trying to evade the net. Out of her loyalty she has still not turned me in. Out of her credulity she has also made my life a ruin. It has cost all this; the last apprentice has gone—but still I believe I can win. Someone can win sometime, thereafter everyone can.

17

I come into the third-floor studio on the Bowery. The look of a place abandoned for a summer. A little dusty, but how dear it is, this old place; here I have made all the sculpture of the last five years, all the photographs and prints, the thousands of drawings. This place that I redeemed from darkness and the grime of a century, painting it over and over. Even the fourteen-foot ceiling, the one thing I could not do alone; going at it with two boys from NYU in the heat of early September, the three of us painting and drinking beer, becoming friends. It is that same time of year now; the summer is over, the fall is ahead: Europe, shows, speeches.

I go first to St. Paul to see my mother and my aunt, then I stop back in New York only a day to join Petra and fly to Amsterdam. There is so much to do, so little time. And here's a pile of mail that never got forwarded—bills, even. Here's old Con Ed—pay it right away. Pay everything you can, get this all straightened out before you leave.

I see the chasm ahead—I'm nearly broke; the money for this trip is about all there is left in the bank. Building the lavender barn has wiped me out. It happened so gradually, like the stages of a gambler's hopes; you throw in some, you throw in more to cover the first loss, recoup. But there is no recouping, and the barn stands there still unfinished. This must happen all the time in building, but I never suspected. I have nothing left. Selling prints in Europe is pin money; there'll be nothing to live on when I come home.

Sophie has gone to meet some UN guy about helping a friend's nephew, who wandered into Cuban waters sailing and got himself imprisoned by Castro. There will be a few moments to concentrate before she gets back. These are the bills. How on earth did the phone bill get like that? But, whoever made these calls, you're going to have to pay them; it's your credit. Read the damn thing carefully. My hands are shaking with the fury of a culprit finally facing the brown envelope and the cheery blue and white form. Surely setting up a show in Europe shouldn't cost this much—how many pictures could we ever sell? Good God, I'll be paying this the rest of my life. When did I ever call California? Who else has been using long distance? I don't even know anyone in Philadelphia.

The door flies open. The lock's cumbersome and it's impossible to open it fast—it hasn't flown open in seven years. I turn around, startled to see Sophie back so soon. And there are others with her: Janey Washburn, one of my oldest friends, and Mallory, my own younger sister. How delightful it seems for an instant—a chance to say goodbye before I leave for St. Paul. I have seen each of them only once over the course of the summer. There is a stranger with them too—a woman I have never seen before. They look odd, an odd tense look about them—inspiring fear. Is there something the matter with Mother? I wonder. But then I am to see her in a few hours, eat at her table tonight.

There is no time to think, only the animal impulse of terror produced by something in their bearing, body language; the cast of their shoulders, the flinch in their eyes. And no natural greeting—the hugs and kisses and arms outstretched, the laughter that would follow any meeting between us. "I thought you went to Phoebe's to meet—" "But guess who was there? Janey, Mallory." Not very likely, I would think; they both now live in other corners of town and would not be apt to meet except on my account. Which it seems they have.

Whereupon the stranger. A doctor. A friend of Phyllis Gibson's. I remember I was to dine with Phyllis the night before last and had to excuse myself since I needed the time to finish business at the farm. Curious revenge to send me a shrink, not just a psychologist like Phyllis herself but a psychiatrist. That sort of doctor.

Therefore a bust. They have come to make a bust. But they call it "talking." My legs shake. The terror in my mind is like a machine out of order. But I must talk. I must look good. I must answer the trick questions perfectly. Maybe I can dissuade them. A bust is an examination—which I am fool enough always to imagine I can pass. A lifetime of passing tests has never prepared me for the kind that are rigged, for the ones that cannot be passed, were not meant to be. But I can tape-record it. I will have at least that defense against them—for they are four against one and I could never fight my way out of here; the moment the door is closed behind them I realize I am a prisoner in my own studio and may never leave here alone or free again. Fear oozes out of the pores of my mind, from my terrified, shaking hands, which manage to find the machine in my luggage and unwrap a tape. I let them see what I do, putting it on the work table where I had been paying bills, inviting them to sit, using my waning power as hostess, Sophie having preempted that role just as she has either organized or gone along with this—their arrival, the trap. How many phone calls did this take to put together? I wonder.

They begin by worrying over my finances. The psychiatrist has heard from my friends that I am spending too much money. I face the inquisition and begin explaining myself: "It wasn't much money to start with but it seems most of it was spent on the phone. I'll show you the figures." "Most of it's phone bills?" "Well, no, I'm teasing, but to get various royalties and stuff, calling Europe I risked about sixty bucks on the phone to locate about sixteen hundred." I begin again. She interrupts me. I interrupt her: "Can I explain that the money is three months late and the middleman is playing with it for the interest?" The doctor: "One of the things that is happening right now is that I was told, you know, such and such a thing—and here you are defending yourself." "Yeah, I was trying to explain. Because you've cornered me in my studio and I am trying to catch a plane." "But why are you defending yourself?" "Man, when you get called crazy a whole lot of times, you get defensive. Because it's pretty offensive—in fact it's aggression—to lock somebody up. I run my own life and I don't need an analyst or a therapist."

This doctor is much younger than I am, by maybe twenty years, fresh out of medical school. Why not tell her what I think—it might work— challenge it all: "At the next level up are psychiatrists, who have doctor's licenses tantamount to police powers, 'cause they can lock you up and feed you Thorazine. I've worked in the area of civil rights for mental patients"—so does she, she probably imagines (Phyllis, who sent her, certainly does) "in fact since I was eighteen years old. You chickened out," I add, turning to Janey, "but we were all going to go out and save the world together. I worked in St. Peter's Asylum the summer after freshman year. You went to California instead that summer, Janey." Janey sits before me, white, nervous—so are they all; the strain and ambiguity of their appointed task seem to exhaust them. Most of all they avoid contact with me, each staring at me yet refusing to make contact with my eyes.

The doctor: "You two have known each other a long time." "Yup—twenty-seven years or something. Janey likes to brag that we're each other's oldest friends, but she's not a very good friend at this moment." Janey's face is hurt, uncertain. She had imagined in coming here she was doing a yeoman's duty as a friend: one concerned, worried, anxious to help, consulted in crisis and unafraid, staunch. The moment my words are out I regret them.

The doctor tries again. "Kate, some of the things people have been telling me that have been happening to you recently . . ." "Well, they're rumor and superstition." I look around the room; only Sophie has been with me continuously; Mallory visited the farm for a day two months ago, Janey for a day one month ago; the doctor and I are total strangers—what has she to go on? I settle in and ask Sophie to pass me an ashtray. The doctor goes on: "I feel if I were to run down a list of them . . ." "It would be hilarious," I suggest. The doctor: "Well, what I would be doing is—might seem a process of accusing." "You are, I agree." "And I don't want—" "Well, you are. And they are accusations that one is non compos mentis. And believe me, lady, I have a fine mind."

"You're one of the most articulate people I've run across." Derisive laughter. I hate this phrase, I hate the word "articulate." "You mean I speak well; the English language is my métier. But 'métier' is French. I don't know if the word is familiar to you." The doctor: "Well, some of us must have had an education." "I learned it on the river, the Mississippi. You know, it all once belonged to French culture—Napoleon once imagined he owned it and sold it to the Yankee bastards for one million dollars. Can you imagine that as a real estate deal?" The doctor tries to bring me back to concentrate on her issue: "Kate, how can we talk about this?" "Imagine—all the way from Canada down to New

Orleans.'' The doctor again: "How can we talk about this?''—a mysterious phrase like many learned in her training. "I'm just speaking in terms of American history, in terms of culture. You know, we're from the river, the Mississippi; the top of it is St. Paul and the bottom of it is New Orleans. Probably you're aware that New Orleans is French culture. Well, I'm from St. Paul.'' In thirty-five minutes the cab should leave; don't forget the mail on the table. I will be there tonight. I can watch the river come into view as we land, and cry, remembering one landing years ago with Turnbull's biography of Fitzgerald in my lap; I had just read of his ruin, and looked up to see the river again and felt that I belonged to it, was grabbed and claimed.

The doctor umms, ready to begin again. "Does that register on you?'' I ask, trying to hang on to terms that mean something to me before I am swept into hers, the trap. "I'm speaking now in terms of culture.'' "I've never been to that area,'' she says, actually answering my question. "Well, you might learn something. People laugh about it as a hick town, you know, the Middle West—it's a joke at cocktail parties. I've had twenty-five years of that in this burg.'' Janey squirms. We always talk about going home, why I do it, why she won't, but not in this kind of context, not before this sort of audience—so inappropriate. The nervousness Janey always exhibits when I am leaving for home is present perhaps—they all must think if I go to St. Paul today I will certainly be jailed out there, away from them, from their power to "help'' me by jailing me here. Right now. Right here in Manhattan, where I'm easy to visit and they are completely in charge. One feels the possessiveness, that it should be they, New Yorkers, friends, fellow artists, peers in age and interest, who should hold you captive, not others whom they cannot trust. They trust themselves perfectly. Then why are they all so anxious, so guilty before the crime they have undertaken? They know it's dirty pool, have known that since the unsullied ethic of childhood. In college we still knew this, that you didn't turn someone in; blue cops or white cops.

The doctor returns to the issue: "Ah, but I'm wondering how you'd talk about this . . .'' My voice grows definite: "I'm going to St. Paul to see my mother. And I've missed one plane already because I had so much business at the farm. But there is a four o'clock plane. So we can't talk very long because I must leave here at three. So what is it you want to say to me and why are you people here?'' The doctor: "I'd like to tell you that.'' "Good, I'm listening.'' The doctor: "I'd also like to find a way of our talking about it . . . in such a way that I'm not in effect . . . you know, that this is not my reading a list of transgressions to you." Out of this mishmash I relish the word "transgressions"—not bad. "While trespassing in my studio?" I smile. I offer her a cold drink and she responds: "I'm not your guest. I was asked to come here by your friends and family." "Back to Star Chamber," I say, the phrase passing over everyone except perhaps Sophie. "I don't know why we can't talk about this," the doctor goes on in a whining New York accent. "I don't know why we have to," I reply. The deceptive simplistic jargon of the profession, "talk about," sounds so harmless; the moment one agrees to begin one is convicted. "What are you supposed to do here, certify me? What is your name and what are your degrees?" "I'm an M.D." "So you're a psychiatrist?" As I had feared and suspected, she is no mere therapist with a Ph.D. or an M.A. in psychology—this one has the hunting license. "So you could call an ambulance and get me slammed?" "Right," she says. She preens, for the first time now not a little girl, not a junior scholar, not a feminist foot soldier, but a general who could take me in tow as her captive and patient. The wonder, the frisson, the excitement in her approach to me now. Intimidation gives way to power. Her moment. "Well, Jesus Christ, I'll just call a lawyer." "But there's no telephone," the voices chorus around me. I turn, furious and in panic, to the others—the phone on this floor has been disconnected all summer. Looking at Sophie, I wonder how much she knew. I know this is hopeless, but I start to explain to the others anyway: "I'm on my way to catch an airplane and she shows up with you guys. Look, Sophie said to me—and I guess she lied—that she'd been going to see some high-mucka-muck Palestinian official in the UN because we have a friend whose nephew got lost and arrested in Cuban waters all the way back in seventy-nine. Sophie was at Phoebe's enlisting this man's help." The doctor intervenes to clarify: "Sophie said she has a friend who's in jail." So Sophie did at least mention her excuse to the posse.

"Who arranged this?" I ask. Sophie's voice: "I called this doctor last night and I spoke to Phyllis also." "How dirty, behind my back." "Yes, Kate." "How tacky." "Yes." "Kate," the doctor begins with patient exasperation. The others chime in. I dread the return of the doctor's jargon and babble—let's get to the point. "Well, what's the subject?" I challenge her. "Am I going to get committed?" "The subject is why we're here," Mallory explains heavily in a patient euphemism, "what we want to say to you . . ." "Why not just say it? Go ahead, I'll get a match.'' I cross over to the front nearer the door—the chairs and the opposition are near the back of the room. Only Sophie is smart enough, has instinct enough to notice. The way to the door is still clear.

The doctor de-escalates to civilian terms: ''Kate, you feel your life is going along smoothly enough, despite money problems and certain vicissitudes, such as, you know, money problems, right now?'' ''I paid all my checks today, I don't owe anybody hardly anything.''

An optimistic view of things, but my affairs are mine, not hers. The doctor tries to place me in the usual way: ''Would you please sit down?'' ''I prefer to talk standing up.'' ''It's making me uncomfortable,'' she moans as if my freedom of movement were an offense against her. ''Please sit down''—an order. ''Well, I have all that mail to attend to—I'd like to read my mail instead.'' She asks me again. I accede, protesting: ''But I don't think you understand, I'm very busy—I have a professional reading to do at the University of Minnesota tomorrow night, and I have to type my manuscript. I also have a couple of gigs, paying ones, at the University of Missouri and at St. Louis, on the river both of them, and I want to get out of here because I have a plane to catch. Because I'm earning a living.''

''Kate,'' the doctor keeps insisting in her little voice, ''Kate, what if . . .'' ''What if what?'' I turn on her, this kid, this nuisance, this obstacle. The others butt in: I should listen. The doctor explains that she finds it hard to ''deal with'' this because . . . Everyone talks at once. The doctor finally announces her name, Dr. Pulp. It seems to suit her. ''What if, God forbid, you made a mistake, what if there are things that you are doing that are endangering yourself, not at this moment but in general, what if there are things that are fucking up your life?'' ''Look, this is really a kind of theater. You're a doctor, I'm a doctor—a doctor of philosophy. What is it you think I'm doing that is fucking up my life? And what does Dr. Phyllis Gibson think? Because I am too busy to see her for dinner—I was supposed to go over and have a good chitchat with her. But I got these goddamned horses.'' Exasperated laugh at how they have complicated everything at the farm and how this morning's plane to St. Paul was missed because the two imps of ponies got away out of the fence and ended up in the backyard again.

''I get the impression it was hard for you to leave the farm.'' ''You're damn right. It's a beautiful place. I love it—it's my home.'' The doctor persists: ''Okay, what about your life do you really hate the most?'' Of course it is the very accusation of insanity that has brought her here: "I don't think there's anything. But I must say it pisses me off when people start saying they're 'worried' about me and pretty soon they get a real strong hand on me. I was beaten up in California when my big sister Sally had me slammed."

My little sister Mallory sits in uncomfortable glory in what is her bid to jail me—will this create family balance? I wonder. Mallory, who is so skittish herself, the flighty actress sister now sitting in judgment as part of the tribunal. Family feeling and squabble venting itself: I am still angry with Sally for turning me over to a machinery she could never control once she had set it in motion. It was probably never her plan that two hefty ambulance drivers would pin me to the floor of a parking lot; having threatened to break my right arm, they seemed to be making it good on every bone of my body as she stood watching. So did Sita. So did Fumio.

The doctor oozes succulent self-satisfaction: "It's a terrible position to be in." The one who commits another—how often has she already partaken of this dirty business? This "terrible position" phrase becomes my clue: this youngster is really going to try to bust me. I look at Mallory—next of kin. They would need her signature—there could be no success without Mallory. The doctor follows her bone: "What in your life would you most hate to part with?" My freedom, of course, but I prefer not to mention that. Instead I make it the next gig: "I have professional commitments, contractual obligations." Try that shtick— it's a reality; the airline ticket home is my only payment for the reading in Minneapolis. Then Europe, then the end of these screwball American rituals of psychiatric medication, therapy, the junior high school quiz I am presently subjected to.

"Your professional reputation, is that what you mean?" "Yes." "Of all the things in your life right now, the thing that you treasure most is your professional reputation?" Absurd question. Sophie is here in the room. The farm, even the silly horses are dearer to me than this absurd phrase. "No, that's just the immediate problem. It's past two o'clock and I have a four o'clock plane. Unless my watch stopped—does anybody have the time?" It's confirmed by the others.

"The only thing I'm concerned with right now is I don't want to be a no-show tomorrow evening," I tell her, Princeton on my mind. "I understand that happened recently," she says. This is the wedge; this story has made the rounds—you could be put away for being thirty minutes late at Princeton. I begin to explain that I did go and I did speak, but there was no contract, the thing arranged by a friend. "The money was allocated by the university and it went through the women's center, who are acting as if the grant were their own funds and absconding with my fee." The doctor: "I understand there were problems . . ." "Can I finish? Petra and I were driving down to Princeton from Poughkeepsie, which is a three-hour drive. We called to apologize for missing the honorary dinner, which turned out to be a chicken sandwich at the women's center." General merriment. I go on justifying myself to the cabal—because it is Princeton that has got me in this mess. Since I have never missed a speech or even been late to one, the word spread: more gossip. Gibson probably heard, even Washburn, then Mallory. Sophie at the core—but she knew the reason I was late was simply because I had followed Princeton's own set of directions. "But the women's center held a little consensus—now remember I had phoned ahead, had warned them I'd be late—that means I'm okay under a contract. But they had decided somehow that I'm a no-show and so they folded up tent. I'm just a block away and they're saying it's over. I did talk before a few students and two faculty witnesses, and the dean has, I think, agreed that I have fulfilled my contractual responsibilities."

"Kate, what if you're wrong?" "I was—I made a mistake on the road. But speakers never have to drive themselves to speeches. Unfortunately Petra doesn't drive." "Kate, what if you're wrong, what if there's more to it than just the wrong turn? What if there's something going on with you?" "I should have requested a plane, to tell you the truth. I should have asked for the Command Airways flight into La Guardia and students to meet me there. But I was dealing with friends. Every other time I've spoken at Princeton they always came into New York and picked me up. So I wouldn't be out there bollixed up on the New Jersey Turnpike at five o'clock." "What if you're wrong?" "What if I'm what?" "Wrong." "Well, then, I'm wrong. Are you right?"

The others are restless; they had expected more. I go nearer to the little doctor. "What's your first name?" "Marilou." "Where did you study?" "Wellesley College." "How old are you?" "Thirty-six." "That old, really?" I say, surprised; the coy adolescence of this person had made me wonder if she even had time to do a degree in medicine. "On a good day I still look thirty," she laughs, again the child.

"Kate, I'm getting worried": the doctor returns to her guns. "I'm getting worried." The ominous word. "And what are you so worried about? Sophie's worried that they'll bust me at home, and I keep saying my lawyer there already got me off an insanity charge, which is a tough rap to beat.'' Irreverence clearly won't do it. "My mother just wanted me to take lithium, but she still had me committed out there—come on, it's an outpatient drug.'' The doctor aims and fires: "It is for people who are cooperative.'' "Well, if I'm not cooperative you're going to slam me, is that what you're threatening? Jesus Christ, are you going to make me miss lectures? I need the money—how dare you? My mother awaits me; maybe I should call her up and have her ransom me.''

Good humor won't do it either—let's try the coin of reality. "Do you charge? What are you charging? Are you charging me or them?'' General mortification at this grossness. "We're just presenting . . .'' Mallory explains in an embarrassed voice. "Well, let's figure out who's buying it. Who's paying you?'' Wonderful moment of confrontation. They clearly haven't gone into this. Washburn, Sophie, and Mallory have never laid eyes on this person before; the detail of which one of them has employed her has not yet been broached. Only the doctor keeps her cool: "I had assumed that Mallory would,'' the doctor says blandly. Of course, next of kin, the power of the signature for commitment. "Well, what are you paying her?'' I ask, looking over at Mallory, who is entirely uncomfortable. "What does she charge per hour? What's your fee?'' "That isn't important right now,'' Mallory says, rising above the occasion financially and assuming her full powers. "Well, who found her?'' "Phyllis,'' the others chorus, having taken this for a guarantee. "You're taking up my time,'' I say, "and you've hired her to do it for you. What is it you're really paying her for?'' "Kate,'' the doctor's tired, patient little voice goes on.

"Mallory believes in astrology too,'' I point out. "I'm an age-of-reason type.'' Mallory assumes her role as the employer: "Kate, none of this is the point—the point is, what I mean is, the point is your condition . . .'' "My condition has changed drastically in the last couple of months: I've felt better. I don't have diarrhea and I don't have hand tremor.'' I have it now though, but to be this nervous at the threat of force is hardly unusual. "She's saying she has the power to commit me to an insane asylum against my will, and all my civil rights will be abrogated at once.'' "You can go voluntarily,'' two voices say together. "I'm not going anywhere—there is no forced hospitalization'': reciting the law, imagining it is obeyed. "But if you go voluntarily''— Mallory's voice hesitant, full of diabolic purpose—"to a hospital.'' "I am already going voluntarily to a good doctor,'' I say, hoping my blood test might satisfy them, "and out in St. Paul, I'll get another blood level.'' "We can postpone the lectures,'' Sophie urges. They are now beginning to spring the trap. "Stay here with us,'' they say; we'll put you away. "Goddamnit to hell, stop doing this to me.''

My inner clock dictates that thirty minutes have passed and it's about time to turn over the tape, and I do so before their eyes though they fail to notice. Then I make the apologetic motions of one getting ready to leave. I have my speech in Minneapolis tomorrow night on my mind, plane schedules, luggage, my mother. "So, since we are all tired, and seeing that I have to leave . . .''

"Kate, do you understand that we're here because we love you?'' A chorus seconds this sentiment. The doctor doesn't know me from Adam. "It sounds like a disease—to have people love you who are paying money to hold you up when you're trying to catch an airplane.'' "But we're your own family, we want to talk'': Mallory's voice. "Mallory, anyone who ever got locked up in St. Peter's Asylum was locked up by their relatives—who all claimed they loved them. Actually, in those days, they used to be a little more forthright. They just put 'em away. They'd put a woman away 'cause she wouldn't wash the dishes. These were farmers. I took care of those old women who had been put away. And the light dying in their eyes. You bet they withdrew. They withdrew into utter fantasy, really mad, no kidding. Couldn't connect with reality at all anymore. Why should they? Twenty years ago''—the doctor keeps trying to interrupt me—"they'd been dropped off there.''

"Kate, let me tell you what I predict will happen if you don't get treatment at this time.'' "Yeah, go ahead.'' I wonder if I can put up with the negative forecast, the evil fortune-telling, and then live with its effects; treat it as a warning even—if they will just permit me to leave in peace. "I think you'll have more and more difficulty over the next couple of weeks and couple of months.'' I try to take this humorously and fail. "Missed lectures and—'' "We could make a bet on it. I can promise you I won't.'' "Let me finish what I'm saying. . . . I mean getting paid and doing it in a way that makes you feel proud of yourself.'' Mallory bursts in: "Why is it that people who are close to you and are with you for long periods of time when you're taking lithium say you're wonderful? You're very lucid, Kate. But when you stop taking lithium, then . . .'' "They like you when you're down. Of course, they never worry about your depression. I was once near suicide and only one person cared, Washburn, my oldest friend.'' A smile for Washburn.

The doctor begins predicting again: "I think that over the next couple of weeks and months you might miss lectures in a way that's humiliating to yourself.'' "I promise not to.'' "Well, it makes no difference to me,'' the doctor informs me in her childish, querulous voice.

Which goes on: "If this happens—if in certain ways you fuck up lectures, and your professional reputation—'' "Then I'll pay for it, I'll deal with it then. I'm in charge of my own life.'' "What if there's a chance that I'm right, an outside chance that I'm right?'' "If you're right, then I'm wrong. Do you want to bet ten bucks?'' Ladylike embarrassment.

"What if you end up presenting yourself in a way . . . that you really don't like?'' "Then that would be my fault. But right now I'm in a hurry 'cause I have to get to a plane.'' "But what if that happens?'' "I'm getting sick of this intrusion, this repetition—do you mind if I read my mail while I listen to you?'' "Actually, I would.'' "How much are you per hour? Maybe I could hire you to let me take care of my own business—do you see all that mail? Could you turn around? Look at this, hmm, Barbara Chase-Riboud is going to have a party on the twenty-ninth. She's a wonderful sculptor and a writer, did that book on Sally Hemings, Thomas Jefferson's mistress—I want to be at that party.'' "What if,'' the doctor goes on, "in the next couple of weeks . . .''

It's time to find out the truth. I turn on the doctor: "Please, I don't like to be talked to in this way. You're threatening me with assault. I belong to something called NAPA, which stands for Napa, the hardest joint in California, the worst asylum. It also stands for Network Against Psychiatric Assault. I'm a member of that, indeed a founding member. And you aren't just taking up my time, you're threatening me with assault. You're threatening me with forced hospitalization, for one thing.''

Now the moment: "It's true that I do have that capability but I really don't want to do it.'' Then I know that she will. That this was planned all along. The bitterness, to look around and see the others—Sophie, Mallory, Washburn. "I really don't want to do it.'' The lie becomes truth. The relish of domination in her voice. Power—she has only waited to do it, like Superman in a phone booth. I look at her: "You should be ashamed of your collusion with the state.'' "I really don't want to do it.'' "That's lovely''—gambler's humor—" 'cause if you do I'd want to slug you. And if I did I'd lose my last card." "Whatever happens, whatever happens, Kate—don't slug me." Heavy emphasis.

The doctor gathers herself together to apply reason repetitiously against delusion: "What if you really fuck up in the next couple of months?" "My darling, I have lost my credibility thousands of times. I'm a free spirit. I lost my credibility with my family because I tried to save a black man from an execution by hanging. By the way, he did hang." The doctor, conciliatory, placating, flattering: "You've done many many important things in your life." "This mattered to me—to stop a lynch. I thought it was noble. They thought it was expensive." "You've had an incredibly remarkable productive life." "I work in a lot of causes besides the women's movement." "That's for sure," she chimes in, stroking, fawning. "I was thrown out of Iran, but that's a place you'd want to leave in a hurry. They are executing people now— have you seen my little piece of paper? I wrote a petition on Iran—that's what I've been doing over the summer." Laying my petition on her, just the sort of thing she would evade. Doing it at all was regarded as eccentric; to actually read it would be a waste of time. To humor me, Sophie offers to fetch one.

Around me the agitation builds. Never mind the law's promise against forced hospitalization, they've gotten around that or can ignore it and simply count on a hospital ready to receive someone involuntarily. They are going through with this. Watch out now, let the animal in you save itself. There is no phone here—all along I've been painfully conscious of that. And that there are too many of them in the room—enough to overpower me, lock the doors, prevent me from leaving. Unless I stick near the door and know my moment. Then I could reach the long arm of the phone to Petra or Civil Liberties or Sheila, who is also a member— any of those on my side. If I could reach them. There is a phone upstairs at my neighbor Michael's, the other artist in the building and a good friend. But they could trap me there too—I need a really public phone in a public place—Phoebe's. Good, I even have the change.

Washburn chimes in, "But I don't want you to go to Minnesota." "Wash, you never want to go to Minnesota; you're afraid to go home and I'm not." I am hungering for the moment late this afternoon when we'll land, see the river at last; it will still be daylight—I've planned it. Then the river road, then Mother's meringues and strawberries. "No, that's not the reason," Mallory explains as if to the slow-witted: "We don't want you to go at this time."

"So where is it you'd like me to go?" And then the long slow

sentence, Mallory's voice: "We would like you to go to the hospital."
The moment of truth. The friendly sword. "Well, I don't think that
under my civil rights you can force me into a hospital." Mallory alone,
her voice somber with responsibility: "We don't want to do anything
like that. We really would like you to see what's happening." I do, all
too clearly.

Sophie has a brilliant idea: "What about this?—you and I stay in New
York and see someone. I've told you before that I think it's a bad idea
for you to go to St. Paul. Because first of all, you're under a lot of strain
right now, and the pressure of moving here . . ." "The moment you all
go away I'll feel great," I answer with cheerful honesty. "Perhaps you
will. But I also think you should have your lithium level taken here
where there's a doctor you could continue to see if you want to." I see
the way: they'll bust me over a lithium level; detained for a meaningless
test, since I have taken no lithium to test for. "I don't want to have it
done here. I want to have it where my attorney is." Panic rises in my
throat. The doctor's snide voice: "Don't you have an attorney here?" as
if it were a charge account at Bloomingdale's, the bourgeois baggage of
doctors and lawyers. My attorney here is the ACLU person in White
Plains—I realize I'm pretty far from help; indeed I was safer at the farm,
wise to stay out of the city. That's why they picked the city. Sophie's
odd behavior when we came in the front door downstairs, the sense of
doom which I imagined presaged the phone bill, all the loose ends
before a trip. These were my last moments of freedom.

"Would you do it for me even . . . ?" Sophie's voice, so very hon-
eyed. "Would you stay here for me?" "No, not for anybody. I'm going
home to see my mother. Sorry, but mothers always come first." I laugh.
Now Mallory, very much the actress; grave, a silence around her
words—the lover has played her gambit—comes forward with the grandeur of kindred: "Well, that's what we think, too, and we don't think
that Mother should have to deal with this right now." Her performing
voice, the voice in the movie we made together years ago in our downtown sister artist days. But how deliberately insulting. I am now too
pestiferous even for my own mother. Jesus, have they called her,
queered my visit?

Suddenly I realize I haven't even told her I wouldn't be on that first
plane—the one I missed this morning by cleaning up my desk and

paying the bills at the farm. These creeps are not going to make me miss the next one; I have an eye on my watch and know just how long it will take me to throw the mail in my bag and be on the street and into a cab. Money, tickets—I have everything. But Mother may be expecting me to land right now—call her. Damn, of course, the phone is off. So then, here is my excuse. Play it like the most innocent scatterbrained filial piety—but here is your exit. The doctor's voice goes on meanwhile: "Let me tell you about how I feel about hospitalizing someone against their will." "Oh, yeah? How do you feel about it?" "Terrible. I don't want to do it." "Then get off my case. Look, lady, I've got to call my mother . . ." Seeing my out, the door—I am alone on this side of the room, the side where the door is. The staircase. The street.

The tension builds for the final assault, for once they begin they will need a telephone, too, unless their ambulance is prearranged. But I must be gone—out of this building. It would not embarrass them to overwhelm me here in my own studio, but Phoebe's bar and grill would never do. Thank God for Mallory's bourgeois sense of propriety, a hatred of publicity before the regulars at Phoebe's, an actors' joint where Mallory lived much of her life before she moved uptown. "If this is going on much longer, I really must call Mother," I say, playing for time.

Later, the recriminations and hard talk of madness—how I have brought this on myself and will not be released until I accept every condition they impose. All lectures have to be canceled, they cannot be postponed and, of course, you can't go to Europe. Maybe for years—we have to be sure you are stabilized, travel is out of the question. I will be someone's ward. Mallory's or Sophie's. I see my life freezing into arrest and the depression that follows it, the shame, the very real possibility I may never be free again. You never know how long you will be held. Neither do those who turn you over bound. That uncertainty, and my own "poor attitude": the very set of convictions that make things go hard for you inside. To feel as I do about drugs and shock and then to become a prisoner of both—no way.

18

Run. Get out of here. Already my legs are saving me, they will get me out the door—the way is still clear even as the others begin to figure it out. But the animal has got access to the door. A burst of talk from each of them. "No, Kate, now listen." "I really have to use the phone." "Let Sophie call, Kate": Mallory's voice big and bullying, again as one talks to a nitwit or a naughty child. "Back in a minute," I say. The fresh air in the hall, the wind of the street in my face, free, my legs carrying me strong into the world. How they shook running down the stairs, but that terror is past; I could walk right out of there, my own studio, which was danger, and into the street, which is freedom, safety. How strange the reversal. If you have your purse, and it has some money and you hold on to it very tight, you are better off out here on the Bowery with the bums than in your own studio with your drawings and your nearest and dearest. "Loved ones": peculiar phrase—give me strangers and the bartender at Phoebe's, dealing out dimes for the phone right under the jukebox speakers and in full view of the street. The plate-glass window where any one of them might appear at any moment in pursuit. Petra, please answer and get me Civil Liberties.

When I left, the tape recorder was still playing on the table, recording nothing but silence for a moment, then footsteps, a little traffic, sighs of dissatisfaction at my escape, then settling-down murmurs. And as the group regroups someone asks where the toilet is. If Sophie has gone to pursue me, that leaves the doctor, Washburn, and Mallory—having to find a telephone to carry out their plan. Mallory and the doctor lament my wayward disposition and Mallory makes one perceptive comment on my fear; at least she noticed. Then Mallory speaks melodramatically about my tragic and progressive illness, predicts that it is chronic, irreversible, a degenerative disease; notices the tape recorder and turns it off.

At Phoebe's things are not panning out; I've been unable to reach the American Civil Liberties Union and it doesn't look as if Petra can do much in view of the fact that she finds this "upsetting." Mother has just disappointed me terribly on the phone by withdrawing her hospitality. I cannot stay in her house. "But I was having dinner with you tonight." "No." "Mallory called you?" "Yes." And since I am "that way," as she puts it—news Mallory must have furnished—she does not want to see me. I swallow and allow it all. Why not?—what can you do against another person's assertion you're crazy? A mother's love is infinite, or so one comes to imagine; here is proof this is not quite so. Well, I can stay with the women from the bookstore who are arranging my reading.

Sophie comes down the street to try to persuade me to stay. They can cancel my reading. The hell you can. "Look," I say, "you don't cancel engagements and keep your reputation." She's for canceling not only Minneapolis but St. Louis and Missouri University as well. "Please stop talking like that—I need those lectures." "Postpone them." "You don't postpone; it's not like that. They have a week of activities and set up a lecture—it happens then, not some other time. There's publicity, university permission and funding, halls to reserve for a certain night—this stuff isn't postponed. If I can't come, they will have to get another lecturer." "Then they will." "Precisely, and I'll never pay the phone bill." "It's not as important as your health." "It's far more important; it's the real world." "You're not in the real world now, running off to St. Paul when you should stay here and relax, rest and get well." Everyone defines things their own way. "Bookie was even coming up from Florida to be with you"—an idea that seems to move her a good deal. Why would they bring an old friend, an old lover even, back to New York all the way from Florida, where she is living in an ashram with a bunch of religious fanatics, if they didn't have it in mind to bust me? Bookie at my bedside with spiritual aids and holy texts—what an absurdity.

"We are only acting in your own interest, because you are making a fool of yourself and we love you." We walk the three blocks down the Bowery from Phoebe's to my studio, all the old streets full of bums, and the remembered corners of old friends. Fumio's corner is just here, there's where my old friend Stimpson used to live, there's where Mallory lived before she moved uptown. Everyone moves and I stay on here in the anus of the city—I love this street. You used to be able to borrow ten dollars on a Sunday morning from five or six different lofts on this street; it was full of my friends, even family. Now how desolate it seems, these three blocks. Really, you are a fool if you have to go to Phoebe's to use the phone because your own studio is invaded by enemies who want to lock you up in an insane asylum. How much worse if these strangers are your own friends and lovers, even your kid sister. You have really lost your grip on the town and the neighborhood without a circle of folks you can trust in this hard city. Only the money in my pocket befriends me now, buys me a cab to use the ticket on a great steel bird that will leave it all behind.

Looking over at the corner, I see that trouble is not yet behind me. Mallory's roommate is parked out in front of my house. Very odd. And what's my friend Martha Ravich doing here too? "Hi, Martha, what brings you over here?" "I've just got to say that I think you're making a big mistake—I know 'cause I did when I went off the stuff. I quit taking lithium and freaked. Then I crashed. I wasted months, nearly a year. I couldn't work. Don't do it." They have set her up to tell this tale. I could stand here and discuss it: her experience, mine, how we both hated the drug and fled it, the shrinking business and what it called us. But there is something unauthentic in our talking here and now—she feels it as much as I do, awkward because she is ashamed, unwilling really to take part in this setup. She has seen someone behind me coming out of my building; she withdraws. The little doctor emerges, Washburn, then Mallory—nervous yet triumphant.

They did it. They must have done it. Called the white coats. Time to get my luggage and go. I bring down the bags with some help from Sophie, interspersed with further pleas that I stay. Mallory officiously moves my bags from the pavement back into the doorway. I move them out again, coldly watched by a whole circle of people who could so easily help me into a cab. Sophie could drive me to La Guardia in my own car, but she won't, all of them insisting I should stay. "It's dangerous for you there—more dangerous than here." "No one I'm going to visit is going to throw me in the booby hatch." "Yes they will. I know Mother, I know Sally," Mallory warns. "How about you, Mallory?"

"No, you've absolutely got to listen to us." "No, I've absolutely got to get a cab or I'll miss the plane." I flag a cabbie, who pulls up and permits one bag on the seat and then mysteriously refuses to take me. This happens again, but the cab had only come to a stop before it pulls away again without me. The next three hardly even slow down. I look up from the exhausting work of getting a taxi in New York only a little before rush hour to see that Mallory is signaling the cabs away. Pointing to me, then shaking her head and tapping her temple in a childish gesture. Meaning crazy. Goddamn. She is actually deflecting the ones I flag with a gesture that warns them I am mad. It is somehow the cruelest thing anyone has ever done to me, the most insulting, the most maliciously dishonoring. I can scarcely believe my eyes. Of course they will not stop—she and the others surround me. I need a cop.

In the heat of this afternoon, with the fear that an ambulance is on its way to take my freedom for however long, or forever, and with only a cab to save me from missing my getaway—and they do this. I once saw a woman abducted on the Bowery and called the police while watching her screaming and fighting from my Bowery window as she was put into a car. To know the same helplessness here—among these—damn right I need a cop. Forget the taboo against asking police assistance, the rule of our lives downtown: you never call a cop to help you against your friends. Look at what is being called against me—the white cops. I need a blue one. Civil liberties logic says call the police; only if you persuade a policeman you are in your rights can you ever win in an illegal bust. Though forced hospitalization is against the law, the Mental Health Act, it is practiced anyway and very successfully. The only way to enforce the law and secure my rights under it is to have a policeman present and quote it to him and hope he concurs. My small word against a doctor, relatives, friends, all eager to turn me over to the mercy of the ambulance drivers and their brutality on these occasions. If nothing else, I can insist that since I will not go willingly, the drivers be prevented from handling me.

Another cab refuses me. I am really angry. Even more, I'm really scared. I do something very difficult. I shout in the street: "Help, help!" Mallory and the rest are mortified. Unembarrassed by what they are doing in deflecting cabs, they are socially embarrassed by my shouts. One doesn't shout in the street. I compound it all by not only shouting

"Help" but shouting "Police!" as well. A squad car at the stoplight. They hear, they turn around. If I had to shout until the bums themselves called the cops for me, I would do it. I feel their sympathy around me, their understanding, men who have been busted and hustled all their lives, many of them acquaintances. But when Michael's wife, Linda, my neighbor from the fourth floor, comes out of the building and I call to her, she doesn't turn around, refuses to. Yet I am sure she can hear me. So they have queered my neighbors for me. That means they have borrowed the phone and called the ambulance. Then they really have done it.

"Officer, I'm trying to catch a cab because I'm late for a plane. I wonder if you could help me." "We don't drive people to airports, lady." "Of course not." "But I can flag a cab for you." "Thank you, that's all I need." The friends, of course, fade into the background and I make no issue of how they waved the cabs away. And then it happens. The ambulance arrives. A siren. One ambulance inside the aura of that siren. Then another siren and another ambulance. And then a police car accompanying the ambulance. Its siren. Another siren and another police car. Two ambulances, three squad cars. The fear I have lived in for over an hour descends now like a plastic bag over my head. It is very hard to stand, not to tremble, not to weep, not to fall apart, become hysterical and scream—epithets, recriminations, everything. Hard not to run, just the mere run for your life. Just what they want. You must stand there, tight, firm, hard. But easy, too. If you have ever stood for civil rights, you better make it now; this is your life you're saving—do a good job of it. It's also for every other quivering soul who ever saw these bastards coming, who ever felt the noose drawn around by their near and dear, the treachery of relatives, the betrayal of friends, the righteous malice of the lover who has now, finally, in this move, in this absurd card game of sick and crazy, achieved at last the perfect blow to smite you, the perfect set of handcuffs, the most willing and agreeable jailers.

I can't win. The thing of appealing to the police is too long a shot. The ambulances bring their own police cars. It will go on as it has in the past. I'll lose the trip home. I'll lose the trip to Europe, Ireland. I'll lose my freedom. They can keep me in there for months, and when I come out I'll be broken. Lose even my friends; if I ever get out I'll never want to see these people again. Mallory and the doctor enter into consultation with the drivers—their forms, her license, the proper destination. I turn to talk to my cop. Out of the corner of my eye I notice with astonishment that they cannot even figure out where to take me. Their first choice doesn't take involuntary subjects, too nice a joint. That means we go where the drivers want. And their ambulance says Mother Cabrini. Not on my life, no Catholic hospital, thank you. My policeman is young and black and very handsome. His name tag says he's Kelly; I love it, black Irish, like my old man. He is everything I like in a man and has a sense of humor. The last gesture of freedom, the need of calm—I find a cigarette. He lights up, too.

While we smoke, apart from the others, I explain the situation in terms of a family misunderstanding into which a psychiatrist has blundered. "That one there is my younger sister. I'm a writer and someday she'll be a wonderful writer, but at the moment she is trying to have me carted off in a loony wagon. The law, you know, forbids forced hospitalization." He nods. "I'm trying to catch a plane to St. Paul, Minnesota, and they would like me to go to some hospital. They're so disorganized they're not very sure which."

The other cops are over with the drivers and the doctor. Kelly's my only hope. "Let's see your ticket." I find the ticket; my hands locate it in my purse, a miracle of will against terror. I present it. He gives it a look and nods. "You gotta ticket to ride." Even a smile. The Beatles song floods over me like heaven: "She's got a ticket to ride and she don't care, my baby don't care." I transform his smile into a wink: a code. All the codes of the world, the arts and music, all the jargons and argots—versus all the middle-class hysteria in the doctor's voice, in Mallory's. Washburn is abashed before the two ambulances. Sophie has made herself scarce, watching from the staircase, appalled.

Did they call twice? Both ambulances are from Mother Cabrini. Clearly they did not choose and call a hospital, merely dialed the police emergency number. And they are now stuck with whatever hospital's ambulances arrive. Tough city hospitals, Catholic hospitals, neighborhood hospitals, whatever hospital had a bed free when the call came in. "They got the name of a hospital on the truck," Kelly says with a very real disgust, "but they're a separate outfit, the ambulance company. The hospital isn't responsible either. Those guys there aren't even union. They could break your arm—when I say they aren't union, I mean they aren't responsible. At all." This is where we are, then. Not with Payne Whitney or whatever their bourgeois faith had imagined in its blind assurance. The thing is embarrassing.

One of the three squad cars departs, the cops seeing nothing in this even worth their time. I still have Kelly. The doctor has the ambulance drivers in her pocket now and is nicely reconciled to locking me up in Mother Cabrini and transferring me when it's convenient. Just overnight, a few days—I can hear them all deciding that's really okay, the main thing is to get her off the street, stop her hobnobbing with cops. Kelly's partner is now in conference with the drivers and the doctor. Kelly leaves me to join his partner.

Maybe that's the end of it. He'll be outranked or something, outnumbered. The bags for my trip, so hopeful still on the sidewalk. It will be like before. This will go on all my life. I have a record. I drift over to hear my fate, hardly noticed until someone asks me if I will go voluntarily. Kelly is at my side. "I will not."

My fate hangs now. The cops in the squad car that accompanied the first ambulance (the second ambulance departing, now that a collar's being made—I cannot be tied into two ambulances simultaneously) are for locking me up. There's a doctor present, a relative to vouch—that's enough. Kelly and his partner see it differently. "If she isn't voluntary," the partner says. The ambulance driver knows that the trump card is called now—an involuntary who knows the law and has a police officer present to enforce it. He backs away from the proposition. Voices of my near and dear beg and beseech and order me to go voluntarily. "Sorry, no." The doctor crumples only because her driver, her main force, will not exercise it. Not here in front of Kelly, who shows no signs of leaving. The squad cars sail off, too.

"Now, do you want that cab?" Kelly asks as the ambulance folds its tent, its wheelchair and stretcher. Will you be tied or ride? they had asked me once, that first time in California. I didn't even know what they were referring to, had actually imagined that "ride" meant I could ride in my own convertible with Sita driving it, and my error in understanding left me beaten to the floor of a parking lot, my arms pinioned to a stretcher. What a long way from that to here, today. Terror gives way to euphoria. "How about that cab?" Kelly asks again. Gallant man, you will think I am really nuts, I suppose, but these people are still my friends, somehow dear to me even now. Because they were before. They may even have learned something. Or they may feel bad about losing. "I've missed the plane I was trying to catch. There isn't another till eight, so I think maybe I'll gather my little flock together and buy them a drink and a steak down the street at Phoebe's. Thank you very much.'' He smiles the smile of a man who understands even this, peace and war and squabbling and making up.

The little doctor is crouched off to the right of the door to my build-ing, seeming smaller and of less consequence than ever. Time to dismiss her: "You disgrace your license. I hope it's the first time you've ever tried to lock someone up—it had better be the last.'' "It's very hard.'' "Shit—don't you ever absorb anything? It's not hard—it's all too damn easy. This time you didn't get by with it; how many people are as lucky as I was with that good cop? Most people don't even know you can call a cop. It took me a long time to learn. Capture is usually so swift there is hardly ever occasion anyway. I was only lucky.'' "You were more than lucky. One thing I'll congratulate you on"—she speaks as if this were only an exercise, a fire drill in civil rights, and she had never meant for it to be more, no one had—"you didn't decompose.'' "What on earth do you mean?'' Is this some psychiatric in-joke? Decompose indeed. "I mean you kept your cool.''

The little doctor has made her inglorious exit. That leaves only us: Mallory, Sophie, Washburn. I rebuke Washburn for her part in this and she leaves. Mallory as always is in a hurry and cannot stay for a drink. That leaves me and Sophie; we could use a drink as a way of making up. I am already beginning to forgive her. When the ambulance arrived, I think, she was genuinely afraid of the violence it represented, the burly drivers and their ways. And the sight of so many policemen must be unsettling.

"They were terrible—I had no idea how terrible it would be,'' she says. It is something of an apology. For, indeed, probably none of them had ever understood the notoriety and savagery of having three squad cars and two ambulances with six ambulance crew members and six policemen all together on our stretch of sidewalk. It made them embar-rassed and squeamish, the publicness. But also the force, the fury of this act of capture, had never quite occurred to them. They had in mind a smooth woman doctor, a feminist, our world; then a nice really first-class hospital, flowers, calm, nurses, white clothes, wealthy psychia-trists, the lull and luxury of treatment. All so middle class and pleasant; being crazy at this rate is nearly a privilege. Ruinous expense, too: it would be my bill and that would be my problem, not theirs. Possibly a suitable punishment for having inconvenienced them for an afternoon.

But cops, the public street, the violence of a crowd of strangers privy to private business, and a slice of the general mayhem of arrest right in the road, the real possibility that I would be subdued by the ambulance crew, tied up in front of them—could they stand that? That I should cry and beg and look at them in my terror and helplessness? All for my own good and so forth. Perhaps it was the presence of the police and their decision in my favor—the knowledge that they were wrong in the eyes of the law and its police force—that may have been the most daunting element of all. For there is a bit of shamefacedness now. Nothing amounting to outright apology, of course. But in Sophie there is a real sense that it was an error: proceeding this way, going ahead and calling ambulances to bring about an enforced hospitalization when persuasion wouldn't work.

As for Petra—who shows up for her own kind of rescue as we are walking up to Phoebe's, all packed to go to St. Paul with me since Sophie won't—it is still all very upsetting but has come to a splendid ending. And on that note we dine.

PART TWO

Ireland

1

I suppose it started with washing my hair, this notion of using the airport as a free hotel. Free, impersonal, a place with banks, postal services and reading matter, food and drink, toilets and spaces to be alone. There is, alas, no baggage department, or at any rate I cannot find it. I am now an authority on both the domestic and the international sections. And it occurred to me, while waiting for the Ryan car rental people to select me the best car of those being turned in this morning, that it would be an excellent idea to finish washing my hair in the ladies' room. Since the hotel's hospitality never extended to letting me finish the job.

While it is a bit brisk here, my heavy sweater will prevent a cold. And they have nice hot water, plenty of towels if the linen roll on the wall is viewed charitably. And where else do you get marble? In fact, the ladies' room at Shannon was rather our favorite spot when Dakota and Petra were here. We admired it extravagantly and found it a lovely place to rest; benches and chairs—you could bring your tea along and spend the afternoon, we'd joked.

No joke now. I'm taking the place seriously. Turn off the well-heeled tourist and on with the downtown artist—this is a great place to while away an interminable wait. Ryan has discovered that they have rented the car I just turned in with my Nikon still hidden carefully under the tire in the trunk, where I so prudently kept it so that a thief would miss it. But alas, where anyone else would, too. This is what comes of letting them unload the car: "The porter will just bring your things around to the desk, ready for the next car." However, the next car is not yet here. And I am loath to let that beautiful Nikon camera float around with strangers.

"Would you phone and trace the car?" "Of course." They are all charm and sloth. I have perfect faith in their integrity and know they will not steal the camera. After all, it has been reported by now. The new custodians of the car, provided they are Irish, won't try to pinch it either. It's just the insecurity of not having it. Worse still, this absurd delay. I have a day's rental left on my last contract; I could be on my way, keep the car as long as I like and pay at the end when I turn it in. But here the day is frittering away.

No matter how I busy myself with sorting film and labeling tapes, I am still marking time. By late afternoon Ryan reports that the camera may not be brought back until the next morning, when the car itself will be returned. How do they expect me to spend the night? I wonder. There is no hotel here that I can see. And I have no transportation to leave the airport.

It is about this time that Patrick appears, sidling up to me in his nice blue airport police uniform. Sent either to help or to harass—it is difficult to tell which. But he is full of questions: When did I come? When am I leaving? Not for a while; I have a solicitor friend, Professor Roach, who will be starting proceedings for dual citizenship. The ins and outs of dual citizenship. Patrick seems to find my papers in order: passport, airline tickets, car rental agreement, and so on. My problem's with Ryan. Who are after all doing their best. They had in fact provided me with a nice inconspicuous car, dull green and pedestrian, earlier today, before the loss of the Nikon camera was discovered. However, it turned out that the key would work in the door but not in the ignition. Patrick worries about my luggage—the mound of it. I tell him Ryan will be clearing things up. I'm sure they'll find my camera since they know exactly who has it at the moment. Patrick finds the vast pile of luggage an indecency. So do I, but I have no idea where to store it while waiting.

Nor do I ever know just how long the wait will be. Up until this evening Ryan keeps me jumping with other plans: Take this car; your camera will be delivered. Wait a bit longer and we'll keep phoning and locate it; perhaps it can be driven to you tonight. Then tomorrow. Then now. Then later. Each clerk contradicting the other.

I am beyond exhaustion: so long without sleep, having had nothing but a cup of tea and several glasses of County Clare milk from the bar.

I cannot find a restaurant yet, so there is only this crazy bar. I have sworn to go by the letter of the law—for in Ireland, airport bars may serve alcohol only to departing passengers and their guests. I have a ticket if queried, a ticket for tomorrow, though I have already told Aer Lingus I will stay longer in Ireland. I can use the ticket whenever I like; they need only one day's notice. Still it's a good idea to stick with milk; there's no point in getting into trouble over those idiotic licensing laws— sometimes it's legal, sometimes it isn't—a maze. Stick with milk— you're tired and it's better for you till you find something to eat. Then see what Ryan's up to now.

To my astonishment they have closed for the night. My God, what will I do, sit up all night on a bench? This is absurd; in an entire day they could not return my camera and give me a car I have already paid for. A thousand confusions overcome me. By evening I have come to sit dejectedly alone at a little table over the solace of a small brandy, compliments of the barman. Half asleep, staring at the passengers about to leave. And the ones who never seem to leave at all, the IRA types with their beaten-down suitcases and caps. Men who will chat you up at the bar, tease you for drinking milk, tell you stories of the States and Boston. For they go back and forth like messengers. And maybe are messengers. Or merely the poor of West Ireland going home to a Boston that has more of their family in residence now than Galway does.

Yet after a word or two about the present Troubles in Ireland, they take your hand and tell you how easy your fingers are to break, how that is the usual thing when you're captured. So watch out for them. Messengers, real or invented. Because in staying you are letting yourself in for something that you neither know nor understand yet. Ireland is in turmoil and it's complicated. Keep to yourself. Watch and learn. Memorize certain figures, like the man at the table before you. An old man in rubber boots. I imagine he is the spirit of County Mayo, my father's county, the one I am headed for at last. He smokes and looks at the floor. Or he smokes and looks ahead. A farmer, he is not flying anywhere at all. He is here to rest, even to think. His whole bearing is in his burly shoulders, a long life of toil that now wishes to contemplate something within itself. There is something enormously moving about him, a centeredness. Also a memory, an understanding that he gives of the years abroad. This figure fills in the gap of the diaspora, explains the time in between. As the barflies who run the political end of it from Shannon to Boston explain another side of things. Uncle Harry in his decorous bars in St. Paul; all the busy masculine intrigue over funds and guns. There is even a sign as you enter the boarding area, warning that guns are illegal past that point and kindly giving notice that you must do something prudent about the one you probably have.

Compared with that cinematic energy, my old countryman is nearly androgynous: a woman's patience and endurance as much as a man's. He is the one who held out, who kept it all together, who saw his people through. This tired old man in boots. A large man, a very fine head. Proud. Mysterious as well. He's Ireland and I've come here to find it, stayed on alone after my friends Petra and Dakota went home to America. Watching the plane carry them away, I felt a disappointment that they couldn't discover the place with me; then a relief, even euphoria. I was alone with it all now, with the famine ghosts of my mother's tribe, with Mayo and the Norman past of my father's. Maybe even my father himself, his disembodied spirit at home here and urging me to roam, to gaze at the enormous maple tree in red leaf last evening and think of writing poetry, filming here with the big 16mm Eclair movie camera Dakota brought over for me, living my own life—time off.

I had to stay, because of D'arcy's prediction. It all comes back to D'arcy, because she said there might be a rising. In the H Blocks prison in the North of Ireland the political prisoners are on hunger strike; they have vowed to starve themselves to death. The women in Armagh jail too. When I arrived in Dublin I was soundly lectured by my sponsor that to go near Armagh, indeed even to go near D'arcy, was poison. Southern Irish women were certain that Armagh was not a feminist issue; the IRA was a masculine organization, and working with them is like working with any other male revolutionary model—you get screwed, brought in when serviceable and dismissed when not. I was here only as a feminist; this was an Irish matter and I am only an American. Irish-American does not qualify; too removed, too ignorant. I was willing to concede that point, but political prisoners are another thing.

As a pacifist I found it difficult to understand why Bernadette Devlin's civil rights strategy and the peace movement couldn't be a better route than terrorism. Blowing up buses, accidental murders, barbarous acts like IRA kneecappings are not only nasty but stupid. When I met D'arcy she challenged me. We were halfway through a bizarre Chinese meal in the only place still open after ten in Galway city, when she started giving me hell for being a pacifist with hopes for nonviolence. I'd already broken all the rules laid down for me by the cautious when I read at Galway University College that night, because I invited D'arcy to give a pitch for the women prisoners, many of them ill, one of them near death now from the hunger strike. The women at Armagh have begun to refuse to wash or to use the occasional humiliating toilet "privileges" of their jailers: a pot to piss in—later the guards throw it at you or on the floor of your cell. So these women, like the men in the H Blocks, were protesting by spreading their own dung and filth on the walls; and being women, their own menstrual blood as well. Finally there were infections. A group of them have now resolved to fast to death.

The hunger strike is pacifist technique, classic even, perhaps carried to further extremes here than ever before. I argued that Gandhi had successfully tried it against the British—why shouldn't the Irish? D'arcy was nearly derisive: "You see where it's gotten us. Men have died on hunger strike for fifty years—there's a whole list of them. If one of those women died you'd never hear of it; they'd bury her quietly in hospital." D'arcy goes on to the American networks, their blackout, the unholy alliance between Thatcher and the State Department. I urge world opinion, the European Court, the evidence of widespread torture against the Irish, reports of bags placed over prisoners' heads over long periods of time so that they lost their balance, their sense perception, maybe even their minds. "After all, D'arcy, these atrocities are so well documented, so well known . . ." "No—we had hopes, too, but we know how long all this has been going on."

"Okay, so what good does violence achieve?" "This is a war, this is an opposition, a people forged in struggle." "If the South—" I'd said. "The South will do nothing; it's a neocolonial extension of the British pound. The only thing new about it is European Common Market money, the recent little affluence. That will make it do even less." "The people," I'd said, "good God, you are one people." "Not anymore— the division was effective." I had said "you." I had wanted to say "we." How easily I gave up this timid probe into my own Irishness. Stick to the question itself, as it might be posed to any human rights advocate of any nationality. I'd been involved with so many of these struggles, consumed with radical politics so long now, that agreement would be automatic and sympathy would be out of principle. But another more personal participation continued to lurk somewhere.

I knew D'arcy put her finger on it. After an evening at her cottage and a thousand bits of information, lectures, questions—Margueretta D'arcy is a well-known actress here; John Arden, her husband, is the playwright—between them they had plied me with books and stories of the Irish political prisoners and the Troubles. And now there's a new book coming out on the conditions in the H Blocks, by two priests, which will make a sensation, since its documentation of torture is irrefutable.

D'arcy started in on the old books, the Oxford editions of Saint Columba, rare books, local histories. We were in their bedroom; Arden had fallen asleep on the couch. I was enraptured by them, by how much there was to learn from them, how magical they are. Their mission, the hard chaos of their lives in this damp hovel full of books, its kitchen floor full of water, its toilet thoroughly problematic. Maybe I could redo the joint for them, paint it, order a few pretty things, bring them steak and wine. What a grand thing it would be to tape conversations with them. There was a book in D'arcy's hands, an old one, the genealogy of her tribe back to the first Norman landings. The woman is like a good witch, like a reasonable version of the cottage woman at the corner of their road who breathed down your throat to wish you luck, a terrifying experience of poverty in her bony hand as she grabbed your arm and stared hard into your eyes. Like Mother Time, like Machree herself, eyeing the immigrant returned after all these years, the eyes that watched your mother's mother from the cliffs those last excruciating minutes out of Galway Bay. When leaving was possibly salvation and probably betrayal, but staying was death. This old woman lived on here, not to buy or sell and claim your land but a cottager still, the very memory and identical twin of my own mother's kin, a Murray or a Tracy or a Feely; years gone by but not gone at all, merely suspended, in this old woman and her man drinking the bit of whiskey I brought. They had a few acres in potatoes and the dole for the rest. And then she took my arm and warned me of the ''thrush,'' a disease of the throat. And so she breathed into it. Yet I wanted more, almost to merge. And as D'arcy and I sat on the bed in what was to be my room for the night, I wanted a few more moments with her too, because I was to leave the next day and the prospect was tearing me in two.

"These are the charts of the families," D'arcy said. I looked at the strange old book; why does she bring this up? "You and I are French names." "D'arcy—I dare say," I laughed. "Every time I say your name I hear echoes of the Three Musketeers." "And here are the twelve families of the Norman barons of Galway." D'arcy of course is one of them. I've always been curious about my father's name; Mother's (Feely) is pure Galway and Irish, but Millett is Mayo and Norman too. D'arcy weighed me like the book in her hands: "Well, if you're Mayo, you won't be in this book. But I'll tell you—if you go away to America tomorrow, you not only haven't seen Mayo this trip, again, which makes it your third time, but if you leave you may miss a rising. This is one of those moments, and you know them too, when it looks like it may happen. There might be progress, a change in this long condition. It may be the only one in our lifetimes."

And I remember '21 and '32 and the talk at home when I was young and the songs of 1916, Yeats's great poems of revolution. I lie in bed after she has left, having shaken all this at me like a flag. There is a woman in Armagh jail tonight who weighs only eighty-nine pounds, with a stomach ailment that may prove fatal under imprisonment. Who wants her to die? Not me, not even the English. Among the men there are many determined on death. It is barbarous. It is also brave and beautiful. Like single combat, the resolution of conflict through a few volunteers so that whole armies may stay alive; in this case, civilian populations. You went to Iran to see the revolution and all you saw was reaction hardening into theocracy. Here it might go up instead of down. This is the Ireland you came to see and didn't, because of others, because of time, because it was all still behind the glass of tourism. Now you could enter it alone, as it entered you. A rising at home—this would make it home. If there is to be a rising, even a ripple, I want to see it, be here, help if I can. D'arcy's right: even the possibility of a rising makes it impossible to leave. And staying makes many other things possible. I have the camera with me, tape recorders, informal bits of history to work on. A car, the land to find and see and love. The people. Ireland would be all mine.

I'm on my way to D'arcy now. And Desmond Roach, the charming professor of law at Galway who has invited me to go on using his cottage in Connemara. Desmond has promised to help arrange dual citizenship for me; my new friend Deirdre has offered to do the research for it in the Dublin Castle records. Desmond is listed as my sponsor in my new Bank of Ireland passbook. "Trust in Ireland" the ad coaxed: I went for it. I have friends here. Galway's only a few hours away; as soon as Ryan has my camera I'm off, tomorrow morning; I could be there for lunch.

2

I would have been in Galway already but for the fact that the transformer for the battery belts on my camera broke. So I was held up for
a few days in Limerick, searching for the right electrician. Not only did
the transformer break but the battery belts look like bandoliers; friends
joke that I look like a terrorist; strangers don't joke, they imagine the
worst. While having it repaired, I decided to stop off for a bit of creature
comfort in an American-style hotel, a place I stayed once before with
my mother; my cousin Roger the travel agent does a big business with
them. But I had an experience there that brought me trembling back to
the airport, so shaken I almost gave up staying on here. The hotel threw
me out. For a book. For D'arcy's book, the priests' report on the
prisoners in the H Blocks.

I'd been filming out at Ennis Cathedral that evening and stopped off
in the hotel lounge to eat a sandwich before bed, leafing through the
book for the first time. There were a pair of young men on a couch—one
heard them almost to distraction if one was trying to read, but they were
friendly and I put my book down to chat with them. They asked about
it. I was cagey, since the book will not be published officially for
another week and D'arcy asked me to read it but say nothing until
publication date. It is a very explosive book, expected to create a political upheaval in southern Ireland. I turned the subject away from this
book to books in general and told them I was an author—which diverted
us all merrily for a quarter of an hour. Then they inquired again about
the book. "If you show this book to anyone, be damn careful who it is,"

D'arcy had warned. "It will not be welcome among your comfortable southern Irish types"—which is exactly how one would describe these young men. "That book could get you in a great deal of trouble, so keep it out of sight." Already I had failed to do this. I am simply not used to hiding books, to censorship, to the notion that anything about a book could be so effective, even dangerous.

I dodged again and said that the book was about the prisoners in the North, going on the assumption that since there have been a great many such books, the very sort of thing an American would find colorful, I could dismiss it as generic. "That's all bollocks, that stuff about the prisoners," one young man lectured me while the other laughed. I was content to be reproved and set straight—what did I know? In no time they were telling me that reports of cruelty are farfetched and fallacious, contending at the same time that those fellows are only getting what they deserve, they're criminals. This is a rather familiar line of thinking in the South, where failing to challenge Britain is a chosen course of survival. But I'd already dipped into the text and its assertions had horrified me. Suddenly I could no longer tolerate their smugness; I showed them the book. "It's pornography," said the first after one glance at a prisoner's drawing. "Torture is pornography," I countered. "The drawing is only of the body of a man who is starving and cold and beaten several times a day." Their girlfriends returned; the conversation became general; I went to bed, rejoicing in the luxury of my room.

It seemed hardly morning when the telephone shrieked at me: "This is the hotel manager." What on earth did he want? And how unlikely that he would need it enough to wake me out of a sound sleep. "Yes," I said, alarmed by his tone, afraid he might find fault with me; I loved my room. "You are not to have propaganda here, nor to distribute it." "What in heaven's name do you mean?" "There has been a complaint." "About what?" "Propaganda and soliciting guests here to political views." "Sir, I was reading a book last evening which two young men asked to have a look at. Surely you do not censor your guests' books." "You are not to distribute propaganda here." "I assure you I am not distributing propaganda and I am also sure that this book is my own personal property and therefore my business, not the hotel's." "You are not to have propaganda here. Do you understand? Otherwise you will be forced to leave."

Where was the kindly proprietor who was so gallant toward my mother, where was Cousin Roger now? I mused; this fascist is ready to kick me out of his hotel because of a book. Even D'arcy would find this hard to believe. Or maybe not. Maybe that's just how uptight everything is now with the hunger strike going into its second month and deaths expected, southern Ireland having to question its neutrality, its ambivalence, its grasp on the old excuses that the rebels are violence and the instigators of violence, against whom little or no violence is practiced.

From that point on my career at the hotel was all downhill. The next morning the manager informed me that I must be gone by noon. Then eleven. As I was taking a shower all my gear was dumped in the lounge: movie camera, underwear, everything. I paid my bill and was waiting for a phone call when the manager called the police—who were extremely civil, even embarrassed, but did take note of my plate number, passport, place of birth, and the telephone numbers of my relatives. I packed my car, locked it, and went out to eat. When I came back and started my engine, the biggest policeman in the world appeared before me and told me to be gone. Where? I asked. At first I couldn't hear his reply; then it sounded like "to the Irish, go to the Irish." Enigmatic. And scary. The plates on my car were now known to the police, maybe others as well, nuts with CBs in a country full of dark roads and assassinations. Should I get on a plane and get out of here? Or change the car to something inconspicuous and even cheaper and be on my way?

So I spent last night sitting up in a parking lot waiting for the airport to open. Ryan car rental or Aer Lingus? To stay or to go? I decided on Ryan. Then this whole day waiting for the Nikon to surface. Tonight there'll only be a bench. Things are not going too well—here only three days on my own and already nearly arrested over a book. Last night there was a white ambulance parked behind me and even that gave me the willies. Because there is one other thing as well: driving west to Galway with my sponsor, Moira O'Neil, who arranged my speech to the Labour Party in Dublin, I made the mistake of telling her I was crazy. Or taken for such. Here in this country where no one knew or could guess. I've been a month in Europe: Amsterdam, London, Dublin—I'd forgotten the bust on the Bowery. But as we rode along, there was by the side of the road a building of terrible desolation, stone and barred, and I knew it for what it was. But I asked anyway, an uncanny sorrow coming over me, so deep and uncontrollable it went on for an hour.

Only an asylum, I was told. The despair of its inhabitants, old women, decades and then hundreds of years of them—women like those at St. Peter's when I was a girl, the very floorboards imbued with urine and feces and blood. And here too, these Irish women, timeless prisoners. And then it was me—I had a vision of myself inexplicably imprisoned there, left forever as the car sped by, as all the cars sped by. This awful building, this hideous stone eyesore. Blind, squat, cruel. It would wait here, but it would get you. It was the prison unacknowledged, infamous; no rhetoric or campaign, it was below consciousness or analysis. The famine house still. As if some woman's soul once could beat every other force: the starvation of history, the criminal acts of the militia, and still this grave of stone would close over her. As if this gibbet by the side of the road were your assignment, ill luck, fatality; you could speed by and take fright and try to tell your friends. And that knowledge would enter into them, that you were singled out, so that when the door opened and the drop came they would experience no surprise, only a certain congruity. In weeping, in the gesture of asking for help, you have only betrayed yourself. So proceed on your own now, no other counsel; play it cool, smart, solitary. Drive alone all day and find cheap shelter at night. Don't give in to fatigue, be patient. Tomorrow you will have another car and be off again, Ireland all before you; you are coming home.

3

Night in the airport, I begin to nod in fatigue, to muse, to dream while not yet asleep. There is a painting of the ancient Queen of Clare. It was all queens then. What if my cousin Claire and I were changelings, what if the old Queen of Clare, gone forever ago, were to make us her heirs? Claire away in Hong Kong, she of the yellow hair. So I of the black, the rascal, would be proclaimed. By the old man. By the rowdies at the bar. By the barman himself, serving me all these glasses of pure County Clare milk all day. The phantom dissolves but the Mayo man sits on before me—all the tired lot of a poor farmer, centuries of it, distilled into the thick of his waist and thighs, the droop of his trousers. The finality and strength of those boots. And the noble beauty of his head, his fine white hair.

Over and over, these images of my father, even in the witty barstool types. Or perhaps against them. He would be gentleness whereas they are bitterness; rebels without reason though plenty of causes. They are furious at the notion of nonviolence; peace is forever away. In fact it is death, it comes only with death. The lure of death fills the room now vacant since the last plane. You can sit here waiting for a plane as if it went from this door to heaven. So the night is different from the day. And the night staff. So different. It was so also at the hotel—the nights were hellish with noises. Here it is quiet. The last reveling Aer Lingus personnel have left, suitcases and goodbyes. All of them have a place to go.

Now the magic starts. Still dozing, I begin to imagine something will happen. Some revelation, some mystery I have waited for and desired. Ghosts will mount the great stairs two by two; the saints go marching in—into a room across the way I have never noticed before. Surely now I will see my father, surely now this is to be my initiation and reunion with him. The lights of the pinball and game machines over against the wall twinkle eerily, still displaying their foolish examination scores. I tried one tonight and it became not what it was—a tedious machine— but an encounter between myself and my father. A driving test no less. And with each error I heard the old chuckle. Not the fury with which he really did teach me to drive but the little laugh he would reserve for a peer—as I cross the central line or make "oil spots": code for loss of anonymity, brushes with the cops. But when he mounts the stairs and enters the last secret room across the way, in the company of heroes, of all the dead family and ancestors, warriors and scholars and artists, then he will acknowledge me. Better yet, our nuptials are being prepared, I realize with a start. And should I accept this marriage, the forbidden, the desired? Outrageous notion. The desire surprises one with its directness, its obvious terror. That would be later, below in the hall, out of the public and international side and at the other end of the airport—the Aer Lingus side. On the way there, each room the length of the long hall would be full of men in formal clothes, women in long dresses. Shall I go, shall I let them dress me? Or should I resist the temptation? For the beings from across the line, the dead and the supernatural, can be enemies, dangerous: traffic with them a scandal to be punished. They have a way, too, of grabbing you, hanging on.

Dreams persist when I am waking yet I cannot shrug them off. They become inextricably mixed in my fatigue, identified with the spot where they occur. Real as the revolving door on the way to the Aer Lingus section, so that it cannot be passed without a shudder. If I could get to Galway, be among friends, this miasma of disorientation, so unfamiliar or familiar only from wine or drugs, otherwise so unlike me, would dissolve in activity, good food, and sleep. I am so tired, have been so long unhoused, upset, chased, terrorized, given the runaround. And must now exert such effort, such patience.

Since there is nowhere else to sleep, I must sleep on the floor of this damned washroom. Then I decide that's too much. Since its bench is too short, I'll find another. There must be a bench in this place somewhere. I wander until I find one just around the corner where Phillips 66 is sold. Dear old familiar sign from childhood—rides with Dad, summer, St.

Paul, and that sense of well-being there back in the forties. How nice that they never redesigned it.

I wake to cold reality, problem solving—difficult to do with Patrick about, demanding I move my luggage. The very moment I can get a car. "It's not safe." "Surely it's safe with the best policeman in Ireland watching it." Minding things is not his job; he is the chief of airport security. I am certainly not a security problem. Our relationship a bantering cat-and-mouse affair, the mouse always certain she has covered her cards, has her papers in order, is just at the verge of being on her way peaceably. Then there are moments when Patrick is surprisingly unpleasant: "You think you're smarter than me because you write books." When did I ever tell him I wrote books? Chatty as we are, many as the questions he has asked, generous as the information I have volunteered: waving my friend Desmond before him like a document of safe conduct, debating women's rights or the Troubles as a game, a pastime for us both, even telling him of my unpleasant experience at the hotel in a humorous way—the adventure of a traveler—trading jokes about cousins in the tourist trade. And even showing him the H Blocks book, feeling on safe ground in an airport with daily flights to New York—I am companionable with Patrick but not willing to lie or disguise. With all this, I never told him I wrote books. Yet somehow he knows their names. One anyway. *Sexual Politics*. Surely Patrick is not a reader. Yet his animosity toward books and authors is a pure fount.

He is the father of four children, he says, that's what he is. He works for a living. Admirable. And suddenly it is admirable beyond anything in my chaotic life. He is a pillar. I congratulate him. But it only makes matters worse: my footloose situation brings out a resentment in him. Would Patrick like to wander the countryside and compose a little poetry? Of course—who wouldn't? But the sight of such freedom brings a snarl out in his soul. Some latent and unfed desire beneath his serge, the years of his careful upbringing so many thousands of miles away from me. I have cousins just like Patrick. All I have to do is remember them.

I have not, after all, lived among Catholics for years. Nor among Irish either, not for a long time. So he is part of things remembered. As an Irish policeman he is so much an improvement over policemen in general they cannot even be compared. And the man with four children moves me. What is he like as a father, a lover, a husband? What is he inside his blue serge uniform, this man real enough to hate a writer?

Who is also so furious with a woman for knowing something. For having achieved a book. How he hates that book, how it threatens all he stands for. He is familiar as piety, as the sanctimonious among my parochial school classmates. Yet he can make me laugh; I can make him laugh. Now if he would just leave off bugging me about my books so I could slip his jurisdiction and make it out of his clutches. Because I have begun to interest Patrick in a dismal, very dangerous way. He has taken the trouble to look me up. He knows that before my speech to the Labour Party I made a shocking endorsement of the hunger strike for the newspapers and television. Now he has only to learn my weak spot. A record. He has only to find out that I was nearly busted for crazy by Mallory and the others this summer, and I'm done for. But the cat assures me my papers are in order and I should either take the noon flight for New York or get one of Ryan's hacks and be out of here. Yes, of course. Relaxed as they are at that office of theirs, they must have my camera by now. So I'll just go over and see about it.

Alas, as usual they are on the verge but have not checked in the car carrying the Nikon. It should be within the hour: cars are due in the morning. They have, however, phoned and had the trunk checked over; the camera is indeed there. Nothing to worry about. Only more time to kill while avoiding Patrick's patrol.

I stand near the counter of Aer Lingus, looking through a high window into the sky. The cloud formations overhead. A wonderful day. Dreaming as the shapes pass, dreaming of flight, airplanes, angels. And I suddenly notice out the window, discover in fact, a statue of the Virgin in one of the parking lots. Only in Ireland would this detail occur. It seems they rebuild this airport every day. Or perhaps they are just beginning it: half of it is still dirt and construction; the other half seems an entirely new creation each time I look. This little garden here, for example; I could swear it was not here yesterday. Maybe someday they'll add some services: a place to eat, to sleep. Perhaps this is a place to eat that I didn't notice yesterday—it must have been shut. Perhaps it's restricted to Aer Lingus personnel. God, how wonderful it will be to get out of here, to be on free ground not owned and operated by the government and the multinationals. Real food, actual places of lodging— better yet, Desmond's cottage. The moors will be a nice change from the crowds at the airport, the periodic surge and then the vast empty halls I must march through—from the Aer Lingus section and my luggage, my bench and my bathroom, up to the international section and sluggish Ryan's car rental. And the cluster of international events such as the drugstore and its candy racks. And the bar and its great foaming glasses of County Clare milk; I know the rules and have had enough glasses of milk here to become a habitué.

The moment I have my camera back and my new rental car keys in hand, I am going to celebrate at last by ordering a Pernod. Before I am on my way. Just out of the necessity of one luxury, one pleasurable thing in this long airport wait, this comedy of errors. Everybody seems to drink at this bar, ticket holder or otherwise. It was the one risk I contemplated the whole time here, since my little half-finished brandy of the night before was a gift and not something I purchased myself. The Pernod would just be a little farewell aperitif. A French thought before I plunged into Mayo and the Norman territories: before the real adventure. It is perfectly silly to have a bar where the public cannot drink; it is as idiotic as the licensing laws themselves.

But while dealing with Patrick one cannot be too careful. He would love any excuse to arrest me, has been trying all morning to inveigle me into one of the little cubicles, functionaries' offices that line the passageway between the two sections of the airport. Where one is neither protected by the crowds of the international section and their publicity nor given the comfort of Aer Lingus itself in the home section.

Popping out of an office door, Patrick insists he has a friend of mine on the telephone inside. "Really, who?" "I can't tell you." "Well then, I don't think I'll take the call," I say laughing, trying to be natural, easy. Patrick at the door of the room, two rooms actually. He ducks in, trying to get me to follow. This anonymous row of rooms, offices, unmarked brown doors.

Always a terrible resonance in this row of unmarked doors. They frightened me unaccountably whenever I went by them. Now I see that they are the state, the authorities, holding rooms. Right in the middle of crowds, throngs of happy travelers, there are these hidden chambers. Look in a few feet: a police office. Only one hat upon the row of pegs—is he alone here then? Busily Patrick offers me a glass of water. The phone is back there; he gestures to the second room. I have no idea who else may be in that room, still less who may be on the phone. I do not wish to be overpowered or surprised; the gorge of claustrophobia rises. Then panic. Then the need to outwit. I back out, closer to the hall, the normal world, observation. There is something dodgy about him; it's a trick.

"It's your solicitor, Professor Desmond Roach." How nice. My legs almost bound to respond. But my gut fright, intervenes. "No problem, Patrick, I'll call him back later. If you'd just say I'll be getting down to Galway this evening and will be in touch. I'm just getting the car now. They have one for me at last." Remember to call Desmond from the road. "You really should talk to him, Katherine." This odd habit of calling me Katherine, like the nuns used to—how it coerces, this formality, this baptismal name. "Am I obliged to? Is this an order from a policeman?" "No." "Then I'll just ring him later." "You shouldn't be afraid." He sees my hands tremble. "Of course not, just busy. Got to get all that luggage stowed. Many thanks, Patrick, for all your kindness. Goodbye."

4

And then I was fool enough to order a drink twenty minutes later, imagining Patrick far away on the other side of the airport. Not because I wanted a drink, only because I wanted a treat, happiness: the little swallow of Pernod to be on my way with, something to please myself with. Idiot. His hand on your arm as it slid forward to collect your change. Patrick. And then to quibble because, of course, you hadn't touched it, hadn't even finished paying for it; were quite content to leave it on the bar untasted. And take your reprimand or hear the rule repeated or change the order to milk. This sophomoric defiance of a silly rule, in a society built on repressive shibboleths of every sort and this the most obvious and everyday and excruciating. Knucklehead.

"Are you going to America this day?" "No." "And what does your ticket say?" "I really can't remember—it's probably open." Open could be a problem for Patrick. So he fastens upon my arm and leads me to the Aer Lingus people, who look at the ticket perplexed and ask me again if I'm going to America today. "There is a flight to Boston still." This is the moment—choose between going back and staying. If I were to leave I would be let off this silly charge. But I want to stay in Ireland. Confusion of ticket agents conferring, Patrick conferring. I am stuck telling the truth, since I want Ireland even on these terms and on no account want to be stuffed into a plane to Boston. Ordering a Pernod without drinking it cannot put one in jail—not with a fine lawyer like Desmond. I have indeed done something stupid in breaking a rule, am willing to apologize, stand rebuked, pay a fine, appear before a magistrate at some time, and so forth.

But it is not worth leaving the glory of Ireland for the doldrums of Boston just for this. Viewed practically, the fare from Boston to New York must be a lot steeper than Patrick's summons. Quite simply, I want to stay in Ireland. I do not want to go home.

Patrick is triumphant. And in earnest—he has collared the car rental clerk and done something possibly both dishonest and illegal by having my contract voided and torn in half. No agreement, no car. In the torn paper my fear, nearly delusionary in its scope and control over me, perceives through the chaos that all my chances are gone. Now he has me. Hurrying me along, mad with his satisfaction. He orders me to follow him, his hand tight around my arm in joyful malevolence. Back to his den. The row of pegs is full of hats. The second of the two rooms is full of officers, the Irish constabulary. And the telephone—like a sacred object to the side of the desk. I am made to sit down beside it. There is another man, in civilian clothes and behind the desk. Said to be a doctor. The worst. A medical doctor? I ask him. Of course. He is blithe, smooth as an advertisement. And he has a pen and a pink piece of paper: official, printed, lines of questions and answers. I am to sign. Just to sign. I know, of course, what it is. And I also have no idea. But I am taken, and in the fears of that moment—the now inescapable fate of it—it hardly matters if I give in to panic and obey, hoping it will go well with me, or resist. Because all resistance is futile. The room is full of men and force.

And then the telephone, their expected call. Patrick is aglow; the operation is going smoothly. The doctor sees his function clearly: he will ask me questions about my health and my progenitors while Patrick talks on the phone. It is hard to hear much, but it is clear he has Desmond on the line. Wonderful. Or perhaps not so wonderful—rather, embarrassing. Desmond will find me a nuisance. I will look shabby in his eyes, having gotten myself into this predicament. But perhaps it will be funny later. We will dine over it and relish the humor of Patrick. The absurdity of being caught ordering but not drinking a Pernod.

Ah, but the doctor. Wait a moment—they have a doctor. Patrick has bethought himself of that already. How would he know to go that route? Surely from Desmond. Who would have heard about it from Moira O'Neil? Remote. I quake in the chair and cannot think. But if Desmond has talked to America—Sophie. Desmond will now talk to me, I'm told. A few meaningless words, then Sophie, her voice—all the way from America. Magical conference call. "Dear heart," I hear myself say, imagining everything will be fine now, solved now. They will help me,

my friends. Then her voice is like honey. But nervous. Everything will
be all right, she says.

It is too much to absorb in this fear. In the room full of big policemen.
In the doctor's opulent tie and his repeated assurances and his urgency
that I sign his pink sheet of paper. I need a light. If I smoke I can think;
I can deal with the shakes. The policeman over there has a light. I get
up to ask him for a match. Consternation on all sides. The muscles of
force clench to attack. I smile and am harmless—only a smoker, sitting
next to the man with the match, looking at the other cops around me.
Terror like nausea, like delirium. Propitiate your captors, make yourself
human to them. So they will not strike you. Iran: the tommy gun in front
of our room all night, the open door, Sophie and I each on our separate
cots, while I scribbled a denunciation of our arrest for the newspapers, to
be delivered in the morning to a man who never came. We were together
then, Sophie deflecting attention from me by packing and repacking our
women's clothing all night. What is happening now? I have left the
scene at the desk, turned my back on it because I could not bear it. Time
to pay attention again. Your fate is between these men and a telephone.

The doctor finishes with a flourish behind the desk. Patrick hangs up.
He is putting me in the charge of the regular officers now. They will take
good care of me; I will go with them. "Where?" "Now then, come
along." They stand. The room is a locked box. Try to leave and you are
restrained, caught. The witch in me whispers "crossed locks." Joan
taken by the English must have felt this, the trickery of the Inquisition
stretching out before her. Where am I going and who are these men?
How is Patrick different from all the civil police? They are the same in
my eyes. Or perhaps they are different. There are so many fears now in
Ireland, North and South. It might be a step in the right direction to get
out of Patrick's control and into the hands of the guardia or regular civil
police. But maybe these officers are not police—maybe they are a goon
squad of some persuasion or other, British or Orange or some IRA
faction who have taken a dislike to me. Maybe their job is to kill me.
The countryside is full of assassinations; bodies on darkly lit roads come
to light in every morning's newspaper. Women, too. D'arcy's committee in the North, several deaths. But this is the South. It happens in the
South, too. But they are the police. So why not—how would it ever
work without collusion from the government?

But if they are just the plain old police, maybe you are only going to
jail. In which case you'll need lawyers; if not Desmond, then some
other. The women in Dublin—you must get in touch with them. You

must know where you are going. If it is only to a loony bin, you must know its name. "Come along now." "But I must know where I am going." I wheedle: "In order to have confidence in your officers, Patrick." "They'll tell you when you are on your way."

I am taken, a cop's hand hard on each arm, out a door and to the runway. Is it by plane then? I wonder, cloudy with tension. Is the night out there the freedom of flying? Not to America, surely; there are no commercial airliners on this side of the airport. The last plane I saw through the window while in tow with Patrick was Swissair. Not that, then; it has left already. Maybe they have their own planes, small planes like my father's—a little aircraft climbing to God, to death out of it all, even Ireland. Ascending and ascending, a smile on the face of the pilot. His face covered with his twenties-style helmet, glove leather, soft and tight over his scalp, the scarf trailing like his grin. Would he be my savior after all or only another killer?

Where am I being taken? Why can't I know? Insisting, civil rights formula, demanding firmly and politely as several men lift me by the arms and virtually carry me. I am ever so willing to go along peaceably but am never permitted this. Or even the courtesy of words. But when they get me out the door, down the short ramp grilled like a cage and onto the tarmac—then I yell. Rape! As loud as I can. Help! I shout. Rape! again. The officers are appalled. I am myself; I have never yelled rape in my life. Though, of course, I mean it in the literal Latin sense: *rapio,* to kidnap, I almost explain to them, recovering my humor. Smiling and cheerful as a precondition to humane treatment. While they prepare to stuff me into a car.

I have already seen the car. Inconceivably small, considering that there are to be five of us inside it: three huge policemen, a driver, and myself, a claustrophobe truly unable to ride in the back seat of a two-door car—which is what this is. Of course they won't let me sit in the front next to the driver: I'm a captive, might run away, obstruct, and so forth. "Look, officer"—his hand is like a vise on my arm—"you are very big; I am much smaller. You are frightening me. Unnecessarily. Stop, simply stop hurting me and I will be calm. All of you, as a matter of fact, are far too excited. Let's everyone relax." They actually do, a little. "Now relax your grip on my arm. I perfectly understand I cannot escape you and am not trying to. Please relax your grip and stop hurting me." He does. He apologizes sheepishly. I like him. We will go now.

*   *   *

And having procured the concession of smoking, and the slight indulgence of a window open upon two inches of fresh air, I begin my journey with them. Having no idea where I am going—to death or jail or the hell of a madhouse—I begin my journey squashed between two enormous policemen with enormous shoulders, waists, and even thighs. Conquering my fear of arrest, prison, even death by putting my arms around their shoulders, as if it were a football afternoon or the night of a homecoming dance and they were buddies, boys from home, chums, not even dates who grapple but comrades in sport or Irish revolution or peace between the sexes. As we bowl along I make them sing with me—"Boola Boola"—because in my fright I simply cannot get another song to come to mind but can explain this one to them until something else occurs to one of us. Then we ride through the calm of County Clare, for I have coaxed them into telling me: we are headed, they say, for Our Lady of Clare. A lovely phrase.

A nunnery. I laugh. "Used to be, anyway. Now it's a rest home." "I could use a rest home." We all laugh. "I'm running out of money and this, I assume, is free?" "State-supported." "Excellent." "And nuns?" "Right." "I grew up with nuns." "Didn't we all?" We all smile remembering in the dark. "But once you're grown, you're not likely to miss them." A laugh from a big chest next to me. In fact, they could be restful. The company of women—I'd like that. The big one adds, "Chaps there, too, of course." "Different compartment, I hope?" "Right." And they drive me along, your true gnarled old IRA type at the wheel. Weedy little fellow grizzled but honorable I fervently hope. To be the captive of four men is disconcerting in the extreme; they could deliver you in any condition and get by with it. But surely this one wouldn't be likely to stop the car and pull a gun on you. I chat him up, too, just to be sure and then lapse back into the embracive company of my oversize bully brothers.

As the miles go by I decide to enjoy and imagine. In this way abbesses must have traveled the countryside after nightfall: two bodyguards, the mother superior's profile elegant and serene as her chaise went along these roads. What will it be like, the company of my quiet rest home nuns? For this may really be a hospice, so old-fashioned, quiet, and full of books. They have promised my luggage will follow; I have plenty to read in it. The Eclair movie camera to study, forever to learn how to load it perfectly. Really just what one needs—rest.

5

 B ut when we get there it is a barracks, a jail, a stone fortress. A gray
Bastille lit by institutional police state lamps. The car hums on while one
officer reconnoiters inside. My heart sinks: another betrayal. It is either
a jail or a prison or, still worse, a real madhouse you will never get out
of. Nineteenth-century, West of Ireland; they could starve you or beat
you or murder you here and you would merely disappear. Enter here and
you are buried alive. The cops seem almost to understand this, but
pleading is to no avail. The harsh light by the stone entranceway, the
gray stretches of institutional pile. The silence, the hum of the motor.
The malign intent of the place is clear; its detail is hazy. A barracks, a
prison, the worst bin of all. The mad politics of whose side these men
are on: do they imprison rebels here or is it a rest stop for terrorists,
revolutionaries, men of violence, the cruelty I felt like a cold draft from
the airport loungers who might be IRA? But whose army are these? The
secret army—is this their rest and recreation spot, asylum, whorehouse?
Is there an Armagh wing in this? Would I be among women or thrown
to some male dogs, jailers worse than my policemen? As the police
bring me through the doors I already regret their departure; they at least
did me no harm.

I am terrified anew. Locks, there are locks. Once past the door you
are finished. And bars on the windows. Hell and forever, this place of
darkness. The sound of keys. And the pretense of a hospital. A nurse,
thank God, the sight of a woman. But hard. She'll just take your bag and
all. I'll just keep it with me. Wouldn't you be more comfortable? Not

really. And if you'll just sit there. A spot where I would never sit: too far into the room, too far from the door, the hall. And the sight of her as a witness to whatever He—she refers to him as to a god—might do to me. After a very long time of waiting and knowing that whatever he is, he is master here, in total control of my life, and I his prisoner, hating whatever trappings of office, state, or psychiatry he will wear—he arrives. Young, handsome, bearded. Natty. Vienna transported to Ennis. I still sit in the chair by the door, my purse in my lap—my last possessions: money, cigarettes. He would have me sit nearer, across from his desk. The procedure. To hell with your procedure; it is simply this that I refuse to partake of. Thereby losing points, looking more abnormal. But the claustrophobia, the general terror of being a prisoner in a darkened building in the countryside of what is now a foreign country in the midst of war and turmoil I do not understand, knowing only that I may never be free again, may never come out of here alive—all this makes it impossible for me to move from the door. I look at him and hate him. As much as I fear him.

He hardly looks at me and drawls: "You're high." High means drunk where I come from and I have not had anything to drink in several days except for a drop of brandy yesterday evening. "No," I say, dizzy with fear. Am I being accused of boozing? Is Patrick's infernal Pernod my crime? "You're high, sure you are. High as a kite." Then I remember what high is. Not ordinary slang, but psychiatric jargon. Manic. Speeding. I remember Mother's doctor used that word, sitting on the grass one summer evening at the university after I had refused to see him in his office in the hospital, where I could be locked up. The next morning he had her sign papers to commit me. Yes, high—I remember high. "As a kite," he repeats, relishing the word. "No, but I am afraid," I say. "But why?" "Because I have been brought here by the police. I have been arrested. Having committed no wrong. Not having been charged with anything. Because I do not know where I am or when I will ever get out." "Ha. Well, you are here for your own good. Now I want you to explain to me how you got here." This is absurd, but anyway: the rental car, changing cars, the Nikon camera being left in the trunk. Waiting till it is returned by the customer who had rented my first car. Patrick. Desmond.

"Why did you want to change cars?" "I felt mine was both expensive and conspicuous." "Why conspicuous?" The hotel. The H Blocks book. Spilling the beans again, complicating it all with their damn

political embroils. At least if they have wards for rebels and reaction-
aries I will land in the right one. Now he presses in with questions: "Did
you feel you were being followed?" "I felt it was possible." "Who are
you that you would be followed?" "Only because of the hassle at the
hotel. Actually I just wanted to go on down to Galway." "Why?" "I
have friends there, things to do." "What?" He is amused. "Film. I
have along a good deal of equipment—in fact my problem seems to have
been that I had too much luggage for one person alone. And when
delayed by Ryan"—remember to explain they are the rental car
people—"my luggage became conspicuous. I came to Patrick's attention." Does he know who Patrick is? "The arresting officer, the chief
of security at the airport." If arrested by the police, why am I in a
madhouse? Aren't they different systems? "Why did you stop taking
lithium? We have a report that you went off lithium in July."

Amazing international system of mental policing. He knows this about
me. Telephone calls. Desmond. Sophie. My record. The room darkens
in despair. The nurse bustles in her cupboard across the hall where she
stores everyone's belongings. "Actually I went off it in May and didn't
tell anyone till July, whereupon they decided I was going crazy. I was
tired of hand tremor and diarrhea and wanted to live an existence without drugs." "Ha." "I refuse to take any here." "Ah ha." "I think that
is my right." He raises his eyebrows, sits up. I go on: "I am not a
citizen here." "You are under our jurisdiction just now and will do what
we think best. Nurse—give your things to the nurse and she will show
you to the ward. We have been in touch with Dr. Foreman. And our own
Dr. McShane has just returned from America, where he has been doing
work on lithium. He will see you in the morning."

I sit on a little chair by the door overcome with shame. A fool.
Arrested by the police into a madhouse. You will be lucky to stay alive
in here. You are the very smartass type they like to drill holes in and call
it experimental surgery. A place like this is sure to give electroshock—
you smell that about it even as you enter. You will fail to cooperate and
the electroshock will be your punishment. If it were just a matter of
having lithium crammed down your throat, it would be easy: take their
pills for two weeks till your blood levels satisfy them and then hop skip
out the door and throw the pills away. The way you did with the
Thorazine from that fellow in California. Did he really believe you
would go on poisoning yourself to the end of the package?

Busted in Ireland maybe for good: wry expression. This is the last bust of all. You will be buried here. Only twenty miles from the Cliffs of Moher, the great line of sea and spray—just over there America. That it should end like this, this misadventure. To be on the rebel side and end in a madhouse; how it dwindles. These are the prisons for women—it's your line after all. Like a fate it settles over me as I am led down the hall. Home in an awful way.

6

The ward. A place of poverty: worn yellow chenille bedspreads, dingy curtains, a crucifix, Jesus displaying his bleeding heart for thirty-five tired female captives. Most of them are elderly, some snoring already even though the lights are still on and it is the hour of the toothbrush and the toilet. I exchange greetings with the women on either side of my bed, mates now. Wary of leaving the room alone and being ambushed, I take advantage of the group tour of the toilet. The stalls without doors. The sorrow of its squalor and chill. My toothbrush is in my luggage but I can still brush my hair with the hairbrush in my purse. Even this feels better. The importance of appearance in crazy houses, its political significance: uncombed hair is never paroled. And the small comforts of it, too; I envy the toothbrushes, the washcloths. But I still have my street clothes whereas the other women here have been imprisoned so long in bathrobes that they have the complete institutional look. Also the shut face of poverty; this place is state not private, the end of the road.

It is horrible to see women in their thirties here, but for me it is the older women who hurt the most. Having no hope, likely to die here. Years of institutions now behind them. Unwanted, alienated, cast out so long. Decades of these gray places. Or relegated here just at the end; son and daughter determined to disencumber themselves. Between their empty charity and the state's prison there was nothing, and so you have this file of old women. Old ladies actually, still careful in their toilettes though liable to snore and disturb a dormitory obscenely devoid of privacy. Still, the gesture of the freckled old hand turning on the faucet is the gesture of a lifetime conducted with a certain grace and dignity, a beauty. The beauty of a fragile but firmly preserved humanity here in this shoddy hell. This infinite nightmare, where one is forced to stay alive only to watch day after day bring you less and less and closer to death. They are already aged past their years, these women; forty looks like fifty-seven. I feel like a college girl among them and they regard me as a youngster, calling me Katie, my child name.

Weeks later they will see my picture in a magazine story on the speech I made to the Labour Party in Dublin. A lifetime away. I see it and cannot believe it, a wave of shame washes over me; would that one or the other existence had never occurred. I cannot still be that person. Interviews, portraits. They call out excitedly, "Is that you, Katie?" Proud, delighted. Until that moment and after it as well, I am only their Katie, the one who cheers them up, who insists on learning the Irish pipe she brought with her, takes instruction from any woman who still remembers, jigs and amuses, inspires laughter. And when the nurse is out of the room, invigorates the spirit of rebellion and noncooperation, talking back and asking questions, having opinions and complaints. Getting their stories, giving support. Making the place as amusing as possible under the circumstances, as full of laughter and camaraderie and respect as it can be. Even persuading the nurses to be nurses rather than guards.

I have begun my life as an inmate. Even my purse is gone. Promises I will get what I need from it. Money? Cigarettes? You know your weakness and you cannot live without tobacco. A little while, as long as the money for it lasts. Without it, you'd freak, be "disturbed," get solitary. Shock. Flip. How many cigarettes are left in my pockets? I wonder, sitting on my bed, counting the possibilities of getting through the night. Maybe I can get out in the morning; maybe this is some Irish notion of a night in the cooler for a drink one never even had. Idiot to have let yourself get caught. Somewhere a Ford Escort is going through the night—you could have been on the road. And how do you contact anyone now? How do you get out? How do you get help? When it is quieter here you can see about doors and windows and telephones. The room only half lit now, the nurses down at the end softly knitting, of all things, Aran sweaters. A bright green one. Would you knit one for me? I ask, chatting them up, taking the liberty of getting out of bed. Shhh. I must hush, it is bedtime.

They have only now finished doling out a whole sackful of pills. Things to make you sleep, they croon. "Mary, won't you have one for sweet dreams?" "What are they?" I ask. But there's no telling. "The powders," they laugh. "The medicines." "Who makes them?" "Ah, the companies." "What's in them?" "What they should have." Nothing is ordered for me yet, which the night watch come to regret, since I parade between the file of bedsteads as if staying on my legs were safety itself, on watch in another vigil.

As the hours go by, the sleeping bodies become everyone I have ever known. I am inside a film where Fumio lies there and Sita just down there—an old woman transported here by death or age, or frailty, a mysterious figure down at the end by the nurses. I feel an enormous compassion for this prone shape, both for herself and for her as an emanation of Sita. I walk the aisle, looking at the faces in the beds. Are they people I know? Girls from grade school, women from the movement. Resemblances. Some yes, some no. Generalities. Or as strangers then, being here, embrace the spirit of each, these marked beings; acknowledge each soul, its sanctity in this charnel house. And keep on learning the place. While you tarry here the time is precious; absorb it all. But figure it out as well, find the exit, explore.

When the nurses lose patience I retreat to my bed. But I will not rest tonight. I must wait it out. To sleep here is to assent to this thing. Lay out your cigarettes. Line them up, count them till each has a personality, a flavor of its own, a moment of its bloom and perfection. This one for coffee—if there is such a thing. Throw in a French Caporal for afterward, then put the rest aside for emergencies. This one for dawn thoughts. This for the end of the night. Already I need to pee again. And there's no leaving this room; I suppose if I tried they might catch me, fancy I was escaping. Solitary—I wonder where they keep it, which rooms are the locked ones. I would like to venture out and explore but I dare not now. So with infinite tact and quietude I pee in the empty water glass by my bed. A perfect job. This little success amuses me. Tired beyond all expression, afraid beyond any hope of rest, my mind plays games. As the room itself fascinates through the night, changes and re-forms itself as if films were being projected upon the walls. But from where?

From the other side of the partition. The practical operator in me would love to explore that, that source. Walls that take on images like the walls of solitary in Herrick, that first bust in California. And here I can summon everyone I know or love or ever have: Fumio, Sophie, Dakota, and Petra, flashes of biblical epic movies, Charlie Chaplin and Paris afternoons in fleapits, my father. A presence here, a protective force.

Desmond will come; he has to since he knows about it. Are there forces at work already to free me? I have only to stay awake and not give in to panic, make no sound. If you speak out loud, if you scream, it's all over. It is necessary to be very stoic. And the place is full of mystery. Come upon it with stealth then. That Sita is here, for example . . . Not the real Sita, but a similitude. Like the Egyptian figure in the baths of the Mayo wing in Minnesota, a servant in a head-rag, the lowest of the low; we have been together in Egypt. And it was Sita. A countess thrown among the poor. Sita is dead now; she may appear as anything, show up in any form to console me. Here she is mercy herself, that very old woman down by the nurses, so ancient she may die tonight. Little gurgling noises, for bed a strange contraption with rails around it. For her to hold on to? For her to be contained and restricted by? I inquire in one of my little runs up the ward, worried that she may indeed be dying with the two phlegmatic, overweight nurses beside her paying no heed at all. One would almost think she was in labor: the little cries, the hunching up of her thighs, her legs drawn up in bed. Birth and death: opposite yet similar paradox. If her bed were to be drawn through the wall behind her into the next room, cell, whatever . . . And if she were transformed upon reaching the other side? Freed. What if Sita were to rise from this deathbed, resurrected? I should go and see. I should explore the next room, make sure. Making my way softly, first finding the bathroom again, then farther a little ways. The ward's wall should end here. Yes, there is a room, a solitary cell is it, a judas window? No, only a small empty room with a strange red glow in it. Nothing. No miracle.

There are no miracles. There is only this place. Clearer in the dawn, the first lovely light—gray on the white of its walls. The corridors go nowhere but to locked doors. Downstairs, for I even made it that far on cat feet, my hand comes upon the bars in a window that will open four inches and no more. Built that way. This is it. A cold chill on my back under the cotton shirt. My sweater and trousers are upstairs on the ward bed; having no nightclothes, I was to sleep in a shirt and underpants. If you could get out of here you'd need trousers—be sure they don't take them away. And money. But that they already have. Buy cigarettes as soon as you can or you really will freak out. I take my hand from under the window sash, remembering all the IRA men warning how it could be broken; they could break it here. What if they caught you at this?

I make it quietly to bed again to watch the day come into the transom overhead, a huge compartmented skylight. Really a lovely thing. For one section of the building is old and despite its present shabbiness and the deliberate ugliness of its current regime, it has something still of its original grandeur in certain architectural details. Like this skylight which invites flight. Dangerously, ominously, recklessly shouting out for angels, for broomsticks and wings. The sky as the only solution. Like their drugs. Avoid all the damn drugs, too. The rest of the ward are night fliers. After the nurse comes around with the little pills of happiness, they ascend in choirs and hit the sky. The routes of their travel so urgent and wonderful that their presence here throughout the day is merely an impersonation—like the bodies snoring in their beds. You must be on guard against that temptation most of all; the urge to fly is great and wonderful; beautiful and white and ethereal, the wind on your face and wings, already an ache in your arms.

Have another cigarette; it's time for the next to the last. Morning has already come. The light is back and with it safety, daytime behavior. They can't get by with as much. This place will have to assume some semblance of a hospital again. The nuns must be around somewhere behind the lay staff and the doctors. Get a message to Desmond. And take another look around, know the lay of the place. Returning from the bathroom and the window at the end of the hall, studying the misty landscape for bearings, I notice a plant. A geranium in a pot, badly in need of water. I clean it, remove the dead leaves, the old blossom, pinch it back, bring it water in a glass from the bathroom. In its tired earth is whatever little hope there ever is: poor reminder of the farm, of the world outside, of Ireland now shining green through impassable windows.

7

Now consciousness returns: I did sleep awhile. This unbelievable place, these absurd events. The sorrow of gray morning in the windows, the incomprehensible bustle, as if an army sergeant were overseeing the making of beds. A nurse in the corner of my eye; next to me two inmates working as if possessed. "The bottom sheet this way, the top sheet that way, the blanket stretched tight—watch now, Katie, you're next." I have no idea how to do this. Others cover for me; one manning my bed from the opposite side, teaching, showing; another at my shoulder, correcting my errors; the nurse bellowing for speed. They can't mean this, I think, it is hardly six in the morning—what is it we rise to? An hour's wait in another room, my stomach growling for coffee, watching the mist out the windows give way to Ireland behind bars. A wave of despair.

The room itself is large, ugly, shabby, the plaster falling from the ceiling in one corner, bilious yellow with the Sacred Heart staring down from the wall. The usual Sacred Heart, the one in every home and refectory in Ireland, the one in Catholic schoolrooms in St. Paul. To be imprisoned with this bad picture . . . Make the best of it; let it remind you of piety, youth, the good intentions of those who love this image. Barf. And yet it does its work, exuding both good and ill: submission, lack of initiative, the old habitual obedience and futility; as well as sympathy, a bond with all those in the room, a tribal icon we share with our jailers.

The women chirping in their chairs, one in particular, a night flier, I imagine; where did she go last night, London, Liverpool? The nearly British accent in the old throat, the fine ways, the taste for tea and umbrellas, the well-worn little suit. Real clothes. Later I learn her name is Rosalind and she has a room all her own, one of the unexplored rooms down the hallway which I mistook for solitary cells. It is a delight to hear her, compared with the others, so morose in their various poses of dejection.

The hopelessness of it all, seeing the old woman, Mary, before the cold hearth; solitary, proud, arthritic, Mother Ireland herself thrown into this rubbish heap. Try to do something, ask if we can have a fire. The hearth has ashes—they must use it sometimes—it's freezing damp in here. Where's the coffee, for God's sake? Agitate carefully and pitch in. Finding a napkin, I put it over my arm. Think of what my pal Bill Rivers would do, waking up in a joint like this, or Edward Jackson. Both are black, the one a painter who is also a magnificent cook, the other the convict I corresponded with for years in Folsom, where he poured the coffee for over a decade. A place like this wouldn't faze them; they would reach out and adapt. Arrange that napkin, set the tables; this may encourage the notion of breakfast. Or at least prepare the way for the appearance of coffee. You're nearly out of cigarettes, so don't stew but make yourself a contributor, cheer this place up. I prepare an elegant table. But the staff do not take well to this at all; I must sit down.

During the moments of my restaurant comedy I am happy, have beat the system, have turned capture into amusement, have become the perfectly amiable inmate doing the best of time. Have even transcended the jail altogether and converted it into a superior eatery. And becoming these two men, remembering and assuming their selves, I look upon it all philosophically, as they would; the meanness and chill of the place is a joke. Thank God for knowing them, for being able to reach out and touch their male humor, their cool, and their blackness. To change gears into a black male self, distant and remote as that should be—yet because of them it is not. Our rapport makes it easy for them to come to my rescue here, for me to assume their attributes and airs, to turn the catastrophe into an occasion to be happy, to play. I have begun to relish serving, to delight in it—waiting on the women, bestowing on them what they need and want. In mockery and reproof of the staff, with their bully manner and their absolute refusal to wait upon, to give, to serve, even to dole out. What comes from their hands is thrown. Their very entrance, so long awaited, is an invasion. For they storm the doors.

Every activity they direct toward us is calculated to intimidate: the door never opens, it bursts. And then their shouting, for they never condescend to speak, only bellow. They take care of me and my cheery restaurateur persona in no time.

I may not set the tables. That is their job and they will not have help from patients. Patients only wash dishes. Sit down and be still, a big nurse thunders at me. I cannot be the friendly spirit of the Mississippi, an imaginary American black gracefully dispensing ironic hospitality, Jim Millett's sassy tomboy running one hell of a good hash house. How obdurate and unimaginative they are—I had amused the others, woken some out of their stupor. But at least there is some sign of life now in the room. Coals are brought in and over the course of an hour and a half a fire is finally installed, a small coal fire to sit about. And then at last the tea is slopped in, horribly watered with milk. Jug after jug consumed in no time together with rubbery white bread, nothing else. If you're not quick, you don't get any. There is no coffee. I wasn't quick enough for the bread. And I've chosen to drink my milk in one cup and black tea in another, a very unorthodox procedure which will distinguish me here. I have taken my things over by the fire, where those who have finished sit. I would make my rations last, sip the tea when it's the right temperature, while smoking and reading the paper. In this way I avoid the staff, who are everywhere cheering on the inmates to eat faster and faster so everything may be taken away from them and they may wash the dishes.

"Teas, ladies," the matron shouted as she whammed into the room, her disciples putting down the tea jugs while she called out one inmate's name after another and ordered them to take their pills before her eyes. You do not get the teas without the pills. She is still calling as the jugs are packed up. She has not called my name. I read as if undisturbed, a lay person here by an error, a civilian. Of course I do not look up. Didn't I tell the doctor with the little beard last night that I would not take drugs, that this was my constitutional right? If she calls my name I will repeat my little formula from the American Civil Liberties Union. Not that that will do me any good, but it's a spell, a ritual, something you must say to have said it. So when I hear my own name called in this place and the beefy face of the boss nurse is staring me down, I mumble my excuses and then wilt before her ringing command. "Swallow that right now." "What is it?" "Your medicine." "Would you explain what it is called?" "Prescribed." "No, I mean what is the substance, what chemical?" "None of your business." "How can I swallow something when I do not even know what it is?" "Swallow." I pretend to swallow. There is really nothing else to do.

And then wait. My mouth still, afraid until the moment I can spit the pill carefully into the little pocket at the top of my Mexican shirt under my warm but rather dingy Aran sweater. Safe. Evidence—that I did not even throw it away, only saved it to explain, demonstrate, prove that I was given no choice. Because some help must be coming. As soon as I can I will have them call Desmond. Maybe they'll let me call him myself. Write letters, too, just to make certain; start wheedling your pen from your purse. Begin first though with cigarettes: if you have cigarettes you can outlast a siege; if not, you're in trouble. And so I beg for some of my own money, getting a five-pound note and brandishing it like a pirate; I want all of this in cigarettes. Laughter and consternation—this is an enormous sum of money. "Good, I want an enormous number of cigarettes." "You'll be cheated," from inmate and nurse alike. "No I won't—you wouldn't think of cheating me. You have seen the amount, we all know how many packages it will buy." "Well, then, when someone is sent to the stores." "Where is the store?" "Main building." "And where is that? May I go myself?" "Indeed, you may not."

I am tormented with curiosity to know what is outside this door. At the end of this hallway there is another lovely skylight, even more complex than that in the dormitory. One saw it for a moment while being led here, an exquisite piece of work; must make the building eighteenth century, later perhaps, way out here in the West. And the nuns once held this place as a hospice for the sick. What is it now, what sort of prison for the state? So many questions to ask them. Where are the nuns, for example? Still here—there is one in charge, and a few others as well. Most of the rest are lay nurses, nurse's aides. And the doctors? They are the state. Try to orient yourself, try to figure the place out: where you are, how it's run, how you get out of here on your own if you cannot get help. The others, they would help me if they knew where I was; the women here in Ireland, the women in Dublin. But they are in Dublin and you are buried alive somewhere near Ennis in Clare.

Outside, the green of Ireland in mist through the windows. The soul breaks itself on the glass, yearning for the road, for the country, for the trees and the shrubs, the gray stone walls and lanes, the sound of happiness in civilian voices, normality, freedom. If roaming in Ireland was freedom itself at the start of this adventure, just to be at large outside these windows would be luxury. That chance is all gone now. You will never see the place, it will be outside these big unopened windows forever. Windows that will slide up only four inches and no more; I have tried the ones in this room already.

They are setting chairs in a circle. What game is it this time? This morning before breakfast we were lined up on chairs in the hallway, the chairs not next to each other but one behind the other. Like the dining room chairs my sisters and I lined up to play train in childhood; moving from chair to chair was moving from coach to coach. But the game of coaches here is only waiting to be seen by the doctor. One after another we proceed to the big sitting room, the dayroom. This room for the day, the dormitory for the night; there are only two rooms and the bathroom—which has no evidence of baths, only toilets and sinks. All of us waiting; the ones who have been inspected sit inside reverently in their chairs. The doctor is God. Or the devil. But we are reverent and querulous. Old Mary complains of her cold, Rosalind cannot sleep, Ann has a running nose. Only physical complaints are brought forward, though he is a psychiatrist. He is even the great Dr. McShane I have been warned is taking on my case as a lithium truant. And he prescribes.

Then the doctor from last night arrives in an immaculate and utterly radiant suit. It must be tailored, must have cost a fortune; the shoulders are cut perfectly. His shirt is spotless. Materialist dandy—how I detest this man. He steps forward as in dancing class to draw my blood. A great deal of it, it seems to me. Isn't that more than you need for a sample—not a lithium level, of course, since I have not taken lithium for months—merely an ordinary blood sample to contrast to later specimens when they have forced lithium upon me? "Vulture," the old woman next to me murmurs. "Vampire," another one comments. They must know him, the procedure; do they weaken you here through large extractions?

McShane marches around, cheering up the ladies, making himself popular. His method is a canny performance: sorcerer to the witches, winking at irrational statements, humming and laughing and lining us up before him, performing before a row of women in his baggy old suit. He is in on our secrets, patron and privy to our obsessions and complaints, our bugbears and specters, our ambitions and hatreds. Distrust him more than the other; "this werewolf," I hear myself whisper. An old woman nods. Curious locutions, but they seem to work, to suit the occasion. Another language is discovered, rediscovered.

And now the little chairs are lined up around the fire, oddly resembling kindergarten. But this is a row of old women, the chairs larger than kindergarten but the atmosphere otherwise the same. Institutional, an enforced childishness and dependence, a great emphasis upon being "good." And we are all good in our row. Except for the pill hidden in my pocket I am good, too, frantic to learn the rules of this joint and shine my way out of it.

The teacher has come, or whatever she is, civilian clothes amid the bathrobes, the fresh air of one from outside. She is Miss Strong. "The boss's daughter," an old woman says to me behind her hand. "You are in Dr. Strong's place." Yes, of course—I heard that last night; from the admitting nurse, from the night aides: "You're in Dr. Strong's now." Like a rattling last laugh in a thriller. And here comes the boss's daughter to have a look at us in the morning. To spread charity and female goodness, to dispense a feudal kindness upon the peasants of the manor, as nineteenth-century ladies visited their cottagers. What has she in mind? She calls it a class. We will be her class. Will we indeed? I look at her sidewise; she will have some young social worker's point of view but she is after all a Strong, his daughter. The same force and omnipotence, only more insidious. They even live here, Strong's family inhabiting the main convent, an eighteenth-century manor house, like colonial nobility. But what will the class be? Everyone's name. The names a little picture of western Ireland, Mayo and Galway and Clare.

The names fascinate me, so I hardly listen to the rest. I think to myself, what if we women, outcast and refuse but representatives of all these clans and tribes—what if we were a conclave of our own, what if the class could really be a meeting of us as it pretends to be? Naturally it degenerates at once into petty complaints, variations of things recited for the doctor. Then rebukes, admonitions on our lady teacher's part. Then we are to write our minds, inscribe our thoughts on a piece of paper. Splendid—does she really mean it? I wonder, itching to make this a powerful declaration of being held against my will and in violation of my rights. I hand it back to her thoroughly satisfied I have expressed myself, pressed a button which will help to free me, done the best of magic. Later I learned that the pieces are brought out of the room and over to the other side of the hospital and torn into bits. I inquired the purpose of this cruel hoax. "Why, to protect the patients, we are protecting their anonymity; the papers must never be read by anyone." Meanwhile the women themselves and the clans convened in their names—the Learys and the Murrays and the Joyces and the O'Connells, names I gaped to hear, each one a revelation, a piece of the map, a chunk of history, a living legend—all now fade back into their chairs. And the day's lassitude begins. The torpor of the hours before television, the hours with television, and the hours after television.

The newspaper makes the rounds. I have read even the livestock section and all the houses to rent or sell, Common Market veal and beef, secretarial openings. Faces stare out the window or more often at the floor, at a bench or table. The teas come again, and the pills, for which the teas are merely an excuse. Lunch itself is only another tea, pill. The tease, I begin to call them, appalled at how little real food is ever served here. White bread and milk-watered tea. For dinner a rasher of bacon and an overcooked egg. That's pretty well it. Starvation of a certain kind; enough white bread to blow you up into fat, never enough food to fill or satisfy. And always the pills, the chemicals you must fight on an empty stomach. Or a stomach with nothing but white bread balled up like wet Kleenex. You need better food to fight off chemicals. They do give you oranges—start going for them.

"Teas, ladies, teas." The big nurse shoves and thunders through the door, interrupting stupor or conversation or frolic. And another pill makes its way into my pocket. What will happen when they draw blood again and you're found out? You can make your stand. Do your "You can't make me swallow the unexplained" thing. Or maybe there will be help sooner. Try the nurse again about the phone. "We have given you money, that's enough for one day." "But where are the cigarettes?" "Calm down, dearie, they don't go to the stores till afternoon." "May I make a phone call?" "Tomorrow, love. Sure now, today just behave yourself." I have seen the phone; it is between the dayroom and the dormitory. I even picked it up once and tried to get outside, but of course it has no dial, is connected to a switchboard on another ward. I could not find out any more before a horrified nurse seized the instrument from my hand. I must call my lawyer, I explained, amiably.

"Sure, darlin', sure, now you run along and don't let me catch you touching this again." So there is no way out.

But a bit down from the phone, where we waited in our chairs to see the doctor this morning, just there is the one hopeful-seeming place, a row of windows that looks onto a small parking lot. Cars come along a road through what seems to be the hospital grounds: wooded, lawns, trees, a bit of digging and planting here and there. A sign announcing that some local contractor has got the grand big job of repairing the wall; probably newfangled security devices, too. There are dogs at night. You hear them through the windows as you lie in bed. But that little road, that little turnaround, hardly even a parking lot—anyone could come for me. Outlandish rescuers like my tutor from Oxford whom I saw only a few weeks ago. What if she were to come, stately in a rented black taxicab, English and hard to argue with, the perfect lady, gentleness itself but determined to scoop up her erring pupil. Miss Eliot, I murmur, staring out the window. What if—the car approaching, the figure descends: a nurse being delivered to work, an aide, a gardener, a woman who makes the evening gruel, the night nurses in pairs. I am hardly missed in the dayroom, having obtained permission for the toilet. I hover near this row of windows and if noticed, I am just cleaning the plants, a very quiet American who has taken on the plants and makes herself useful. Afraid, then hopeful; release like heaven, the sweetness of it. The horror of more days here. How do you hold out? How to stay sane, not go racing right over the edge? So near it is, so hard not to succumb; the place is built to make you surrender. Hold on, be quiet, wait. One holler, four cuss words, and you will never get out. Solitary. Shock. Transport to another can. I stand sentinel before these windows for hours, imagining anyone: the women from Dublin, Desmond himself. It is too much to imagine Sophie.

I remember her only in a book. A volume of Irish verse I happened to have in my purse and now regard as a Bible, since it is the only book I can lay my hands on, nearly memorizing every poem. Eroticizing them at times, politicizing them at others; a curious religion of love, of rebellion and uprising. For I am too stubborn to let Sophie go. To believe in her betrayal and admit defeat. She must be somewhere still. No, not loving me as I love her. But simply because I will not cease or desist from loving her, she will not escape me. I will make her an idea—which I will not swerve from or betray. And my fidelity will be so steadfast, so enormous it will conquer. Knowing she has helped to put me here gives me only two choices: to abandon her as she has abandoned me or to transcend the whole thing. With a crazy charity, a greater devotion, like courtly love, a religious retention of faith, hope, mercy. For once inside, I have forgiven everyone—never forgotten, of course, but forgiven. It has happened before: my sister, Fumio, Sita— all of them had connived against me and I insisted on continuing to love them all. To deal with their invincible ignorance of prison and despair, I would have to forgive them gratuitously. With a sweep of pure goodness only religious jargon approaches.

But you are in Ennis in Clare now, in Strong's power. So find some writing paper, start trying to get letters out of here.

It will be the usual lined foolscap of grammar school effusions. It will be difficult to make an impression on paper like this, but try. "Tomorrow," I am told when I ask for paper. Even paper is forbidden. You are incommunicado here then. The only hope is to do what they do in jails. So I start off in secret on the mean little brown sheets of folded toilet paper. Good enough for the H Blocks lads, I figure. The women at Armagh write on this, too. D'arcy has shown me examples of how much can be said. "Five hundred words, I'll bet it is," we murmured as she unfurled a sheet slipped to her on a visit. Now it's a question of whether you can smuggle your words outside. Are there envelopes in that purse of yours? I'll bet there are. Make a fuss about your hairbrush or something and get inside the bag again. But you must also get your address book; you can hardly use that while they watch you. Arrange to sit down with it, do a little song and dance about how messy your bag is, how long it takes to find something. Then let them be distracted by another patient. Go over these addresses carefully. First try the women in Dublin: Deirdre, Nell, Charlotte. And then there is your friend Monika in Amsterdam. You have to work at this from all sides. You cannot just sit—you must devote every moment to getting out. Otherwise you get scared, paralyzed with fear that you will die here, be here for years, a figure in a window somewhere in Clare near Ennis. If you've really done all you can for the day, go ahead and delve into trivia like learning the rules here, let yourself lapse into television or the cheery radio voices that transport you, popular music, watering their damned plants. The day is nightmare unless you work.

8

The windows at the back of the dayroom giving onto Ireland. Vigils before them: the distant green, the mists of morning and evening. The other windows from the dormitory. Times after dinner waiting out the hours before bed with matchsticks. Counting the ones left, striking one, lighting the cigarette, then burning the flame before the windowpane until the wooden stick is nearly gone. Each charred stick another dead Indian in an imaginary game of Sierra Madre. Still in my embroidered Mexican shirt. Do the matches signal to anyone, does anyone know? The first night I even thought I heard the sound of drummers, the flicker of torches—crazy with fright, I fancied my immurement would cause notice, attract help, conjuring some grand band of Irish rebels waiting outside, their drums a signal I was watched over and would be rescued. Only a matter of time and the dignity of proper measure. Then I got some sleep and woke up to reality. Days ago.

Today I took things into my own hands, without waiting for my money. When I found the route, I should have lain low a few more hours, gotten the nurse to dole out cigarettes or candy money or an emery board—anything to get into my purse, which is locked away in a strong room with everyone else's belongings. And their clothes. Because, of course, I still have my clothes; they have never taken them from me. Probably because I have nothing else, was not turned in by willing relatives with a suitcase full of nighties and underwear. So I remain in my clothes, able to make this gamble even if it means washing the same pair of socks every night. My suitcases are still at the airport

and I am a foreigner; perhaps these considerations contributed to bending the rules. I am the only one here not in a bathrobe. With my clothes
and money I might have made it.

Even without money I could have gotten as far as Ennis; it is only two
miles. A call to my lawyer, Desmond, and I could take asylum at the
Old Ground Hotel until this is cleared up. Sit myself down in that lovely
country inn and order coffee, register, begin charging things with the
credit I have here—former guest, tourist, even writer—and one call to
Desmond to straighten this out. Because, of course, I know it is against
the law to escape these joints—I was only availing myself of counsel,
since it was never permitted me, and by my laws it is my right. Just to
sit in the lounge by the peat fire and wait for the call to go through to
Desmond for legal advice.

So under what authority am I being detained? What doctor signed me
in, with the collusion or permission of which friend or relative? There
must always be a next of kin in the United States, in my country. How
have they arranged it here? By telephone? Well, I have only to get to a
telephone myself. Just to sit in the lounge and wait for coffee to come
while the switchboard puts through the call. Only that. Then Desmond's
voice. The pause and then the laughter—the thing a ghastly joke for
which one bears no ill will. Of course he'll help—he'll say: "Now this
is what you do, what we'll do." Quick and full of good sense, till a plan
is outlined and concluded. And then we'll have all the charming talk
about the fun over lunch, the cottage on the moors, how I must meet his
wife, how there's just the place in Galway now to hear music. Out along
the coast. And do I know the French restaurant there, did I try it? The
owner's a friend of his; it would be the perfect place for dinner and then
the pub for the tunes.

I turn away smiling. And the manager will be there to say the room
is ready and there are sandwiches in the bar. Probably Pernod too, but
all one needs now is human kindness. Special thanks to the women at
the switchboard, the faces of goodness. My hands no longer shake, I am
saved. Back in the human race and among the civilized; returned from
those buried only two miles away.

And so I didn't even bother about the money. It would take too long and
complicate things. When I realized that the door had been left open for
the moment and that my clothes were proof of lay condition, made me

not a prisoner but one able to walk the grounds, were at least a ticket to walk, I walked. Quite as if it were an ordinary thing. Heart in my mouth and beating right through my gullet.

The energy of fear. Adrenaline in need of control, for it would otherwise let me run, make me run. No, walk. Look about you as you walk, get the lay of the land here, find the gate, follow the road. How it resembles the Hudson River; the lovely grounds for the public to see. Away from view in the back wards behind me the screams of nighttime, the bars of despair, the odor of cheap food and poor washing, victim flesh gray and hopeless in confinement. Only a few hundred yards away is a charming flower bed I never saw out the window, lush lawns, great eighteenth-century stone buildings. Even one of those old ruined towers where legend says they used to imprison witches during the persecution. The place where I was confined is for the most part undistinguished concrete. Being outside it now, I can finally see it.

The buildings get better as you go along. The fine places are for administration evidently and Dr. Strong's private residence. There are a few old men who seem to come and go as they please, pensioners, I suppose. Would I achieve this dubious status in twenty years? I wonder. Just keep walking as if this were a constitutional. Smile at the people you meet. But not a crazy smile. Figures in the landscape, a patient or a guard, the difference a subtle matter of clothing. Will they spot you? Become invisible. If approached you must be an American; ask the age of the building, pretend you have a car in the lot. You have a clear path to the gate, which is under reconstruction, being refurbished. But just now it is lunchtime and even the masons are away. Go to it; you got it—go.

Out on the road a moment's indecision: should I hitch a ride right to Galway? This is a main highway and the distance is only thirty or forty miles. But with no money? It's too much to chance. To hitchhike with nothing but the clothes on your back, no money, no passport. And if caught you would be open to the legal charge of escape. Whereas if you only go into Ennis to contact your lawyer—hell, you have an argument then. Okay, Ennis. I notice a woman driving into a courtyard across the highway. Instinct would keep me off the road, and if she would give me a lift I wouldn't be spotted and run down between here and the Old Ground; I could make it. But she is a student driver; this building is in fact a driving school and her teacher, she says, does not permit her to take passengers. Very well, on foot then. Hoping my American accent,

my story about taking a walk and losing my way, were all in order—
there are telephones in her driving school; she would only have to lift a
receiver and the guards would be after me in force.

And the way seems long, though it isn't. Along the highway up to the
gas station it seems very long. Closer, then at the bridge where you
catch sight of the town. And then it is no longer far, it is near. An old
man approaches me, a fresh young woman, each saying hello. I am
already in Ireland. The Old Ground is only over this bridge, past the
ruined abbey; then take a right down a fine old medieval street. There at
the end, across from the cathedral, the Old Ground Hotel. Its wonderful
white plaster walls immaculate. The freshly painted black trim, the
drive past the door, flowers. It is easy now—you can see it, smell it, feel
it. You are there even if you are only approaching the bridge. The rest
is the cathedral city of Ennis; you know this town—one of your favorite
places. It is all over, it never happened, you are merely on a walk, a hike
maybe. Trembling with happiness, with nearness, with success.

When the car pulls up. Full of them. Big nurse and another one in her
civilian clothes and the one with Swiss badges. I am forever examining
their badges to reassure myself they are nurses and not merely jailers.
Today the one wearing badges has a rope. "Really, rope, dear lady,"
I protest. Big nurse tries to tackle me. I keep explaining that I am not
escaping, only trying to reach my lawyer, and since I have not been
permitted to write or phone him I am merely taking a walk to the Old
Ground Hotel, where there is a telephone. I won't resist; there is no need
to hurt my arm. Only after thousands of promises is this accepted.
Watch out—after the rope, the straitjacket. It is absolutely necessary
that you talk her out of the rope. Joke her out of it, for her sake too.
"Tell me now, how did you ever come by such a thing?" "It's for my
pony," she admits. She always keeps it in the car. I laugh and they do
too. Deliberately calculatingly charming them. We ride along cramped
into intimacy. Our laughter is nervous, a bit ashamed. We are all in bad
faith; my appeasement, their overkill. The idea penetrating them ever so
slightly that I might not be that crazy after all, but it's doctor's orders
that I'm inside the hospital. With a lawyer I'd be a real nuisance.

"So you thought you'd take a walk, Katherine?" "I did. I didn't
realize you'd object. The door was open. I was never told that I was
locked up and forbidden to leave." "Leaving's against the law even,"
the big one says from the front seat. "Perhaps you'd let me write a letter
one day?" I venture. "If you're good, the doctor may take you off

orders; right now you're incommunicado." And when I get back things may be worse. They will certainly guard me better, maybe drug me more. Maybe solitary now. Shock—would this induce them to shock for punishment? Jesus. Talk faster, be merry, not too merry, but extremely good-natured, stupidly foreign, innocent, a naïf who took a walk. Ask about them, their lives, their training; admire. We are back in the gates—the hope is lost. The idea that I had intended to escape to a hotel and a phone call to an attorney amuses them no end. How thoroughly American, how quaint. I sit in the back seat, fighting off claustrophobia and a hundred related fears of what comes next, and play for them old selves still around for reference: the well-mannered foreign student, the carefully brought up young lady from St. Paul. Harmless, touristic, obedient. Fending off the retribution that will follow once inside the walls. So that I will not be stuck in there where I could be struck, beaten, given solitary, shock.

And they've been fairly decent about it. Of course I lost my clothes. That was the first thing. After the doctor heard, I was jumped by a gang of women and divested of my trousers. They might easily have asked me to remove them. The story given out is that they have decided my wool trousers needed mending at the cuff and a dry cleaning. Dry cleaning takes them two weeks. Then I was awarded a bathrobe. But since the only top I have is a shirt and sweater they have decided these must be worm over the bathrobe rather than under. Otherwise, since I have no pajama bottoms, the bathrobe might open to reveal my legs, a dreadful thing. So with my long Aran sweater over a bathrobe I troop about now far more eccentric than the other ladies. And I therefore have an even smaller chance of getting out, since clothing and appearance are everything in a nuthouse.

9

Tonight big nurse found me out. After the lithium pill was duly given and received (in time the blood count would tell them if their own vigilance had not observed), she noticed. Waited until I swallowed— and then her instinct grabbed for me and found the pill still in my cheek. I could swallow then or confront. I decided to confront. The speech about civil liberties, about forced medication of unexplained substances. Carried away with my case, I demonstrated the tablets in the right-hand pocket of my Mexican shirt. That was it. Swallow or else. "And you are to swallow this, too." "What is it?" "Thorazine."

Prescribed, one supposes, since the breakout. Although here one hardly knows, since pills appear to be meted out with such abandon, especially by the night shift, who have bags of them. Cellophane bags with pills of all colors, doled out at night as delicacies, the older women and the more depressed eager to accept them as tickets to sleep, to dreams—dreams advertised as wonderful by the dispensers. At times I imagine they are testing drugs for manufacturers or catering to drug addiction as a subterranean way of life here, the night life. The things of the day are not the things of the night here at all, the night staff a different breed, meaner, further inclined to have no contact with the patients. Unlike the maternalistic scolding habits of the day staff, who treat us as defective children, the night staff treat us more like convicted felons.

And now there is a fairly hideous Thorazine syrup I am to consume in the evening. Pretending to myself that it is brandy or Drambuie or some Irish liqueur I haven't come across in the outside world. Drinking it slowly, trying to avoid its odious taste and convert it to booze or pleasure or a treat—anything but punishment to darken the mind. Mixing it with milk or drinking it in alternate drafts while the night nurse bellows that I finish. Defying her, pretending to like it. By God, she forces more upon me. Prescribed? Who knows, by a doctor, by her whim, who knows?

I only know that it will take more oranges to beat it. More coffee if I could get it, or straight black tea. I begin to eat fruit like an athlete. To save it in my dresser, to go through six oranges a day. I begin to thirst. For, of course, Thorazine is thirst. The women talk of another drug here—Prolixin. As for Thorazine, it's not watered down with orange juice as in America. This is straight shots, big shots. What is it? What is it doing to my mind? Thorazine is hallucinatory. I hardly need that while trying to maintain my sanity against this place. But what is Prolixin?

I have lost the sense of being the quiet one here, the nearly invisible being at teatime. Only noticed at the very end, then she takes her tablet obediently. Polite, nondescript; even the accent and the foreignness go unnoticed, since she never says anything in the nurses' presence. Out of sight of the guards she is the life of the party, amusing and clowning and waking up and occupying the listless, learning their stories, finding out about the place, discovering who is getting shock. Always the battered-looking ones, utterly terrified, who either know it is punishment or try desperately to tell themselves it is for their own good. But in the telling, the truth hits them in the face as they talk. Mostly they are silent and tremble, their hands a Saint Vitus' dance over the chenille laps of their bathrobes; their faces red, their tongues difficult to control. Other tongues, too: the Thorazine tongues that swell and thirst constantly; most of the day but a quest for liquid of some kind.

Ann's husband put her here, Mary's in-laws, Margaret's own mother. And the visits, even the visits of the culprits, are cherished, awaited, loved, hated, feared. Boredom and necessity together.

If I could get the dope on this place, the drugs and the shock particularly, then Deirdre's friend Charlotte, who is a member of the Irish parliament, could look into it. Just the sight of our peeling paint and the jaundiced walls—the diseased look of the plaster in that corner of the ceiling in the dayroom—would incite a committee.

There has recently been a scandal over Irish loony bins; maybe we could get some mileage out of that. Just "mileage," of course, since what is really wrong, the drug—the drug as healer, as official method now—is insidious, the true evil. Generally the drug is advocated because it pacifies and makes work easy for the aides and nurses, the guards. Actually it does a great deal more, all very contrary to sanity; it induces visions, hallucinations, paranoia, mental confusion. Nothing could be harder than to maintain sanity against the onslaught of a drug. The bin itself is insane, abnormal, a terrifying captivity, an irrational deprivation of every human need—so that maintaining reason within it is an overwhelming struggle. After a certain time many victims collapse and agree to be crazy; they surrender. And withdraw. And as time goes by, they cannot or finally will not return; it is too far, it is too unrewarding, it is too dubious—they have forgotten. And they limit their lives to their own minds, the diversions within them. The woes and gratifications of some carefully wrought fantasy, built like a nest out of the tatters of what was once a life but could be no longer.

Odd how the shape of an institution, its intention and definition, affect its inmates: felons remain sane in prison, because it is prison and not a loony bin. The very purpose of the bin and what all understand by its meaning predicate madness. To remain sane in a bin is to defy its definition. The general understanding is that one does not get there till crazy and one gets out only when well, that is, cured and purged of craziness. And what is the cure—fear? Is the danger of endless captivity supposed to motivate one into reason? For me it has the opposite effect. The more I am afraid I will never get out, the more anxious I am. The more eager to find a way out, whether it be telephone or mail, friends or a walk to the hotel. And now that escape has failed me I realize I have sunk deeper here, lost points, will be watched as a jumper from now on, drugged harder. I have come to their attention, need closer supervision. Another attempt, and it would be more than your old brown trousers that you'd lose. There must be "quiet" rooms in this passage. There is shock certain mornings.

To keep your mind, assailed here on every side by the place itself, you will have to fight the drugs now. You have defied the guards, drunk their stuff as cheerfully as if it were booze, it will be a game for them now to drug you. Since you are too afraid to sleep at night, the issue of when—if ever—you will get out of here becomes more crushing then. With time alone, you pace back and forth to the bathroom, trying to plan, trying to figure out who, if anyone, could even know you are here. D'arcy, Deirdre, Moira, the women in Dublin. Desmond. If he knows, why doesn't he do something? Why doesn't he tell the others? If Sophie knows . . . and she must—she was on the phone through some amazing conference call at the same time as Desmond and the cops at the airport and that stuffed-shirt doctor. A tailor's dummy with a paper you do not even know if you signed, let alone what it was—scared, rabbit-scared. Now all these days later—how many days?—count, try to remember what day you were busted. They took you right here, installed you that night—the little beard and the good suit. McShane you saw the next day. The next day—how do you remember it and the one after? By what was on television? By counting your packs of cigarettes; you ordered a carton but got only five. Why do they cost twice as much here? Never mind—do you have enough money in that purse to keep buying ciga-rettes? There is never enough time to count it when they let you have it. Remember to work that out—some of the money is in traveler's checks, or the Bank of Ireland. Fool, you now have a checking account in this country and can't use it; this joint is never going to take checks.

Forget it—who, who could help, come to the rescue? Desmond—I cannot believe this of Desmond: a rebel, a freedom fighter. But a law-yer. Then the women, but do they know? Sophie—would she come all this way? Mallory, having seen the error of her ways? Absurd. There is no help from America then; only Sophie and the family would know and a few friends—who will decide from what they've heard that I'm in exactly the right place and getting wonderful care. The Irish women then—which of them? Whoops, the night nurse. Just finishing, touch of diarrhea. Yes, of course, I'll get right back in bed. No, I'm sure I won't need anything to sleep. No, really. No. And the needle jabs your rear like an insult and the white stupor comes over, fast so fast, and then more of the terrible dreams.

The dreams of Prolixin. Like a white club it comes down and for a little while you are unconscious. Then it begins. I am totally conscious, horribly awake and yet rigid, locked in the dream. There is no way out of this fate, the same dream over and over, only worse. More certain. It starts with the back windows of the dormitory, which even in daytime haunt me. As does the skylight, the passage to heaven, the route of the fliers. For in the dream one is tempted first that way, to join the others and take the night flights, the pills taken willingly for those moments of ecstasy when, as in a pre-Raphaelite painting, the old ladies of the ward rush like angels through the skylight and then disperse into the greatest freedom of all, autoflight, da Vinci's aspiration fulfilled in their gray nightclothes escaping through the hatch. And if you give in, if you don't keep working to get out of here, that is how you will go. Up the hatch. Feel the air, the breath of freedom, riding the clouds and winds, witches on their night ride. Don't, don't. Stay on the ground. They buy you with this. But you are already inoculated with the nightmare toxin, so you won't even get off the ground. And you will never get out of here either.

Then the windows onto the trees, the view of the back fields. You will be a face in one of these windows. Years. A face like aging paper—old, then older. Looking out. Mute. Helpless, a cipher without method or manner of communication. Silent, like an illusion. A reminder of hardly anything at all. Just this white figure behind glass over the years. It will beckon less but the face cannot refrain from its appeal, its last gesture no one will ever see. These windows look out only upon a few trees; there is no path there even, only a gardener, the dogs at night. Far away in New York, America, the people she knew will lose count, forget, be told first that she had a medical illness as well, pneumonia perhaps, a broken arm. Months, then half a year, then a year and a half. The doctors reporting but with diminishing punctuality. Friends hearing that the condition is incurable, madness has won; she is best off there. The people in the hospital are kind, she has everything she wants, she loves Ireland. Arrangements will have to be made about the farm. A shaggy mess of neglect and sold for a poor price, but what else can be done? No one has time or inclination to tend the place. And that art colony business was daffy, the sort of deluded scheme that is to be expected in the manic type. Everything was left most untidy. Years ago. Now only this face in the window.

You are in the hard lock of Dr. Strong now forever. You are in the hands of the Church you ran away from so long ago, down the stairs out of the confessional onto the streets. The stone arm has you now, those same cut stones. Despite the presence of the state it is finally Rome that has you prisoner. Ironic shiver that it would come to this; that you could evade your heritage this far only to end up here, a cripple and infirm, an aging crone among the nuns, all your little American freedom fighter business quite over, women's lib and other notions crunched like cellophane in the strength of this stone force.

Rome barks like the dog at the end of a fairy tale read once upon your father's lap, where the little boy or girl, the quester, enters an underground chamber, and there atop a chest is a great snarling dog. In black and white in the book we read together; he read the words, I read the pictures. The pen-and-ink illustrations drawn fierce and terrible. You are there now, descending every rung until you reach the last barred door and there is the dog. The Pope. A dog enthroned. Fangs. Alive, buried alive in the stone rooms, the stone corridors, the barred doors, the teeth that guard or bite. That rivet you into a small space underground without air or light. Dark it is now, farther down, and the games begin. Oh God, not the games, not the dials, not the horrors of the last one. I remember the last dream all over in this one. The dials like the dials on a gas meter but worse, harder to interpret and more erratic, inscrutable. The winged skate like a token in Monopoly. The dials spinning are expenses and then become time and then become death itself and I watch my death and gasp. If they spun the other way? But no. Spin spin and the winged skate comes like fate, a portentous and shining little emblem. In this figure, senseless yet full of meaning, I study my chances of being freed, of being killed slowly by years. Still hanging on to hope as it drains away. Spin. Faster the winged skate. The dials. Finally the last figure, the Pope in hell. He is there and I am his prisoner in hell. The robes, the miter, the throne. I hate him utterly in this dream. The Papacy, not even the Pope. Surely not the jolly TV Pope of the upper regions but the shadow Pope, the Pope behind the Pope: the historical truth, the figure through the ages, the Popes of the Inquisition, the holders of hellfire and the stake. And I am found out. The final laugh. Witch and pretender. A Joan, a heretic. And they have me now.

I am in their dungeon and their jail. From this room—if you refuse the skylight and stand your ground, wanting out, wanting the trees outside and the roads—from this room you will go to another. To solitary, then cell after cell, farther and deeper, until this last game of all, the dials and the skates. The shiny little Atlantic City figure of a winged skate, the token in a Cracker Jack box, emblem of some pinball machine, mechanistic allegory of fate. And the ugly little gas meter dials, like dials in cheap rooms in England where you pay a penny for a few hours' warmth. They swirl, moving the way electrical dials swirl around when klieg lights are on; fast, faster. You never know which dial registers which thing. Just as when the company lets you read your own dial—since you do not understand it, you cannot cheat or foreknow—so it is here. And the red figure of the Pope on his throne, waiting like a spider below a grating, down down, dizzy into hell—they have made me dream this. This is their punishment, their lesson. Every night I will be tortured thus. And if I resist they will tie me down to inoculate me with this horror, this eight hours of hellfire. Exhausted into the gray light of morning.

Waking to our great sad room of waking women, each a prisoner in her mind and body. The heart flutters: perhaps today, surely today, it must be today that there will be news. Word. Desmond. Today they will let me phone. If not phone, then write; a far smaller opportunity, of course—so humble, a stamp and real paper. All that is written on toilet paper, in emulation of Armagh and out of the same necessity, all that is stored up and ready. But for nothing. Not without stamps, not without their permission or someone to pass it to. I cannot keep the letters in my purse, since it is in the possession of the staff. And my little bedside dresser is also unsafe. So, like all the other women here, I have adopted a shopping bag that goes with me everywhere and is guarded all the time from the guards but left about continually among the women. There is nothing to steal; I give my cigarettes away and include sharing them in the ration I count on. But I always know where the bag is when the door opens loudly upon a nurse. Today—something must happen today. I cannot stand more of these nights. In the day I can think, hold on to my mind, resist Thorazine and the other stuff with oranges and milk and bread and hard tea and determination.

But not the nighttime, Prolixin. Asking the other women to repeat the name of it for me and what they know about it, I suddenly remember it is mentioned in the H Blocks book—it is the stuff they force upon the prisoners in northern Ireland. One of the strikers' demands is to stop having Prolixin foisted upon them under the pretext of testing it. "An experimental drug developed in England for use upon schizophrenics." Political punishment, sadistic control. Old women here show me blisters on their backs from the stuff, years of large doses. Something has to happen today. The windows onto the service road, the little car park— there, someone will come from there. Watch for them or they will be turned away. The doctors will say you are resting, better, doing nicely. Must not be disturbed, have requested no visitors.

10

My religion of Sophie, the religion of love. Irrational, mystical, screwball. Never mind all that happened, even the voice on the airport phone turning me in. That was only ignorance, not malice. Transcend this betrayal, all betrayals. My notion of her is still the force, the idea, that sustains me here. All the long hours of the night, the lengthy tedium of the day.

With others who might rescue me, D'arcy or the women in Dublin, even the family I imagine at times coming to the rescue—that fantasy— with the others it is only rescue they could achieve. From the idea of Sophie, I derive the power to endure. A phantom probably, her echo in every line of the slender volume of poetry I carry about with me. Someone else's poems, someone else's love poems, someone else's love. The poems may not even be about a love; the drawings that accompany them are ambiguous to say the least, stick figure nudes, rather reminiscent of the H Blocks book. A keen acquaintance with what is acceptable along this line makes me sure to keep the illustrations away from the nurses. The poems are not really the issue, merely a jumping- off point for me, for the constancy and adoration they evoke. The poet and the illustrator are both women, so I have enlisted them, against their intentions probably, as a pair of lesbian muses in charge of my powers of recollection and dedication.

You escaped the Church to fall into the religion of love. Then art. Now back into this martyr's cult again: practiced in an insane asylum. Where better?—these are the hardest jails. All those years of medieval and courtly love poetry for undergraduates, Genet's prison romances—now this. And there has to be a Sophie. Like Santa Claus? Just consider the meaning in the name: *philosophia,* love of wisdom, learning. An adopted name but therefore all the more significant for infatuation. She may even have found someone else by now; there are always the admirers—the colony is depressingly full of them. It hardly matters. Since it is the idea of Sophie. She is not even here and I may never see her again or not for a long time—it could be years—yet the Sophie I can summon here is my boon and help and staff, my succor. And if I reach hard and am very good at it, my salvation.

Balls. You know it too; remember the other times, loving Fumio and Sita, still loving them, despite the hell they had delivered you to, the doctor and the indeterminate sentence and all. Because if they came to visit they might get you out? No, more than that—because if I did not preserve my faith in them I lost my faith in living, in life itself. Freedom was emptiness if it consumed my every illusion. Illusion—you said it. Sure; ideal too. It is the forgiving that makes this experience transcendent, worth it, enlarging instead of diminishing. It is *caritas.* Carrot and stick. No, too easy, it's the enlargement of sympathy, you keep some of it afterward—though most of it is lost. Living down the shame, living through the depression.

Because once you're out the really hard times start. Yes, and then you get small again, deny, squelch that sympathy, pass as sane and well adjusted or shaky but conformist. And the other victims vanish from your mind. Noble causes are simply envelopes asking for contributions—while you are obsessed with just paying bills, the little concerns of those around you downtown, or how to get the tractor to run at the farm, meet the mortgage, hold on to things, grasp and clutch. And your eye narrows again. You never did enough for Michael; then they hanged him. When did you last get a hundred dollars together for his wife and kids? They're going through something terrible down there.

Everything recedes. Political prisoners become file folders in your file cabinet, references in lectures, arguments by the fire over martinis if you can find someone to pontificate to. Then I fall through the trapdoor again and discover the dungeon and its values, its sworn truths, its charity and clarity and generosity, its eternal faith. The faiths and affections, allegiances that transcend all, trespass heaven, turn the night into day with the glare of their virtues. Then you get out, you go normal again.

And you love Sophie? Yes, uncritically. I can even call it passion since it's senseless and sensual. It is now time to think about her, to obsess, to recharge my battery with the light of this illusion, hope, invention. Just by remembering her neck, the back of it, that line, which I can see perfectly even here, though I never had sense enough to photograph it. The lines of her shoulders, which I have drawn so many times. And for the mundane, I can recall her ears, which remind me of the old Gerber baby food ads. Or her foot—her right foot where a bone was broken years ago, leaving it imperfect. I stomped on that foot this summer. Inadvertently but during a quarrel. To make amends to it in my mind is a meditation adequate to remove me from this banal room and captivity. Loving itself is a sanity, the rest is madness.

II

The blur of days in this place, I no longer know how many. Hours marked only by the tease of tablets, the cheat of the watered tea, the fat rubberoid slices of white bread. The turning on or off of lights, the troop from dormitory to dayroom, the barks of nurses that it is time to get up, make the bed for inspection. Time for the toilet or the pills, time for bed again. The television is on or off, the radio blares or is silent, the newspaper is a week old or yesterday's or today's. Get hold of it and copy the date for reference, consign it to your shopping bag. November a gray silhouette out the window. Was it October they caught me? When in October?

Years have passed already in preview. Always the same room, these chairs. The same women or replicas. If you play it cool, miss solitary and shock, you could vegetate here in this same routine—deprived of everything you want in life, of everyone you know or love—for years. Provided you keep your temper and never raise your voice. Do that once, and you go the hard way.

You could be a great little scholar in Miss Strong's class, her therapy circle. Scribbling pompous civil liberties briefs on half sheets of lined paper once a week to provide amusement before they're torn up to protect your identity. You could be the life of the party when the nurses are out of the room; agitate and foment rebellions that never take place. And by asking questions and getting the dope, you could confirm all your worst suspicions of this place to no purpose whatsoever. In years you might even learn to play the penny whistle. You could compose hundreds of letters on toilet paper, even write your congressman, while fighting off lassitude and despair, amend a lifetime's turpitude in correspondence. They would never be mailed. You could beg a phone call every day for thousands of days and never get one. Today you even forgot to beg. You are growing docile, adjusted. Out of the wind and the rain, housed and fed for nothing. You are growing accustomed.

The day you run out of cigarettes is the day your passivity ends. Passivity, not pacifism. That lost out a while ago, when they discovered you weren't taking the drugs. And then you had an attack of honesty which was little more than bragging. Pacifism doesn't brag. Because the big nurse wouldn't believe you'd gotten by with this, you had to demonstrate your winnings. Civil disobedience is not a childish hoarding of tablets in a shirt pocket, followed up with rhetoric about your rights which you must have known would cut no ice at all. Her look alone could have broken your jaw. And her big hands pummeling at your cheeks till you swallow the pill. And then the punishment—a big dose of Thorazine. You have started your career in drugs. Back on lithium—extended to Thorazine. The doctors ignore you; no further observations, just chemicals now.

And it is harder every day to stay straight, to keep on worrying about the date, the phone, the petitions for stamps. So tired, so sick of trying that I nearly ask to stay in the dormitory mornings, needing more rest, pretending to an illness. Watch out—they might treat it. It is actually so boring that even the terror wears thin. The roar of television, the noise of twenty people in one room with no occupation for an entire day, day after day—the noise alone could drive you nuts. You get sick of Nelly's screaming, Colleen's incoherent chattering to herself as she fiddles with those damned ugly little machine parts on her card table, some unexplained sweated labor farmed out here. One vapid television program after another, nearly every one of them British vulgarity—how appropriate to beam it here for the most crushed and negligible of the Irish. An allegory in that. Relish it for a moment and then the mouth turns to ashes. I wish I could throw up. Lie down. Disappear. Vanish. Nice time to vanish—in a way I already have: Who knows where I am? Every woman I met in Dublin believes I left the country mid-October. Only D'arcy knows I was staying in Ireland. Desmond knows; maybe Moira O'Neil heard the final disposition, too. That means they have consigned me here. Best place for her and so forth. Your goose is cooked. So you'll have to start working your way out of here, talking them smooth, working on good behavior—anything. With your record, an escape? Anyone can reform. No, somehow I can't. I just hate them too much. Toe the line and be pleasant, but I won't kiss ass here. It'll be a while then, but I can hardly stay awake to think about it. Drugged rainy afternoon. Hard even to give a damn. Daydream, it's daytime.

The night nurse is CIA. I can tell by her swooping nose. Like the front of a jet, like a bird's beak imitated by a fighter plane. She and the other one, too. I had thought the other one was Mary Quinn, my high school sweetheart. Watching the two of them sitting up in the dayroom this evening, I had felt the strains of Derham Hall; watching this nurse and seeing again the wonderful black hair and fair skin hypnotized me. With the first evening shots of Thorazine I even felt the rhythms of high school again, its gestures and call. Mary Quinn's long black hair, the sweep of that long black hair along her cheek, past the pure white uniform blouse. To fall enamored upon the serge of her uniform jumper and its crest. That time again, its music—never remembered until now. Sitting in the dayroom, refusing to go to the dormitory, insisting on staying up as long as possible. Or as long as possible without punishment. Being an adult who smokes and likes to do her thinking late at night, after state television bows off at ten. I had succumbed to the dark nurse, staring at her out of my drug, half in love with her. Standing up to draft after draft of the horrible stuff that, alas, is not booze. Being sly, teasing that after all, it was only Irish Mist, wasn't it? "Sure indeed," they said. "Now it's time for you to go to bed."

And the charm turned off, the swoop nose took over; efficient as a cop, she had me in the dormitory in no time. Lying in bed, hearing her on the phone. For sure she is CIA, not even chemical company like the others. CIA with the ambassador in on it, forces in America. Then I must have somehow become a pawn in the Irish political puzzle and she would have me kidnapped and murdered in an American government plane on the way home. Her scheme, on orders from the agency. I lie in bed full of Thorazine and tremble, imagining. A bag over my head. Transported in a car trunk. Then just bludgeoned on the plane. Dear God, don't let me fall into the hands of the Americans. Was the CIA with the Ayatollah too? Lie still as a mummy in the sheets, a mannequin asleep, a wax model with "Perfect Patient" engraved upon it. You must never provoke them and you just have. She suspected you with Mary Quinn. Her partner. She smelled the queerness; this they must hate above everything. So she has arranged for you to be spirited away. Maybe to America. New York. A wave of homesickness, tears. The airport here, the airport there—they'll kill you in a back room. No, on the plane, another kind of plane—military, secret, government.

If it were just escape you'd go for it, jump out of bed and follow anybody. How funny to escape via the CIA. But that isn't all of it, unfortunately; that is only the official program. There are ten minutes somewhere along the route where they will have you alone, where you will be blindfolded, in custody, confined somehow, a car, a gangway, a fuselage. And it is during those few moments—most of the ones involved will be unaware of this part of it—that you will be strangled, stifled. Fabric pulled over your head, in the dark, tied, dying. Claustrophobia is the fear of death, this death—when you are in others' hands and they can do something, anything, everything to you. Maybe they would, maybe they wouldn't. It would be the unauthorized segment of the trip, the covert action, the hidden agenda.

And so I lie here afraid of her, of her hushed tones on the phone. Afraid of her intentions this night particularly. Because it is this night they will do it. And then she comes toward me. The needle. Damn, not this again, the nightmares. Yes—even this is better than death. If they do this, only this, they won't do the rest. No, fool, they do this so that you will be unconscious when they remove you. You may wake up in a sack or in a plane going home. Or dead. No, I will not let her. But she is fast, already the sting. Move and she breaks that needle in your flesh. Out fast as a bee sting and the long nightmare begins again.

This is not a dream. Dreams bore me; I have always been careful to skip dream passages in fiction. Other people's dreams are tedious to me and I never remember my own. But this dream—is not a dream: a nightmare, a carnival of hell. Again the windows and the thin old white face, my future. The organization that put me here: police, psychiatry, family, property, religion, state medicine. The web. Drawing tighter and tighter from one bin to another, one trap evaded after another, but here there is no way out. You will grow old here. The face that is my own future, the face seen in the window looking onto nothing, unseen. A recluse. The iron mask. Daily descending to hell through the dials and the skates, the diabolic roulette with the red Pope devil at the bottom. Over and over.

The morning is relief, because I did not die. Exhaustion at having nearly died all night long. I must somehow avoid the shit in their needles, this drug I still feel even in my bone marrow, stiff, ill. Worse each morning.

Desmond? What became of Desmond? He could not have put me here and left me. To the doctors' discretion, to the end of the world. Dear God, impossible to believe that of anyone. Desmond, you loaned me your own house. Is it not immaculate? Did we not even fix the window in the freezing rain, faultlessly? We left whole cupboards full of groceries; the key is under the eighth stone on the left-hand side; there are thank-you notes everywhere. What happened, man? And Moira O'Neil? If she knows, and if she has told them, the women in Dublin? She could be the link.

But will they all just hear that "she had a breakdown"? It looks really serious this time; it's happened before; yes, several times in America. Hospitalized in California and Minnesota where her mother lives. And she was nearly put away a short time ago in New York by her younger sister, who simply couldn't face the prospect of seeing her go abroad in that condition. Yes, of course, all summer long; her friends have been extremely worried. Really, she shouldn't have traveled in that condition. We'll just have to wait and see how it turns out, whether the doctors can help her or not. Of course, it's Ennis and rather old-fashioned, but they have a man down there who specializes in lithium. That's what they take for manic depression, and the thing is she'd been on it for years. The problem is she willfully stopped taking it. And then, of course, fell apart. Sophie, the woman she lives with, is most concerned, is sure they're on the right track by putting her back on the stuff. It's really pretty harmless, usually an outpatient situation. They don't need to be locked up unless they go off the deep end. And that's just what happened. If they can get her down off this high—that's what they call it, mania, they call it being high, like booze; probably is, no idea myself—they can have her back in shape in a couple of weeks perhaps. But you never know. If she doesn't respond to treatment and cooperate. Well, that is the trouble, she won't; she thinks it's some kind of civil rights issue and she'd far prefer to have a lawyer than a doctor. That's what happened when her mother put her away, years ago, committed her actually, since she wouldn't cooperate. And wouldn't you know, a whole gang of lawyers marched in and helped her get out? Her mother was beside herself because she went off without the treatment. And then they fall into these big depressions and want to kill themselves. Oh yes, she's been through that too. By this time they've usually run through every cent they had in the world, and all their friends and whoever loved them have had it as well. Because they really are just dreadful to be around. So they have a great deal to feel sorry for themselves about, and that's the time they start thinking suicide. Then they'll give in, maybe, and see the doctors. But when they're high like she is now, then they want out and they'll live their own life, thank you. And see, what did she do?—she got herself arrested at the airport. Yes, that's what I'm saying, she got arrested. Well, for hanging around and talking funny to a policeman, that's what. Some long involved business about renting a car and her camera was in another car or something. But you can be sure she was misbehaving somehow for the Shannon police to take her into custody. Of course, before they did they called Desmond—she gave them his number as her lawyer. And right away Desmond talked to America, and Sophie filled him in on the history. So fortunately the police could turn her over to a doctor rather than book her and she's safe in the hospital getting excellent care. It would be a terrible shame if she were really arrested—can you see that in the papers with all the trouble women have already? Charge of vagrancy and sleeping in the lavatory— we don't need that now, do we? I ask you. So we'll just wait till they say she's well enough to travel and they can put her on the plane for America down there in Shannon. God knows she's near enough to the airport. And that's the end of it.

Respectability, there is always respectability to deal with. The insane asylum is better than jail because it is not reported; it is not even spoken of. An intimate and shameful secret generally kept. You can scarcely put in the paper that someone is locked up in a loony bin—it is too sad, too scandalous; it would be below the belt. Whereas jail would be grist for the mill, hilarious, wonderful. If the Armagh women refusing to wash are tragedy, this could be farce. I grin and remember my Shannon ladies' room ditty: "Six old ladies locked in a lavatory, they were there from Monday till Saturday—nobody knew they were there." Singing it as children titillated by the naughtiness of lavatory. Singing it to myself here crushed by the squalor of this toilet. It still has its rebellious nonsense kick.

Whimsical maybe, maybe just plain crazy. But how do such notions and pastimes get you here, a prisoner perhaps for the rest of your life? Is there that much harm in an antic thought? All that nutty stuff about the first night here; the transom, the skylight, the night fliers, little old ladies in their bedclothes floating out the trap into the night air, compliments of their pills. I'd had enough pills in here to be at least that dotty. Can that: you had nutty thoughts before the pills, without them. How about Sita rising from the dead through some screwball operation between rooms, some passage through the far wall, exchanged for the very old lady in the last bed who gasps and wheezes all night, so you decide she's either dying or giving birth? Radical disorientation. Bullshit—it's madness.

And for this you must sit here, wondering if D'arcy or anybody will ever come and rescue you before the farm is sold and you are buried alive behind some back window invisible to the world. Seems steep. Of course, madness is worse than a crime; crimes merit trials, counsel, stated sentences if convicted. If acquitted of crime, one is free to go. You will never get acquitted and, as a matter of fact, you are not nearly as innocent as you claim. Because you were daft, thought daft thoughts, said daft things. Daft is mad, is a terrible and frightening disease to the world. People have been totally unable to cope with it, now or ever. Your madness is their possible madness. And it must be stamped out. It is all the hidden fears of the mind in losing itself.

Anyway, you looked funny because you had too much luggage, because of all that impossible movie gear; if you'd had just two suitcases and been a little less picky about your rental cars, had the wit not to leave your Nikon in the first car and then not been so stubborn as to wait around until it was found before taking a second car—if. If. Listen, what about your paranoia—afraid of being tailed after the H Blocks book business at that crummy hotel? Plus you thought you could get something cheaper and smaller—so why not just get in the cheaper and smaller car and wait for the camera to be forwarded to you? You could have trusted them to do that. Because I saved for two years to buy that camera. So instead you wind up here. Combination of your bizarre behavior and your bizarre circumstances: too much luggage, having to wait so long for another car because something had to be retrieved from the first, and so on. But all that's made more bizarre when you chat up a cop, thinking to get by with hanging around too long in a public place. No, you asked for it. In their terms you sure did. And if anybody should be aware of the world's prejudice against lunacy and loonies, you should. And should take that into account the way blacks calculate for racism or women take rape into consideration when traveling at night.

And so forth. You're handicapped, or a pariah or something, and you should get a little smart about it. I hear the voice of my elder sister, the lawyer, in all this, especially in the phrase "get a little smart."

The day wanes into the afternoon. Staring out the waist-high windows into the car park, begging for paper or a stamp. A phone call is again "tomorrow"—the promise given as if it were sincere. But it is always this way. With time assurance has only grown more vehement, more persuasive. And more a lie. It will go on forever in here. Already one's thoughts become contained within these walls. Save for fantasy: Miss Eliott's arrival, Sophie stepping down from a car through the wind, Mallory's raucous voice sounding cheerily through the hall—well, how do you like Ireland? And you smile and say something entirely without irony. And then you find you are smiling at a greasy wooden table in a room full of shabby women, a crucifix, the Sacred Heart, the horrible sideboard full of counted forks.

And you dream of witches by the fire, uprisings, the whole gang of us building the fire high and higher and defying the doctors and nurses and the nuns, even the Pope. An insurrection of the mad, the wretched of the earth in an incendiary fervor. France in the moment of passion. Our pitchforks, knitting needles, oranges, an uplifted chair. Old Mary, Margaret, Ann, Rosalind, Bridie, and Colleen—a determined circle around the fire, heaping on coal until the room is hot, hellish, grim. More than extravagant because the coal is rationed sternly and it is cold here always—we will make it hot, hotter than a fiery temper. And play at coaches and horses and bridges—one can't say crossings—the old game of the witches where every move is a riddle, a cognomen, a parallel phrase with secret import directing the outlaw people through the dangers and persecutions of the past. Now played again here in language as symbolic as the tarot, pressed again into service to avoid the dangers of the present; directing our warfare, our escapes, our moves and maneuvers. Tonight, now finally, toward confrontation. After all the years of silence and the sidelong glance. Who better than the mad-women, surely the hardest witches of all, the most sat upon, those with the least to lose? Crossed sticks, the voice says in my mind, for I do not hear the old lady say it aloud. I do not need to, I am on the wavelength. They are initiating me. Crossed sticks—make fire. But no crossed locks, I murmur—prison leads to the stake.

These are the puns of our history, encapsulated in phrases by which we recall, realize, and redirect. I was between crossed locks and taken, was given the fire of Thorazine. Minor torment. Nevertheless material assistance in putting the question. As always, the question put has no answer. If it did it would be less useful in torture, in irrational torment. My own question is the old one—will I live? It is never answered. My own version of it is, when will I be released? But we have done with that—we will stay here by the fire and build it higher, we will take our fate into our own hands, we will form a fellowship, solidarity. We will not let each other down, bend or betray. United, we will refuse to cooperate at all. There are not enough of them to control us even with their drugs. And we will not opt out with the drugs. Or the promises either. For they will try to separate us, divide and conquer. Tonight. We begin resistance tonight.

12

I go to the dormitory for more cigarettes. Tonight, begin resisting
tonight. This will be a long night and it's only six o'clock. The gray
giving onto darker gray, the light going its hopeless way one more time.
I walk back along the hall, past the door where I made my getaway. And
there is D'arcy standing by the water fountain. "Good God, how did
you get here?" "Shh, I don't quite have permission. I thought you were
here—they lied and lied to me all over the system." "D'arcy—thanks,
I can't say how much." There is no time to embrace. In a second one
of them will come, will catch her. "I thought this is what they'd do with
you, where they'd put you. It's so near the airport—you're not the first
foreigner who's disappeared into this place." "This is hell, D'arcy, and
we are in it." "Shh. They have no idea I'm here—we must talk fast."
"How did you get in here?" Is this her fate, too, the general thing with
troublemakers, rebels? I wonder, remembering the old women about the
fire in the dayroom. "We are all witches here, D'arcy." "Right, but in
a moment they are going to pitch me out. I just snuck in here. They have
lied and lied to me all over their bloody system—this was just a guess."
"And I'm walking by, out of the coop for a moment—isn't it perfect?"
"Take it easy, there'll be a nurse in a moment. But at least I've found
you." "You should meet the others, the rest of us—they'd love you.
We could build the fire high; you could spend the night." "John's
waiting outside—we really have just a moment." She is leaving. "How
can I get out of here, D'arcy?" "Now that we know where you are, we
can make a start on it. It may not be easy; it was very hard to find out

where you had disappeared to. Desmond's wife told me you had an accident in Ennis. I thought of your car." "An accident?" "Damned silly cover-up. I looked for you in all the hospitals. Then I thought of this one." "This is no hospital, this is a jail. They've never let me telephone you. Or Desmond." I am beginning to realize about Desmond but cannot believe it. "Will you tell them in Dublin, D'arcy?" "Of course."

A nurse appears and pounces on D'arcy's arm and shoulder: "You have no business here." "Yes, she does; this is my friend Margueretta D'arcy. She's here to visit me." "Oh no, she isn't. How did you get in, missus?" "Through the door—it was open." I admire D'arcy's cool, in fact I adore it. The door was open for some night nurse coming on and D'arcy just trailed her. Into this place where they might never let her go. Lovely. Guts. Gap-toothed she is—one of us, a witch, a high witch. If only she could stay with us tonight we could break the whole bunch of us out, empty the place. But she is manacled by the nurse, the big pushy one, furious. "D'arcy—remember." "Don't worry; we'll do everything we can." Her goodness, the wonder of seeing her, the miracle of her appearance. No one else has ever braved hell for me this way. Against the rules, without permission, a guerrilla visit, a surprise attack. That she was there, even as I hear her hustled down the stairs as I am hustled back to the dayroom. Where the fire is not very high and may not get high either.

The world comes back; out there still are phone calls and letters, offices to visit, influence and energy. That route rather than this one where the prisoners sit listless, needing to be roused with the old conundrums. The old speech, the bridges and horses: they can get you at bridges—beware of bridges. D'arcy said only one witch was burned in Ireland, at Kilkenny. But the questioning must have spread far. Still we were safer here, are now. Is this not a people who would have a Joan in a Bernadette? Watch the old woman in the corner, old Margaret—she is posing the riddles now. Remember your answers, or let them come from beyond and past memory, the collective unconscious, the second sight, whatever metaphor—for these are the tricks of poetry, the rhyming, the finding of similitudes and parallels, duplications and dualities, even dupes if you err. Full of Thorazine, an extra measure. Find an orange or sit by the building fire and fuel the flames. Smoke out their damn room, stoke the coal until we all disappear up through the chimney.

*   *   *

"She's restive; she needs another dose tonight again, Prolixin too, or she'll not sleep a wink." It must be tonight. There will be signals we will see out the windows, the torches, the sounds of the drummers. Tonight of all nights, beware the skylight and the potions spread out in cellophane, in their fists like candies. Tonight you must stay on the ground. So if you stay up you may miss the pills—just keep smoking and be quiet by the fire. The other women gave in, went to bed, obeyed. They will not wait with you. Perhaps they may not even want to leave, have given up. Rescue all you can but if they will not hang in, there is nothing you can do. Still the sorrow at leaving them, losing them, failing them. Now as the nurses sit and watch you, guard you, figure when they'll take you off to the other room, the dormitory, and stop this nonsense. Waiting for the dose to take. "My God, Agnes, it's the third she's had now—wouldn't you think she'd be knocked out by now? Well, they can do it over next door with the needle once we've got her in bed." Dose after dose and there is no joking about it now, no sport this time, simply poison. Horrid straight, horrid between sips of milk, horrid no matter how long you take to swallow it while they badger you. "Quick now and we're off."

Hold on to the world outside through following the news, remembering friends, planning the bureaucratic ritual of your release, composing letters, schedules, alternatives, balancing your checkbook, remembering details. The horses at the farm must be put on fodder soon—the grass is gone now; we must find a hay farmer. Think these thoughts and make lists and look out onto the green beyond the windows where there is Ireland and do not weep.

Never mind—D'arcy found me; took the trouble to come here, got in, broke the rules. Endangered herself. For I believe that to enter this place unauthorized is to risk something. Was D'arcy really here tonight or did I imagine it? So hard to tell the difference. In the hall before the windows to the car park—just as I had always foreknown rescue would come that way. If they knew who D'arcy was they'd cheerfully lock her up for good. Then John would wait forever. I incorporate John into the witch fantasies. The one permitted male, the sorcerer, the broad figure in white who wears a coat and whose face is puffy from incarceration. Much like Agatha here, who in her age and continuously narcotized state has come to resemble a man. If John is here as Agatha, who is D'arcy then? My eyes rove the room but can find no parallel for the

nonpareil. My God, then she was here. It happened. There is no opposite number here—the clue. That would mean that she has left John here
in Agatha for solace while she is gone. Moreover, it is evidence she will
return. That is the clue, the answer, the guarantee: you may go to bed
in relief now. You may be sure D'arcy will come back for you. "Yes,
yes, I'm going. No, I don't need any more of that stuff. I have found the
answer." "Isn't that grand now? There'll be something for you when
you get into bed. Unless you're very quiet. Just like the tomb. Lovely,
that's a good girl." I grin into the dark: I will get out of here someday.
And then the sharp burn of the needle and the hell begins.

You accommodate, you learn what to avoid, whom to placate. And the
pull to be solid with the oppressed, the moral imperative toward solidarity, meets the pull toward making yourself agreeable with the guards.
Yesterday I discovered that there is a little kitchen available to the
patients who wash dishes. The staff kitchen really, but if you are good
and smile a great deal and are very pleasant, there is real coffee there.
This must be the coffee they gave me that first night—when was it? How
long?—you must know; you must always know the date. You must
count the days and keep a record in your night table. If you no longer
know how long you have been held, how long you have been imprisoned, how will you ever get out or help yourself? What will you say
when you are asked? Suppose that help came and you were unable to tell
them when you were taken, the day of your arrest—it would dissolve all
this horror into nothing. Forget it—make up to this bully of a nurse and
admire the coffee, the glass jar of instant coffee. Would she make me
some? Would she really? Or could I make it myself? Oh, I'd love to.
"You can come here again if you are good." "But sure I am always
good": the brogue to amuse them. "Ah, but ya take walks now, don't
ya, Katherine?" "Nothing but a wee small walk it was," this with the
grin of an eight-year-old. "And a great mistake it was, too," I add,
perfectly serious, swallowing my own meaning while they take theirs.
    If I keep this up, do I get a phone call? No, that is doctor's orders,
they say. And they seem to be leveling with me. It is the doctor who has
decided I will speak to no one, write to no one. Then how can I make
anything happen—just wait for D'arcy? They will go on frustrating her
at every turn. The system is huge, a nationwide bureaucracy. And
maybe she is unable to interest anyone else. Then, too, she is busy with

the women at Armagh, and she lives way out in the bog without a car and has damn little money. Maybe she has come to the end of her road, too. So the only thing I can do here is try to talk to one of the doctors. But they are never here. If one draws your blood he does not speak. If you meet one in the hall, he isn't yours or he cannot talk to you now; you are to see the nurse, who tells you to see the doctor. You are to remain on your course of medicine and try to guess how long or how much Thorazine and Prolixin and even relatively harmless and familiar old lithium. Lithium is called Pryabil here—I invariably think of a little bird having its beak jammed open. Many of the drugs here have different names, so it takes a long while to figure out which is which. And Prolixin is still a mystery to me. How does it produce the sores on Margaret's back? Why on earth prescribe something with these physical side effects? Or such psychic traumas, nightmares like mine?

There is shock always in the background. Enid has it. Delores has had it since she was eighteen; she is thirty-five now. The last time she was out she found a young man to marry. Then he jilted her, and they put her on shock again. Perhaps permanently or perhaps she will get out after a year or two, fall away and be captured again, and back to the empty look and the tremor, the blank fright of her presence in the dayroom. A beaten creature, a lifelong patient without a shred of self-confidence left. They have consumed her human substance utterly. It is painful to look at her, acutely embarrassing. To see the fear in her eyes makes one ashamed, near tears, as before some terrible malformation. You count your blessings: They don't give you shock. You have even discovered coffee. You are learning to make yourself agreeable when you forswear your vow never to speak to the staff, only the patients. The mechanics of a concentration camp and the little payoffs. Cushy it is, soft. Got your smokes and the telly, a bit to read in the papers. If you are feeling responsible you can think of someone else to address with your little toilet paper missives.

Nice word, "missives"—you may be the only one here who knows that word. The root derivation? Let's see: *missio,* probably; Latin; missionary, mission, missile, and so forth. But the phoneme—for that is my interest now, to break root derivation down to phoneme, to find the phoneme key. If only I had the Oxford dictionary. But having all day long, I have time to remember. Incarceration has the curious effect of giving me time to reaccumulate my learning, to remember things from long ago: studies in geology or the course of Alexander Pope's publish-

ing career and the name of his archenemy, Lewis Theobald. The hero of
The Dunciad. Professor Monk's remark about how sheer animosity
caused Pope to immortalize a nobody. Theobald, a footnote forever.
And Jonathan Swift—was Swift mad at the end or only a prisoner? The
Dean on a leash in his Irish-English cathedral—was it not politics? Was
Swift a manic-depressive, so called, a fellow spirit and abused? A collar
and a dog leash the rest of his life. Think about it, imagine it.

No, return to your favorite rumination, the key to language; it begins
with lithium. When they were going to give you lithium and you had no
information about it, apart from that "it works," the Greeks used it, and
so forth, you found all you needed to know through language. Lithium:
root derivation, "litho" as in lithos, lithograph, stone, a mineral found
in stone deposits.

Forget chemistry, stick to language, to the puzzle at the source of
meaning. Root derivation is wisdom; the phoneme, the smallest unit,
the atom, must be magic. If you could find the phoneme key, it might
go beyond the Indo-European group. Take "litho"—it is a root, made
of two phonemes, "li" and "tho." What is the semantic base of each?
Or "Ka," the first part of your name—why are so many Irish names,
male as well as female, composed of this? Is it Celtic? But there is much
in Russian, too. Japanese in its kana, its syllabet: the "ka ke ku ki ko"
series lists all the *k* phonemes and the possible syllabetic combinations.
From root to phoneme to the individual human sounds. Not combined in
syllables but each a unique integer. Do they fall into groups of mean-
ings? Have they emotional or sensual associations, colors? The last
drawings I did at Provincetown were composed to some old Scots Gaelic
sea chantey, playing over and over like a loop while I drew—the warrior
returning in his ships, the great boat of the Celtic world, his queen and
his people awaiting him on the cliffs with torches, the great boat at the
beginning of the Celtic world. "Kishmael's Galley," the song was
called and it was almost holy; so ancient, so primeval, so calling-out it
was in its haunting, nearly remembered tune. Kishmael, like Ishmael:
makes my dad's old quip about the Irish coming from Egypt snap into
place.

What if Gaelic were a link, a missing piece? All the people I've met
here who know Gaelic or have studied it tell me it brings the other
Indo-European languages together; as if it were an earlier general form,
a younger brother of Sanskrit. Will they let me study Gaelic here—can
I get a text? What do its phonemes tell you in place names?—wisps of

straw, bits of learning, consciousness, recall. Without a dictionary, without paper, what can you do? Make notes on toilet paper and carry them about in a plastic shopping bag. Imagine yourself an old woman here. But hanging on to your marbles for dear life.

Imagine anything at all, for after all one is free to do it here. That is the purpose of this place; it was made for you to be mad in. And when you give in and have a real fine bout, they have won. And then they have their evidence as well. But the temptation in the long hours is hard to resist, and it comes over you like the drowsiness of the powders. How do you keep a mind clear that they befoul every three hours with narcotics guaranteed to bring on hallucinations, delusions? When you wake, you will be ashamed to remember them. But that is control, too. And you will soon not know the difference, will lose confidence. Will agree you are crazy, deserve to be here, should stay and take some more powders, and dream again until your brain is gray pulp corroded with the poison and your own shame and frailty before it.

The moments of clarity are the worst. You burn in humiliation remembering yesterday's folderol, your own foolish thoughts. Not the boredom of here, the passive futility of reality, but the flights of fancy, which would convict you, are the evidence that you merit your fate and are here for a purpose. The crime of the imaginary. The lure of madness as illness. And you crumble day by day and admit your guilt. Induced madness. Refuse a pill and you will be tied down and given a hypodermic by force. Enforced irrationality. With all the force of the state behind it, pharmaceutical corporations, and an entrenched bureaucratic psychiatry. Unassailable social beliefs, general throughout the culture. And all the scientific prestige of medicine. Locks, bars, buildings, cops. A massive system.

Have any of them ever taken this shit? Do they know what it does to consciousness, perception, sensation, logic and reasoning? Each little intern should know. But how would they know without ingesting these drugs themselves? And even then, would they relinquish them? With all this money at stake? The vast multinational chemical firms. The network of police powers and state control behind it. It has all gone too far, become a closed and self-sufficient world, complete, hermetic. An antiworld, the other side of the mirror of reason, its opposition and now its replacement. Now you will be examined and condemned by tests of reason themselves irrational, weighed and assessed by rules of logic which are illogical. And the drugs will make sure you fail. It is not the mind or reason that is the issue but control.

I am Pope Joan in the jakes; I smile, sitting on the pot, giving in to it after all these days of resistance. How could you shit without a door? This is how. And if someone walks by, you assume the look of the blessed or the hopelessly mad. Being reduced to this calls for grandeur. Thorazine reveries among the plants or in the dormitory room recall me to armor and cassocks, the stake and the discovery of an Anti-Pope. That dire moment when they have discovered a rebel in the heart of their festivities and celebration, the processions and the golden vestments. And so they have caught you at last; the Pope has appointed you this throne. A toilet without a door. The old priestcraft still ruling from death, from the Middle Ages. Because the secret is that they never forswore that time when their power was full. All present pomp only imitates it; present mundane parish hymnals and rosary meetings and thundering against contraception. The hand that throttles you now is stone and from another age.

Here where time has stopped, here where the face prepares itself to appear in the window, pasty, the dough of despair and rubber bread and too long waiting for nothing. Making itself ready for old age, for white hair—no distinguished Norman streak but the Ma Perkins real thing—yeasty and flatulent and innocuous. Here, the drums will not come, nor torches. No, fool. Not even the flight of the skylight—you won't be that lucky. You wanted to hang on to your mind and keep your feet on the ground. Okay—step up to that back window and make your invisible face the inaudible scream of years. Plead in a void, empty as your piecrust face, unbaked, chilly. Or sit in the jakes and roll about in your phlegm and your sanguine fantasy. Be the Pope himself, if you please—why the hell not? Pretend you're Pope Joan and get torn to bits or whatever it is they did to her. Ought to look that up. Funny notion, looking something up—you will be forever forbidden reference books. The triumph of ignorance: television and narcotic fantasy. So play, romp, laugh little laughs at them; conquer in your mind, rearrange history, play a part.

*   *   *

Suddenly—do you realize what you are doing? Have you noticed your thoughts? Pope Joan, for God's sake. The red creeps up my neck and onto my cheeks. My heart stops. Admit, admit what you were thinking. It's delusion—the mind pausing at the word. You have delusions. You really are crazy. They are right, then. Will you think the thoughts that make them right—these bastards trying to drive you mad? Even if you think them for fun, for amusement, to entertain yourself in hell. Then there is a still moment—it is like remembering sin before confession in childhood—when you realize you have come upon the truth even if you never admit it. You have just now observed your own mind wacky, flipped out, nuts. The way a prisoner of the Inquisition suspects himself of heresy, remembering yesterday's fleeting disloyalty to Holy Church under its torture.

Pope Joan, wow. Delusions of grandeur. How amusing that condition used to be to you as a teenage crusader working in St. Peter's snake pit in southern Minnesota. Reading the case histories, watching for the signs. The arrogance of your clinical, snotty-nosed self-importance. And the credulity before every book in the hospital library, the ease with which you swallowed diagnoses and every chance sarcasm or cynicism of the big nurses. And now you are the saint of the jakes in a nineteenth-century asylum in western Ireland. The realization closes my mouth like a smothering hand. My eyes stare at the humdrum room, the cupboard and the sink stand. I do not make a sound.

Jesus, it's enough to make you pray. Sweet Jesus—experimenting with the idea. Will it come to breathing entreaties to the awful Sacred Heart picture in the dayroom, whispering and sidling up to it when no one's looking?

No, D'arcy is out there. I did not invent her. Yes, but consider, how could she break into all this again, the shock value of crashing the gate being gone? Ask for a phone call. Keep asking—you've got to keep asking. And cut this out, stop wandering in history, stop following the metaphor. Concentrate, for God's sake, go in there and make some more lists, bring some toilet paper and write another letter.

13

When they called me I knew that it was for shock, for solitary, that the moment had come. It was in their tone, a final exasperation. And then it was Deirdre. The overwhelming joy to fall into her arms and hold her, saying her name over and over. This beautiful name which is Ireland itself, the sorrow transformed to delight. I could not touch D'arcy—there was no time and it was too risky—but here we have a whole room to ourselves. Our own room to visit and hug and say anything we like, talking softly—Deirdre whispering, for I have sufficient paranoia to be contagious. "Deirdre, how did you get in here?" We laugh and we cry and get up and sit down again on the little single beds. A tryst in furniture. A night table even, as if this were a private room, some mysterious room accessible to visitors in daytime, a cell at night. Do they lock it? Have they locked this? Deirdre is here; they cannot, would not. I am safe and she is safe and we laugh and smile and sigh. She is weeping too, as I am.

"How in the world did it happen? Are you a miracle?" And we laugh all over again, for I had been expecting merely to see a face. At a distance, but the face of my rescuer. It was almost a vow, that whoever came to me first would have my gratitude forever. D'arcy was the first. Now Deirdre. For a moment there is a sting for those who didn't come and were hoped for. Never mind—Deirdre is new and brave and beautiful. And she has made her way in here.

"How, Deirdre, how?" "I can tell you it wasn't easy. We've had a terrible time getting information. Then Moira O'Neil came down here with Charlotte on the weekend and they wouldn't let them in. Told them that you were not having visitors. As if you were refusing to see anyone. But I said it was a fiddle, sure you'd want visitors, they just wouldn't let you. And I'd try. So I came down and checked into the Auburn Hotel, and I just pestered them. From Dublin, Charlotte kept after the bureaucrats and chased all the official types around by phone. So we pulled strings.'' She laughs and squeezes my hand. ''You are wonderful, both of you, wonderful.'' ''What's even better is that we have a plan for getting you out. Now, it's a little complicated, so hang on. We have to get you transferred to Dublin first.''

''Oh no, not another bin. Deirdre, that's how they run the system—they drag you from place to place and you never get out.'' ''No, no, nothing like that. But we must get you to Dublin first.'' I am in despair at the idea; Rosemary was so happy yesterday at being transferred somewhere, but I heard later that the place was only another bin and a worse one at that. ''The reason it's got to be Dublin is that we have a man there, a very good doctor in fact, who's on our side. The one here is very old hat and would never let you go.'' I must trust her—consider how much they have done for me already. ''You see, they wouldn't just discharge you here. That would stick in their craw. But they would turn you over to a colleague—you know how they think.'' All too well.

''No more of that now—let me sing you a song,'' she says. ''Are you mad?'' I have to laugh. ''No, it's just the best thing and so much more relevant now. It's from the North, from Derry. I heard a boy singing it in a bar once and it went right to my heart.'' It's about a boat and the sea and fishermen trying to make it home. It's about courage and sorrow and poverty. And making it back alive. We just let ourselves cry. Then I ask for another. Planxty's older version of Yeats's ''Salley Gardens.'' Planxty's third verse has haunted me ever since I've been here. Tempting me to stay here, even to cross the border, and go north to the women of Armagh.

> ''I wish I were in Belfast town
> And my true love along with me
> And money in my pocket to keep us in good company.
> Liquor to be plenty and a flowing glass on every side
> Hard fortune would ne'er daunt me,
> For I am young and the world is mine.''

The singer has been too cautious and had missed out, lost his love long ago. But he could still imagine glory. Imagine Belfast being fun or

the site of great celebration, freedom, or ease. This is the same over-
flow, the same euphoria born out of such longing following upon loss.
Deirdre is wonderful for singing this strange little-heard music. What
perception for the necessary thing, the truly important. And only an
artist would stop to sing in the midst of a whispered conference: secrets,
plans of escape, messages. "I brought you bananas, apples." "This
will do wonders against the drugs, Deirdre, ammunition." We laugh
and rock back and forth.

She is hope itself, comfort and joy. "Now what can I do for you in
the outside world in the small way? What do you need? I brought plenty
of books. Some are from Moira O'Neil—there's a whole store; lots of
them are new Irish writers we'd like you to know." The flattery of that,
how it soothes, how it lifts the head to be addressed this way about a
book. "I have some letters, Deirdre, done in the johnny paper way, the
felon's correspondence method—really, they are so bitchy here they
won't trust me even with the lined foolscap insane asylums usually
provide. Stamps, of course, are unobtainable; envelopes." "Don't
worry, I'll see they get mailed." "Good. I'll just correct this address if
you'll loan me your pen." "Sure." Deirdre delves into her purse. "Oh,
look at this, here's a nice surprise. The cops had it." My passport.
"After the cops, I guess, the shrinks." Dear little blue book back in my
hands. "You can be sure it was the first thing Charlotte went for." I had
forgotten even that it was gone. Of course—Patrick never gave it back.
How else to stop you in your tracks? Inside this place I thought only of
locks and bars, not passports. But the sight of the little blue American
book crumples something in me. Then it springs back like crushed paper
or even springy and ephemeral cellophane—optimistically. I have this;
there is hope.

"And they got your still camera, your Nikon." It confirms me. It was
the reason I waited, took the chance, made a fool of myself, got busted.
"Deirdre—wonderful." "Everything else is still out at the airport in
police storage." "If I'd only had a little storage facility myself, this
never would have happened, Deirdre." "Never mind, the whole thing's
a silly mistake. You wouldn't believe the idiocy we've had to put up
with from these people; the lies and procrastinations—thank God for
Charlotte. We're making progress now and it won't be long. Only a few
days more. Hang on now." The nurse is nearly at the door and she
mustn't see the letters. They mean it about incommunicado; they have
told Deirdre that was the order. "This is for Sophie, this for my friend

Monika in Amsterdam. This for Nell and this for D'arcy—but she has been here already and knows.'' The papers change hands, flying out of my shopping bag to hide quickly in Deirdre's purse.

The nurse we had cajoled into bringing my purse and then some tea returns from her other errands to demand the purse back, the passport too. "Now then, ladies, this is exceptional and it must end as well. You are twenty minutes over and the doctor doesn't want any disturbance.'' Deirdre and I cling to each other and then she goes.

Queening it at my bedside table: bananas, apples, oranges. You must keep your strength up. For them, too, now, carry on like a runner in training. Tensing and relaxing, I feel the will returning to my arms and legs—yes, yes, I will get out of here. My friends will save me.

If you get out, what of the others? How do you help them, how do you change these places? What did you do last time? One radio program on National Public Radio—and they were surprised you'd do it. Membership in the madness network groups when you can find them, references here and there, public admissions—not very damn much. Your case in Minnesota helped, as a test case it even helped change the law. But you have done very little. When you offered to talk on mental hospitals as a form of social control to some learned gang at Columbia, who had invited you imagining you'd be a little less disconcerting, they canceled the conference. So now you can just be quiet. Which is surely the usual thing that happens to those who slide through: they never want to discuss it, even to think about it. Next to making it never have happened, discretion is the best thing. The first time—it was that way the first time. What will you do this time? Get Charlotte to bring a tour of the parliament down here and show them where the plaster crumbles in the dayroom ceiling? More funds for repairs and higher salaries for the staff—and they wouldn't change a damn thing about how it is run or what one puts up with.

What then? The patients. If they could talk, their stories of how they got here: the husband who wanted that other child and she didn't and so he committed her for postpartum psychosis; the brother and sister who wanted one woman's bit of land; the husband and priest of another; the son and daughter-in-law who wanted the house of another. The incarceration of another in adolescence for promiscuity, traded over to the mental arm to be retained half a lifetime; the alleged senility of a whole bunch of women who for no reason but being old and poor will live out their lives in a prison that also poisons their consciousness with chemicals they are never permitted to refuse. And there is nothing to do here all day, no "therapy," conversational or occupational, nothing to read beyond the *Clare Bugle,* no television but the nurses' favorites, and no exercise except for the fortunate who can walk two hundred yards to Mass. A privilege I never enjoyed, being a known escapee.

So—when you leave them all behind—then what? I'll tell, somehow I'll tell about it. Each time, these places have taught me compassion and the reality of being in the underworld, the pit, in my own person. And then it disappears and you forget. Twice now. If this is the last time, you must be sure you do not collude again. So you will have to work a new job. This accident, this piece of bad luck, this perhaps adventitious turn of chance obliges you now. You must be an inmate forever, one who will never forget.

But if you are to be any use, you will have to stop equating madness with captivity; that is, stop proving you aren't crazy, since this assumes that if you were, you might deserve to be locked up: you're only innocent if you're sane, and so on. So your mind has to be cold sober, if possible slightly depressed, in order to be adequate or credible. No mania. No imagination, no fantasy, no coming apart. Not till you permit madness, coming apart into smithereens, can you really stand against the bin as prison and punishment. Then you have a case—not otherwise. But you don't even know madness from sanity. And you fear madness as much as the others, would cut it out of your mind like a cancer. Would be surgical about it, lobotomize your own errant thoughts: silly pronouncements, metaphorical thinking, symbols, woolgathering, impulsive urges, double identities, resemblances, similitudes, traces and recollections. All like dirt to be sprayed away with detergent. Say that you were mad, say lunaticking around Shannon Airport—they still have no right to put you here, deprive you of your liberty and even hope. Laing believes that and Szasz and David Cooper. But you don't believe it enough yet. No one else believes it at all. That, finally, is the problem.

The rest of Ireland blurs, speeds by in the taxi to Dublin. Compliments of the government, an entire taxicab to carry me—a distinguished sinner worth this much expense—and the two nurses guarding me. McShane has relinquished me. Desmond has been to visit me with a great pot of gloxinia, looking foolish. "A houseplant, for God's sake," Deirdre said in disgust, still operating out of the Auburn Hotel and a visitor herself that day. "Does he expect you'll be staying for the season?" "How could Desmond have turned me in?" I ask. "I've heard he turned his own brother in for schizophrenia, that's how," Charlotte answers me. "Forget Desmond, he's no help at all." "But he's an expert on civil rights." Charlotte closes the subject: "Shall we agree then that this side of civil rights is Desmond's blind side?"

Now the taxi speeds by the great new factories in the neighborhood, and the nurses reply with a cynical humor to my question about them: these are the factories that make the powders. Ciba is here, churning out psychotropic drugs for the whole world—millions, perhaps billions of capsules as the custom spreads. In six years I absorbed 8,760 capsules of a major tranquilizer in four doses of 300 mg each; 1200 mg a day. Some of it may have come from right here. Eire in the modern world, where the flood of multinationals is coming in fast on cheap labor and destroying the landscape. The last beautiful country in the West. And very lovely it is along the Dublin road, the green of freedom. It's hard to be this happy, to see the sunlight again, to be on the move through such wonderful country—and then to see the prison door again at nightfall. "This is the St. James Infirmary," the nurse says, alighting. An old blues song.

But Nell McCafferty is here and Maere Rountree. And their Dr. Browne, the highest shrink in Ireland, the head doctor. He closets me for ten minutes and pronounces me competent. I am freed. With a signature. And a compliment, which is some reassurance despite my outrage at the entire system. Even, good man, at him. I have thereafter, at Nell's house and at his own, a number of occasions to hector him and his profession. He regards it as reasonable anger, detests drug therapy, is of the deeper-levels school himself and would have me try therapy, to go over the ground about my mother and father and so forth. But he did not really carry that into force. So I was permitted to stay at Nell McCafferty's house and then, when Monika came over from Amsterdam, to travel with her back to the West of Ireland and stay in a cottage by the sea. There I visited D'arcy and tried to kindle sympathy for the Irish hunger strikers by writing abroad to France and America. The strikers' courage was at last causing a great swell of feeling throughout southern Ireland. Not a rising but a gentle transformation from ignorant hostility to compassion.

PART THREE

New York City

1

I am lost in the middle of the city. On Park Avenue and Seventeenth
Street, even in sight of Union Square, but still lost. Home in America
for two months now, winding down. The show uptown failed. Despite
a fine brownstone, splendid rooms, even good frames for the photographs. It was the same exhibit—Lesbia Erotica, nudes and city water
towers, Sophie and the loft with writing in the pictures, little short
stories—that had worked in Amsterdam and Berlin, but the show
flopped in New York. Maybe too far uptown for my audience. Maybe
what did me in was that Sophie wouldn't come. I waited for her to arrive
at the opening, more incredulous every moment that she could do this to
me. She's taken an apartment on Fifteenth Street. And a lover. Sophie
came by the show the afternoon it closed, stayed for an hour, and left.
Then it was over.

The wind has been going out of me for weeks; sitting alone on the
Bowery, I lose my anger. Friends figure I must have ''done something''
to deserve what happened in Ireland. Over Christmas Dakota raved that
I had tried to live in the ladies' room, for God's sake, and I ranted back
about the Nikon and Ryan and finally gave up. Useless to describe the
bin. Or the Troubles in Ireland; everyone is satisfied with the tidbits
from television. This is Reagan's new America. I'm coming from some-
place else. Bernadette Devlin was shot seven times and lived and no one
here notices. Things are unreal now. The streets are still here, but
everyone is changed. I begin to hear the voice of reason all around me:
give up, you're stone broke, you could lose the farm.

*   *   *

I walk the streets aimlessly, as if merely moving can alleviate the suffering of consciousness, the ache of anxiety within the four walls on the Bowery. This is the old lostness from before, the last time; depression is coming on now, will wipe me out. Panic precedes depression, heralds it. It is the pointless frantic energy before lethargy, a last attempt to effect something through motion. All I think about is money. And that I am losing my art, my living, my power to create and enjoy what I have made. Now it is just survival, how to make it through the next few months. There is always the deadline of poverty. So many years before I die—what will I do till then? Lost. The next move is blocked.

Walk faster, go farther uptown, into the wilderness of buildings. This morning I mentioned my debts to Monika, who is staying with me; she was both surprised and dismayed. How gross, how extravagantly American, it must seem to her to owe money on a credit card. Even to owe H. G. Page for building supplies. Her quiet academic life would never incur such expense, permit the folly of owing the telephone company. Being with Monika in America, I can see in her assurance and courage how much my own have fallen.

I disappoint her. In every way, not least as a lover. What a mistake to have started up with her; two cold nights at the cottage in Corofin in Clare, when my loneliness and her goodness deceived me into an attraction that has evaporated entirely now. I would only be friends, which displeases her, insults her. I am obsessed with Sophie, which Monika regards as folly. "She will leave you for someone younger," she warns me gravely. "She already has," I say. Monika is in a constant state of anger with me, which even her patience cannot hide. But when she goes, I will be alone. Then it will start—the battle with death. Worse this time, because there is no possibility of suicide as there was before. I will be dying and yet unable to die.

The only way out is to write: the manuscript I called the Deathbook with all the notes and passages, the fragments from the first bust and lockup, and the attempts at suicide that flooded in afterward, the very record of the end of me. I went up to the farm for one last go, desperate to reconnect with that unfinished thread. This is it, I'll finally do it, I thought. Now was the time, after Ennis, after the bin again. A fight back, a writer's solution to the panic. Fly in the face of it all this time, risk it.

Because after last time I had dared to forget the bin. I had thought I was free, it was over forever. Then they got me again. So this time confront, don't run. Heal yourself. Stand your ground. You have just been sent to hell and jail again, disappeared down the wonder hole, busted again. This time spill the beans and speak, the way you meant to the last time you got out. But then you chickened out—too much to tell, too many to hurt, and then depression. It will get you again and you will go under and die unless you tell your own truth.

I must go right to the Deathbook then; there's a book all neatly arranged. Careful notes, even rough manuscript. The thing is already half done—all you have to do is flesh it out. Now you'll remember, have the necessary drive and anger. They got you again just to remind you— the experience stands like a boulder in your road. Karma has dug it up, you can't hide it; if you don't level with it, admit to it, you'll be blocked forever. A cop-out. You copped out last time and even got away with it, managed to keep on writing, but life won't let you repeat that dishonesty. What happened in those joints is not just a catastrophe but a source. The manuscript is the logical place to begin, the missing piece— it's what will save you now.

But it was gone. Simply gone. Rifling through boxes and drawers on the farm, sweating. All my papers had been moved around to make way for the winter tenant, who was down in Florida for a week and had given me permission to use the house. Turning the storage room upside down each day. Monika was visiting, and finally even she helped. "What does it look like?" "It's a pile of manila folders tied together with big rubber bands: 'Death' or 'Deathbook' or something scrawled on the front in pencil. Be careful, there are a lot of loose little sheets that might fall out when you pick it up." We have tea and start again. My hands shake so that I can hardly manage going through this wilderness of papers: letters, accounts, records, photographs. My wedding pictures, Fumio's face looking out, family members beaming reproach at the two of us now in this desolate and disordered room. University notes, every sentence of my Oxford studies in English literature, lectures from teaching—it's got to be here. And it just wasn't. No, no, I'd say and get up in the middle of the night and go through everything again. Even as we packed the car to leave I was still searching.

So grab something else, grab anything. You were writing about your father, it was coming along—grab that. You have to write your way out. Only work, only writing can do it—can forestall depression. Work will save you, not their lousy pills and telling you you're crazy.

But then the writing wouldn't come. Day after day straining for it. One afternoon I sat at the dining room table and realized my father's book couldn't be written. If I could do this now, it would finally set everything right. It started like rolling off a log; it was a delight. Over the past two years I had already done a hundred and fifty pages, composing leisurely in the blue barn, my table before just the right window, the summer or the autumn scene—sheer luxury. Now I have turned to it for rescue, and nothing comes.

And what finally did come would be impossible to print: scabrous, turgid, furtive, fantastic—you can't publish all that stuff about your old man's balls, the sexual vitality of your parent, really: hardly fit subject matter. Imagine how your mother's going to take this sort of stuff. Failing that, denying it, nothing else would emerge at all. However I strain, I cannot even remember my childhood now. As for the man's own history, I realize suddenly I actually know nothing about him. You'd have to go to St. Paul, talk to the old men who knew him, worked with him. Hardly in shape for that now, are you?

I won't say it aloud, but already I know it has come to an end. The book on my father will not be written. Block has never happened to me before, or never on this scale. To lose a whole book—it may take me years to make another. How will I live? How can I hold on to the farm?

Of course, if you hadn't spent money last summer, you would still have the mortgage money for the land. Instead you threw it into the lavender barn. You owe Page's three thousand dollars on a house you'll never finish. Because you cannot finish anything now—you are finished yourself. Monika is mopping the floor today because you cannot even keep your house clean. You can't do anything anymore. When she goes you will sit there alone and rot. There is no energy in your soul anymore, only this frantic thing in your legs walking, walking: where in God's name are you going? You're finished. You have lost your marbles. And you're broke. Where do you run?

*   *   *

But I know. All along I know. Guessing; not even guessing; knowing to the very brownstone. Knowing long before I get there that I am going there. But not to enter—I will go there just to look at the place. Or if I make an appointment I needn't keep it. If I talk to him I needn't agree with him. How disgusted Monika would be by my coming here: head-shrinkers and drug therapy are mind control, she would say. But she doesn't have my disease. I do.

Now, only now, are you crazy to yourself. Craziness that reeks worse than old socks, more like a ten-day-old corpse. Depression is death, the very tinge and certainty of decay. Paradoxically, depression is when you finally contract the sickness they accused you of as a manic. A delayed reaction, if you will; the internalization of all the crimes of your high-and-mighty time in the suffering of your fallen, dying time. Depression is when you agree with them all and surrender. I am like a starving animal, circling toward the place where I give up my little cudgel and ask for mercy—in the form of a medicine that might prevent this pit, this hollow valley, from becoming my life. Over and over: ten, twenty, thirty more years of this shit.

It's worse, though: it is not only the medicine I hunt but the door, the way back in. As if this doctor could grant me absolution and reintegration with all those I love. And he can; my mother would be delighted, Fumio, Sophie. It is perhaps the only way to retrieve Sophie; she said as much Thursday night over a single cup of coffee at Phoebe's: "If you don't go back on lithium I no longer want to see you."

Of course, it's perfectly easy to tell all these folks you are taking your medicine and then not take it. Even possible to take it and not tell them. It might also have been possible to refuse to take it long enough so you survived and made them agree with you that it was perhaps not necessary—but that was a great deal harder. I tried it and am broke now. I can't write and am terrified. We may now conclude I have failed.

2

I am going to Dr. Foreman's office for myself alone, to save my life, I say, nauseated. I surrender my capacity—proclaimed so willfully, foolishly—to control my fate through my own unaided mind. My mind on its own was not sound. Being of unsound mind then . . .

And here is the remedy, lithium; take it and you are healed. Bullshit. You don't really believe that, walking up Fifty-third Street toward the dreaded, hated, and so desired place. It is Mallory's phrase I hear: "degenerative disease." The whole tragic hush. I nearly laughed when I heard it first on the tape recorder left playing during the bust. The textbook phrase. So actressy, I thought, so melodramatic.

This is the place here. These elegant brass doors. The office, the waiting room, the receptionist just now closing the glass inner doors. "No, there's no possibility of seeing Dr. Foreman today." Clearly he has already left, and they're closing shop. Detestable smell of money— guess what the rent on a place like this must be. Gone are the old days of free treatments at the university clinic. Foreman has withdrawn into private practice—it now costs sixty dollars just to see this man. I wait like a fool while she fusses with her books, finally deigning to look up. "Would it be possible to have an appointment? Soon, please—this is rather an emergency." Her look sizes me up. "Suicidal?" A withered, exhausted figure, but not suicidal. "There isn't anything till a week from Monday." That's ten days away, I think, outraged, and unable to do anything about it.

*   *   *

But they did manage to help me last time, when I was depressed and Washburn finally talked me into going to the university hospital. There I was interviewed by both Foreman and another doctor named Abramoff, an interesting man who spoke of depression with feeling, named it grief, appeared even to know what he was talking about. Foreman was young, cocky, and gorgeous. He was the one who dispensed the pills. When we first met him, Wash and I winked at each other, figuring him for an S.A.E., Sigma Alpha Epsilon, the most frivolous fraternity on campus when we were at college together. Today, when I finally have an appointment to see him, I am astonished to remember our old lighthearted designation; he has become formidable.

Foreman is by no means glad to see me, though my coming at all must be a satisfaction: hadn't I been fool enough to go off the medication, and wasn't I here just as prophesied in serious depression? The punishment, the inevitable punishment of mania.

But it is the mania that really interests the doctors, that must be stamped out. Depression is your own problem; get out of it however you can. Wait out the months, a year maybe, till it goes away. Only you must not commit suicide—that is absolutely forbidden. Your life does not belong to you but to the doctors, the relatives, the state: the social circle. Show any symptoms of suicide, and they'll pick you up like a thief. I show none. Am not even admitting the extent of my depression— only my surrender to the medication, to anything that will give me the will to live. Prevent the cycle of my hell between up and down, sure and unsure, brilliant and stupid, full of schemes and full of nothingness. Failure is a desert now before me—a lifetime of these terrifying rides, this Ferris wheel of the mind. Rescue me, I plead. Without saying that. Saying instead that I was wrong to stop taking lithium and think I must resume, since a serious depression is coming. My manner is saying so much more: ashamed of my hubris, my error. Of course I couldn't treat myself or understand it; the disease is alien, mysterious; they hardly understand this foreign thing that strikes me, after centuries of trying. All I had to do was swallow four simple capsules a day. I would have been all right the rest of my life: my career, my farm, my friends, my reputation. I wouldn't be broke and unable to write. The six years I took the stuff were fine and productive. I did three books in that period and a great many exhibitions. Fool. Fool, to think you knew better. I squirm before Foreman while he regards me, probably amused.

*   *   *

"It was a great mistake—I've made a mess of it," I say. "What'd you do? What kind of trouble did you get in?" "Textbook, I suppose: I spent too much money, drove off friends and lovers, ended up in a hospital in Ireland." "If you flip out in foreign countries they can be pretty mean about it. Like Iran." "I didn't flip out in Iran, I got arrested, remember?" It all seems the same to him. He must have hundreds of patients, and the six months I haven't seen him appear to have quite erased me from his mind. Sitting before him, I feel erased. A defector surely, but in returning a prodigal as well, proof of the pudding. He's not sympathetic, merely recriminating. As if accusation after accusation of madness, misconduct, bizarre behavior, were cure in itself. I want a prescription, not a lecture. My illness now is not mania but depression— he should direct this indictment to the other one, the manic. She would have been delighted in answering these charges, contradicting him, demanding he prove it. The self I am now wouldn't bother to cavil, is too tired and humbled and broken, too sick to fight back.

Capitulate and get a prescription. I was mad to stop taking lithium, yes, manic as they say. There's no point in arguing it; it no longer applies. What applies now is the descent of the one illness I have never questioned—depression. I feel it descending hourly, daily, recognize the vertigo. I am certain of the onset because of the panic, the great heightened fear—which is both imaginary in its monstrous proportions and real as well, since it is the last attempt of the psyche to struggle free before being buried alive in inertia. Panic is a haste in emergency that finds the dime but drops it while scrabbling for the telephone number.

Foreman would be more than right; he is merciless, laying down the law about my disease, infirmity, blight: "No doubt about it, no way around it, Kate, you're a manic-depressive, that's you, Kate." How I hate his use of my first name in this condescending sentence. He calls me Kate, I call him doctor. "Get used to that, you're just going to have to live with it," he says, leaning back in his chair, smiling. "Of course we've got a new name for it now: bipolar affective illness." The boyish haircut, the perfect good looks, his shirt stretched tight against his perfect chest. The walkie-talkie at his belt, the office humming behind him, full of patients waiting. His avaricious assistants are consummately rude to me—a crumpled, has-been writer, condemned by this diagnosis to a lifetime of insanity. Would it were over already; I can't last through another depression.

Now he plays with me: He's not sure I'd be a good patient; I used to reschedule appointments. And haven't I just proved myself unreliable by quitting the lithium and going full cycle from manic episode to this place? "You feel pretty down now, don't you?" He is perfectly at ease, hands joined behind his head. At the clinic you got in if your symptoms were right, but here, in his plush new private office in a smart brownstone, your attitude must be correct as well. Furthermore, he can make no adjustments in fees according to need. "So it's a matter of how much you really want to come here. There are a number of tests as well and they're pretty expensive, time-consuming." I don't have a choice; he can refuse me lithium. He stretches in his large chair behind his desk, bored. It is boring to interview someone who can scarcely talk. I am forced to truckle: "Well, I guess I don't have a choice; as you say, I'm sick, I must have this medicine." "Sure you have a choice. There are doctors all over town; you could even go to the clinic down at St. Vincent's. Bit crowded maybe, but they're okay." Corridors of the poor, anonymity, hours of waiting. Dealing with strangers for whom I am no more than a number. No, much as I detest him at this moment, I will stick with him; because I need him, know him. It worked before.

My sickness is chemical, they say, and the cure is also chemical. They say that depression follows mania as the night the day, though at some indeterminate time. But what if I were only broke and deflated, censured by others and unsure of myself in my art? At odds with my friends, sad over losing my lover, scared of my future without anything in the bank or the prospect of a job? Then I would not be chemically and fatefully overcome by disease—just blue. Maybe with something real to complain about, even if without solutions: new lovers, better publishing prospects, and so forth. Then my depression would be what Foreman himself used to call reactive—a reaction to the real world. Why go to a doctor if what you need is a good publisher and a lover? Because you have been manic, he insists.

So you accept this reproach for your shameful, eccentric behavior—craziness, the flower of insanity, the ugly root of it in your very genetic structure; constitutional, perhaps even inherited. Foreman has decided it's genetic. I wince. "Afraid so, Kate, we're just about certain of it now. Wasn't your father an alcoholic?" My father, whose life I am supposed to be writing, though I cannot, have lost him to death, to absence of memory, of subject, anecdote, anything. God, how my dad would hate this guy. I focus on the man at the desk in front of me, trying not to hear him. My mind wanders off to a vignette I'd seen along

Bleecker Street the other evening, a man and a little girl walking in the snow just at dusk. The wind blew hard and he picked her up and carried her, his face in her hair. An epiphany I forced myself to incorporate in the manuscript, my description belaboring the picture for two whole pages, bleeding with envy of that child in the street whose father so evidently adored her. There is nothing left of my father now: the rebel himself is dead and his sisters disowned me twenty years ago—the Milletts.

I reach for but cannot touch my father, cannot even remember him when I try to write, so much with me once before when I began the book, delighting in the very act of bringing him to life on paper. There's nothing I dare say about my father now, or any of them, the whole tribe. Even Mother—I cannot put her on paper, and she has to be in it. Family: how could you dare address that subject now, unworthy of all of them? Hospitalized again, the taint in you proved again.

You must say you are crazy, say it, kiss the rod. Unless you repent to this stuffed shirt there is no lithium pill, no chemical cure, the precious prophylactic against your ups and downs, the vicious cycle of manic episode and depression. It balances and prevents, keeps you on an even keel. Or at least lithium prevents mania for sure; unfortunately, as he keeps saying, it's less effective with depression—especially if you've already got it. And I have. So it's in for the long haul, with a vague prognosis that by taking it I might just return to normality. You might need antidepressants too, he says, though he's not offering anything along that line. Life under lithium; a peculiar, submerged, slightly sedated, and ever so slightly depressed life. Slow—but passably normal. A low-level tranquilizer, but you could live with it. I did for six years and could work, hating it at times, but in six years one grows accustomed. Give me the stuff—let me try it again. If I start early enough maybe I can head off depression.

Not on your life, not without submission. Say it, tell him you were crazy. So, sure I was crazy. I assent to it all today, all the definitions I had denied in my skepticism, my grab after sanity. Admit it to him: your hope produced nothing. Recite the formula: your classic behavior of talking all the time, going without sleep, living in a state of heightened awareness and intellectual excitement, out of which nothing comes, because there is no finishing of things, the mind interrupts itself constantly. Go on, recite; make no mention of being interrupted by others. Also, you were irascible, antagonistic; no one else was, of course. Mea culpa. You frustrated others; they did not frustrate you. Do a general confession. Tell lies. Truth is a lie now.

Then the assistant snatches you out of the corridor into an office to arrange the next appointment, which will cost another sixty dollars. And of course there will be more to pay when the prescription is filled, and an hour's wait at the university pharmacy. You must return there again before the next appointment in order to pay for and get a blood level. Nearly a full-time job. But better, I can get better, fright mumbles within me as I sit on the bench waiting for the officious summoner to bleed me. Another ironical, utterly exhausted voice, knowing all is lost, finds a deluded humor in it: Your mother will be pleased, and Sophie. You have done what they wanted, finally.

3

Tame I am, defeated. No longer the crone of Ireland raving at them all.
Forget her—that way lay madness. From now on it will be your eternal
disgrace that you said this or did that, the words filtering back to you in
accusing voices, your follies defined in their tones, demonstrated in the
tired disgust of their very manner of breathing as they deliver the withering quotations. What they went through: the anxiety over you, the
embarrassment of you. The problematic one day to the next while you
were off in a foreign country and getting into God knows what trouble.
Or at home and endangering the farm, ruining the summer for the
apprentices. Spending like a fool, wasting time and money and energy;
wasting everything.

All over now: Foreman's voice commands you to surrender, not only
the present but the past. "You were wild, you were wacko, you were
high as a kite." How the hell does he know—isn't Sophie his only
source of information? But he's the doctor you've come crawling back
to at sixty dollars per half hour. For these endless reproaches, couched
in clinical terms like "psychotic break" and "manic episode," the
phrase suggesting a rat at the end of a pincer. "You were just uncontrollable, you drove everybody up the wall, you've gotta realize that.
You had all the people around you frantic—they just didn't know what
to do with you." He looks to Sophie; he has ordered that she should
come with me today, his witness.

She says nothing; he speaks for her, though he was never there
himself and must go by what she told him on the telephone. Months ago,

when I stopped taking lithium and went mad, when she pleaded with me to go back on it. That failing, since I refused, she called him for advice. "You should have been institutionalized right then—as a matter of fact," he thunders.

This is my arraignment. I must be made to admit my crimes before a witness now. I admitted them last week. Why again? Why before Sophie? Even coming here was admitting all: he was right, I was a manic-depressive, had the disease, was its victim, desperately needed his cure. Two appointments later he decreed I bring Sophie. It had pleased her that I went to see him but she had little relish for seeing him herself. She is here unwillingly.

Again he looks over to Sophie. "She was all over the place, wasn't she, last summer?" Sophie nods, deeply embarrassed, her slender arms on the chair rests, her face looking straight ahead. How she must dislike this American emotional vulgarity. Not that Foreman is of our sticky therapeutic "inner feelings" school; he is biochemical, crisp and pharmaceutical. But he must establish the insanity in order to effect his cure. So that I will never stop taking the medicine again, so that I vow and vow again I am the prisoner of an illness, and this its cure. Sophie's face stares straight ahead; I see it out of the corner of my eye from the chair where I am placed. She is here to be sealed into complicity; like a contract, she is hereby being enlisted on the side of the cure, adjunct to the doctor in watchful control.

Does Foreman wonder how long she will be with me? Coming over here, I had the impression this might be the last time I'd see her. Manics always lose their mates, Foreman has given me to understand. Abandonment is the customary punishment for them. No one can put up with a manic, he assured me. And once it's over and you're depressed and diagnosed and repentant, husbands and wives and lovers depart anyway. The damage is done. This pattern is an established fact. So in front of Sophie I am convicted again. All her own sayings are evidence now: her complaints, her fury against me.

I would only complicate matters by pulling my oar and remarking that she was as irascible as I. Why delay the process? I fervently want this interview to be over. Today is the special appointment, the one to determine whether he will truck with me at all. For three weeks I have been on trial, but he is still reserving judgment.

I hear the verdict now. It seems I am a dubious ingrate, probably not worth the effort. This doesn't bode well for recovery; I may be abandoned to this disease. I who was once the star patient at the university clinic, invited to benefits that raised money for its continuation. A well-known figure they could point to, though, thank God, they didn't.

Foreman has his own fine practice now; I am expendable. How prosperous he is, how secure; no blight will take him off, no misfortune strike him. He will go on making more and more money, become more and more entrenched as an authority in his field, rise higher and higher in psychiatric circles and university tenure. In his beautiful clothes and surroundings. The walkie-talkie on his belt: he is so busy, so needed everywhere. The sixty-dollar check I will write in ten minutes will have to be covered first thing tomorrow morning. I am the end; he is the beginning, the future assured. I hate him at this moment, find his bullying beyond anything called for. Sophie trembles.

"You've got to admit the state you were in." "I've admitted it," I say, my voice as crumpled and inaudible as I am, making no difference at all. The question is still one of my worthiness: "Because there's something else I have to tell you—so I waited till she was here," he says, nodding to Sophie. He addresses everything to her; they are the adults, the sane, the whole and hale, his figure vital and energetic in his beautiful suit in his beautiful big chair. A pronouncement is about to be made.

"You have to quit drinking," he announces dramatically. "But I don't drink," I protest. Surely not as he means it; this drinking business is one of the libels against me. "You were drinking plenty last summer, don't tell me you weren't." "I probably was then." Under stress, under attack. "Yes, I suppose so." I have drunk martinis most of my adult life, ever since graduate school introduced me to them; the rigors of Columbia and two hours in the subway made them a necessity I have since enjoyed as a pleasure. A martini before dinner, one of the solaces of life. "But I am certainly not drinking much now. A martini before dinner and a glass of wine with the meal—is that drinking in the sense of 'She drinks, you know,' or 'The problem of her drinking . . .'?'' "It is." He is passionate now; he is doing autopsies at the university, he and his colleagues. And they are coming upon great kidney damage in lithium users.

"If you weren't taking lithium you could drink your head off, you're healthy enough. But not with lithium; you cannot take lithium and drink, you absolutely can't—you should see these cells." Next we begin on the brain: alcohol destroys the brain as well. One shouldn't drink anyway; he sounds like a teetotaler now. "Do you drink?" I ask him, irrelevantly, trying somehow to dispel the atmosphere of prohibition. Surely drinking is a part of life, a happiness, not a contagion of devastated cells. "Socially," he says. "What does that mean?" "When you go to a party you have a drink. You could have a drink once in a while on social occasions—but you're going to have to give up the martinis. Forever."

A little nervous laughter all around. "It'll hurt, sure. Maybe it's part of your life, but you cannot, you absolutely cannot, continue if you want to take lithium. Not if you're going to be my patient. There are other guys will dole it out to you no matter what, but not me." Not him, he has rules. I almost like him for being so fierce about this. I also think that he is pompous and impossible and his method of telling me this is obnoxious. It would be very simple to describe the autopsies and the results of lithium on the kidneys, and then urge a conclusion.

The drug is still new enough that there is little evidence of its effect over a long period of time. Sophie need not have been summoned to hear this. I am the more humiliated for getting an alcoholic's lecture in front of her, not being an alcoholic to begin with.

In fact, when we finally hit the door of the our next stop, the blood clinic, safe beyond bureaucracy and institutionalization, coercion, conformity—all of which have taken their toll on Sophie—our first and concerted thought was to find a bar. "It's terrible, of course, but it seems so necessary just now." We giggle, sitting down in the Chelsea, a first-class drinking establishment. She has even telephoned Marcy from the dispensary, as I have called Monika, both of us creating this time and this place for ourselves, carving it out of the others. We will buy a chicken and a log for the fireplace on Fifteenth Street. But for now what one needs is a martini, and some scotch for Sophie. "Will you give it up, what do you think?" Sophie sips her scotch. "Wasn't he awful?" She shakes her head in bewilderment. "I had no idea he'd be like that."

"And that place, my God, that place." She closes her eyes. Probably the people got to her too, the sad-faced patients; the despair in the waiting room; the hush before the throne; the gorgeous bourgeois fittings paid for by the sufferers. I had been embarrassed sitting with her in the waiting room, embarrassed to be one of the mad among the mad before her uncomfortable gaze. And when admitted, to be flagellated by the doctor for mania, for the sins of the summer, naked before her eyes—at that moment finally she was no longer accusing. He did it for her. All her own insistence that my behavior was outrageous, tainted, unclean: now when authority shouted it, heaped me in obloquy for my sins, I could see her soften, even wince.

I have assented to something infinitely demeaning, which she has been made to watch; in a certain sense, we have been had, both of us. The relationship between us, this vulnerable bond, has been pried open, invaded by another. Not the usual appeal to legal mates and relatives. Two women: fragile, unacknowledged. To keep her, I have accepted her as keeper. He has sent us away to "think about it." It never occurs to him that I give him no argument or reasons of my own, pretend to agree, only because I want a prescription. Months ago, even weeks ago, I would have denied all that stuff—it would have been my word against Sophie's. But then I wouldn't have been in his office begging him for lithium.

In this bar we are only at the beginning, with the surrender of the martini—following upon the initial surrender, the resignation of self back to psychiatry, independence relinquished for medication. And now I must submit everything, beginning with this by no means small daily sacrament of light: the clarity in the glass at evening, the float of joy in a summer sunset—the whole Atlantic is in its clarity, I used to think. Making drawings, abstract spatters and brush lines, homages to the martini. Even drinking a martini while drawing, the first half a very productive tonic.

Though I tell myself I will not give up my martini life, my carefree-artist-downtown-raffish-talker-of-an-evening life, I know I will. I am furious he can dangle the drug they say is the only thing that can cure me, dangle it before my eyes—and then pull it away on the strength of a martini. Beyond question I'd miss it: my way of life a long day's work that led to the happiness of a snifter of ice and lemon and the restful gin before a fire in winter, before the pond in summer. Days when I could work and had a life. Now, in the vacuous nowhere of depression, a drink can still call the end of a day's panic and dread; food, a fire, some solace. Now there will not even be that.

Why do they put you on this stuff before they realize it may eat out your kidneys, the lithium lodging there and retained by alcohol? Side effect after side effect. Autopsies, the gray, hard bodies of the dead.

It's all gone anyway. What the hell. Even Sophie is gone, lost to me.

But tonight I have her, depression at bay for a moment as I go for our supplies, the log we have just enough money to buy after the chicken at the store around the corner. Just tonight. Like the last drink. "What are you going to do, have you decided?" That insistence of hers. "I guess I'll have to quit drinking martinis. And I think I'll quit Foreman as well." "Where will you go, then?" "Maybe I'll try to get in the clinic at St. Vincent's." I do the impossible, almost deciding something out of the chaos of indecision I live in now—seeing the corridors of St. Vincent's before me, charity hospital of the poor, all I can afford and so much more agreeable and honest than where we were today.

Driving over to her place, I thank her with some dishonesty for going with me today, for sticking by me. I ignore her crossness, her bitchiness as we near her house—a fury emanating from her having a date she cannot keep tonight, or as she calls it, an "appointment" with Marcy. Tonight she has elected to spend the evening with me out of pity, or goodness, or maybe even preference. The scale between me and my rival tips one way or another from day to day. The very situation is my loss anyway, since once I had no rival, once I lived with Sophie.

This strange life we lead now—she says it herself, bringing it up, the bewildering painful change, whenever some errand has brought her to the Bowery, and she looks around and sees the house she used to live in. Every board, chair, plant, rug, bookcase, table, the Franklin stove, the little kitchen, the dressing room—I suppose she sees the bed, too. It happens as well, she says, when she looks around Fifteenth Street, her own place, wondering why she lives there. In fact, she hardly seems to; there is never anything in the icebox. The room is bright and orderly; she has a nice fireplace, a fine big skylight, another little room to work in. A bedroom I regard as alien territory and have never been comfortable in, since Marcy also sleeps here on other nights. On my sheets: Sophie has pinched or borrowed two sets of sheets, and put them on her bed for Marcy, for herself, even for me.

I ignore the bedroom for the fire in the living room. The roasted bird. I do not stay overnight, have only a few hours of grace. I prefer the rug before the fire, making love to Sophie that night as if passion could bring her back, aware of passion, able after so long in apathy and numbness, able to feel. One of the few times. For there is no sex in me now either. Only the great rise on that night, her breasts dearer to me than life; the grief of love gone, going. A little while and it will all be gone, I will never see this place again. It will finally be over and she will have tired of me past any further invitation. The passion in each of us only sorrow.

4

Things constrict, they all boil down to the kitchen on the Bowery. I pace the narrow floor there past the sink, the little counter Sophie created over the iron body of a Singer sewing machine. The floor is a dirty brown paint on top of old white tiles, the tiles of a toilet. This building was once a bums' hotel, Liberty House; the word "Liberty" is still in the broken tiles before the front door downstairs. The kitchen was once part of the showers and urinals. When I moved in to pioneer here, to camp out and salvage an abandoned building, it was logical to place the kitchen where the pipes were, in this narrow confine before a window. The window is waist-high, decayed and dirty, and overlooks a shabby balcony. Or something I was always going to make into a balcony: French doors, a greenhouse. Absurd plans now: you would have to remove the window, cut out four feet of brick under it, reinforce and frame again in order to put in French doors. Chilly probably, expensive, ambitious, laughable to consider now. Like the skylight I was going to open up someday, the roof garden—wonderful crazy schemes my neighbor Michael and I would cook up while drinking by the Franklin stove, on nights when he and his wife, Linda, would come down to discuss the newest emergency threatening us: what the city was up to now; when it would manage to throw us out of our lofts. We have only thirty-day leases. There is a demolition order hanging over the entire neighborhood, city and speculators always on the horizon to bulldoze it and erase our world within these walls.

Mother calls—a distant voice on the telephone, worrying about me while I reassure her I am fine, just fine. I am hardly able to talk at all but still swear at her once when she harasses me about drink—do I drink? "No, I don't. I quit. Now they won't let you drink at all if you take lithium." I am taking Foreman's lithium but I have not been back, am holding out against his expensive tests and his complete control over me—at a crossroads, evading him. "Thank heaven you're back on lithium—I've been making a novena that you would." "Really, Mom." "I used to worry about you so much all those years you took it and drank those martinis." "No more martinis, Mom, I gave 'em up." Jovial. Then furious a moment later when she wants to know if I'm drinking now, this moment. Haven't I just told her no? "No, damn it, I'm not drinking or drunk. Anyway, Mother, I never did drink—I mean, I never 'drank' in your sense of the word." "Yes you did, plenty of people have told me." "Who, damn it?" I wonder whom she'll quote, who her informant will be, who in hell is doing this to me, worrying this poor old woman, meddling with her trust in me? Or just simply turning me in. Ruth, it must be Ruth—Ruth can't drink at all because of an ulcer, so she has the most inflated notions about people who do. Sophie—did she get it from Sophie? I am finally angry, capable of a little anger, a little life. Therefore she thinks I'm drunk. I shout at her now. And hang up—the first time I have ever done this to her in my life. Then I call her back and make up, coax her into thinking I'm fine. I can't tell her anything else; I don't want her in on this.

The Franklin stove has been cold all winter. It's too much trouble to cook, I live on soda crackers. The answering machine is set so that I can monitor calls; except for Sophie I never pick up the phone at the sound of a friend's voice, never even write down the messages or copy out the numbers to call back. This is a ghost's life. I won't bother with a fire, am not worth it. But I still sit next to the stove sometimes while reading, endlessly reading. Trash. Junk. A type of book I have studiously avoided all my life: a parade of unknowns, historical novels, supermarket paperbacks. Reading kills the time, whole days are consumed, one after another—just pages. I read when I wake up because the lines of type follow one after another, excluding any other words. Even the silly story helps me forget: Sophie; the bin in Ennis; the disappointment of being back home, broke, a tarnished nut who can no longer write at all. Since I will never write anything again, there is a lot to admire in any piece of printed rubbish. Moreover, the snob in me has completely let go—I enjoy this pap, stay alive on it, mainline it fourteen hours a day. I despise myself for reading hour after hour, stuff beneath attention—but it keeps my mind from straying back to reality: the bills, the horses up at the farm, the land taxes, the mortgage coming due on the new land.

The farm will have to be auctioned—I guess that's what they do. Never mind, dive back into Matilda's nineteenth-century adventures. (Dickens could never hold your attention these days—your mind is so far gone, the very cells are pulp by now.) This piece of junk with the lurid cover, purporting to be about factory conditions in the last century but really an excuse to go on and on about clothing and the heroine's indomitable spirit before the overseer's terrible eyes, will get you through until around five, when you have another opiate purchased with foresight and grocery money yesterday—your one foray outside the house in eight days.

When I think of the farm I shiver. I tried to borrow money this year for the land taxes and couldn't: no one would lend me money. I had never tried to borrow before; the experience was alarming. The taxes were to be paid from the rent on the farmhouse, but the money was already cheerfully eaten up by the horses, their hay. More money went to pay the neighborhood kids to feed and muck out, though they never shovel the barn clean. "When I heard you'd bought horses," Mother said, as if this sealed it—the most obvious sign of madness, for her kind of Irish. My kind of course, my evil Millett blood, was only waiting for the day when I could look at a horse on my land. But she's right. It was crazy. Think of what you spent.

And now the horses storm their barbwire walls and are breaking out of the barn, having spoiled several doors already. It's an old structure—they may manage to kick it to pieces by spring. The beasts are continually angry because of the water situation: the frozen pipe, which is now not only frozen but broken. For two weeks when I came home from Ireland I carried them water in buckets and improvised with a hose from the wellhead. Finally I found a plumber with animals himself who thought it was important and fixed the pipes. Now the kids have taken over again, mucking out and watering in their absentminded schoolboy way, and I was able to go back to town, back to paying Palmquist for hay.

Get rid of the horses, I tell myself, pacing the loft on the Bowery. Get rid of them. How could I get rid of Jim? I love him. And the idea of saving their lives—would you just walk out of it, the promise that entails? If you could last it out, keep them while they live out their lives at pasture. Plant timothy, fence off the back acres, let them wander the woods. Use one to ride your trees. Let them live and go on living— didn't you see a dream in that, some daft Amazon vision in your mania?

Can you still remember that morning when it was all clear? I had just been with the horses, all of them, playing with them. Then I crossed over to the new field we had fenced for them as they began to eat the first field bare. It is still a new field; its vantage and view and ambience were new to me. The grass was knee-high. From this distance you see the place as a unit, the house and barns and the pond. And all that green of the landscape right to left, a thousand shades of green, each shade promising the farm could succeed and be paradise. "The women who lived here . . ." I told myself, almost as if I were beginning a story, something which had already taken place—imagining Amazon figures, golden women.

The summer is with me now like a reproach: its endless possibilities and expectations, that perfect world. Here in winter, in depression, the past mocks and ridicules. That morning in the pasture it was all at hand, like the day we made garlands by the pond. Petra's idea—fey, outrageous. The whole herd by the pond, around the white table, grazing on a nice little sward we had recovered from the wilderness and made into a lawn. The goldenrod just beginning, daisies still, a ring of daisies. Let's put them on the palomino and around Jim's neck, she said, and loosestrife for the big white horse, the lavender against his white. The animals put up with it—they realize their beauty, make no objections. We weave faster, laughing and excited, women and horses united in the garlands, the glory of the flowers against their manes: the antique, lovers, people in ballads, Amazons. This is, of course, pure Petra. Sophie is delighted too. The wars are over. The farm is being what it can be, the secret perfect place, heaven on earth this short life.

We could be that, I thought, looking at the second horse field that particular morning, the sun golden throughout the meadow, the shine of the morning everywhere on leaves and blades of grass. There will be more trees, till there are thirty thousand, enough to maintain the place in the future, build houses for the women artists who come. Groves to walk in, an orchard, and up on the hill to the right a little stone Irish house I always imagine as in honor of my mother, Galway.

The life lived here beyond America, the present century, reality—

whatever. The life of women and trees and horses, the golden morning. Why not grow our own wine? Women in the past lived and held land. Loved it and were free. Look at it there stretching away from this second meadow, the sun gilding the runoff and the trees, the farmhouse way to the right, and the barns across the pond. A vineyard here? The plantations to come, a horse chomping quietly behind me, the others in my vision if I turn, and the land ahead of me across the ravine of the runoff swelling like a giant breast. The hill on the left is another breast, the very earth is warm and comforting as flesh. This moment it is at rest, without the cruelty of winter here, the rust and mud of early spring.

Sophie and I would still have the fall here to come together again, restore ourselves after the whirlwind. I'll go get her, show her this, how it can be paradise, is paradise already if you look. And the horses—she should see them in this morning's light, I thought, imagining that we would be turned on by the sexual presence of the beasts and make love in the warm deep grass, the animals friendly around us, watching. I sensed her unwillingness. It would have been a lovely farewell to the place, we're leaving tomorrow. The worst is knowing this, how desire is not shared anymore.

Then all of a sudden I was filled with a dreadful premonition that the place was mine alone, not ours. I imagine the farm without Sophie and hate it. I did not want it. Because it is too much, because it is no fun alone. I am its slave then. And the only figure at the feast, solitary and without appetite. How would I endure it in the future, this enormity of space? To be old here and alone, a vengeance of solitude: a loneliness crushed by the memory of company, friendship, love. The green leaves are ashes, tedium. God deliver me from this place.

Now it may be lost altogether. The vision failed—but the very place itself may go too. Lose the farm, really lose it? I have never been so scared in my life.

5

Death is everything, it blots out life. Would it would come soon. Imagine twenty or thirty more years of this, an old an older and then decrepit woman living alone on toast or canned soup or cocoa or whatever requires the least effort and can be consumed while reading. All I do now is read. If I stop I always end up pacing the kitchen, this dirty little room bounded by a sink, a stove, grimy windows onto the prisonlike brick building next door; its rooftop is, ironically, a playground covered with an enormous grille which precisely resembles a penitentiary. Refiguring my debts across this dirty floor, scattered with gravel and potting soil from the time I cared for plants. The gay bower of hanging ivies is grotesque now; I scarcely water them; they are dying right before my eyes. I don't even care, haven't the energy or the optimism. Though a part of me is still able to be ashamed. There is so much to be ashamed of now. I was crazy, I am mad; I have an illness that will worsen through my life. I know I can't succeed at suicide; I don't even think of it anymore. Only of death, wanting to be dead. Unable to get there.

I stand by the stove looking at the coffeepot. I have probably been looking at it for hours. Some new glass business Sophie recommended, makes only a cup at a time. Living alone now, I will need only one cup at a time. Don't use that big aluminum one—the metal poisons you. And the plastic one is broken now. Very nearly everything is broken. The icebox over there is empty; and I the gourmet cook who used to feed everybody. I'm still laboriously paying twenty dollars a month to Sears for this. What if it broke too? What would I do? I could never buy another one. Today a man on the phone, interrupting my stealthy explorations into nothingness, managed to sell me icebox insurance. I'm so scared of life I couldn't even laugh. Losing the farm . . .

There is no future in the room where I live, no present. Only the mind goes on. Consciousness is suffering. If I could excise thought altogether, leaving just enough to get through a day's junk reading . . . When I stop reading I pace, and whenever I come to rest by the low table near the Franklin stove, the table we used to eat at before a fire, the past comes back like nausea. Don't remember. Anywhere near this table, and I hear echoes of how I used to hold forth at dinners, in interviews. Thought is nothing but recrimination.

Somehow I must find eight hundred dollars to pay the taxes and save the farm. And then—how remote and impossible—the thousands needed to pay the mortgage. If you had those thousands, wouldn't you be smarter to eat them, and to hell with the mortgage? You could live a year—writing might come back if you had time.

It has simply disappeared. I have been trying to write at the kitchen table, where I wrote all the other books or parts of them. And the table never failed. Months ago it was a day's labor to get a page. Then less and less would come, until now an afternoon yields nothing at all. I play music, walk back and forth—nothing helps. There is nothing there. It is the subject then, my father, my parents, and so forth; strong emotional repercussions might possibly contribute to block. I hate that kind of talk. But of course, something is stopping me. They called my father a drunk and I was called crazy; there was a bond in being outlaws. But now I've capitulated, gone back to the headshrinker, laid down my differentness as if it were a disease and sided with convention. It was the living at risk, the love for that in him and even in myself, that gave the book energy and affection. I've lost faith, let it be stolen away.

At first I could still manage to compose a little. I retyped fifty pages of earlier prose. But now the writing has literally gone. Day after day I try for it, risking failure. And getting only the dry white page. This book will not be coerced. Yet at first it was—even a few new pages, painfully wrenched out that week in the country, one whole day devoted to a paragraph about the heavenly safety of sitting in my father's lap as a child while he read to me. But then the book refused to be written.

Refused. I sat at the typing table back in the loft, with the red kitchen table just to my right—the ashtray, the cigarettes, piles of unanswered mail. Nothing happens. If I can begin a sentence in the morning, doing something safe like washing dishes, I do not sing it along for a while like the old days till the coffeepot is clean or the coffee made, a few phone calls in between. No, sir, not anymore—I run right to the typewriter or a notebook to write it down. But when it is inscribed on typing paper, its cousin or friend or little sister—the next sentence—does not rush to its side out of nowhere, the unconscious, the great goodness of the goddess, or even just good luck. It stands alone, for hours. Pace the floor. Try listening to New Orleans music while you write about the joy of your father's Saturday nights: the little beat of his feet, the tapping of his shoes just walking around the carpet, or letting go a bit on the linoleum in the kitchen. How he was the spirit of going out, the out of adults, the out of "out on the town." This engineer warming his Black Bottom and rehearsing his Charleston; not even rehearsing—he not only knew them, he *was* these dances. Hearing a drum, as black as he was white, a natural man finger-popping, a little hum at the back of his throat. The delight and suggestiveness of his chuckle. Rarin' to go, waiting for his lady to dress, priming himself for his evening while entertaining his kids, admiring his shoeshine, jingling the change in his pocket—this magnificent black Irishman with kinky hair and nicotine stains, dressed up in his best suit. Already unable to resist the dance inside him, his fingers snapping counterrhythms to his feet—"the Wabash Cannonball."

I fight with this stuff all day and get nowhere. There are no words anymore, and this was the thing I loved in him: that he was the dance, that he had music all through him, and good times—quiet or hell-raising good times. The phonograph goes on playing the music that was him, and I love it too. But I have no stomach for it now; there is no fun now. No music. I miss him as I labor to create and cannot. And who would need to create him if he were here, if he were not dead? I am trying to connect with this long-gone outlaw, the paternal line, my male self. Dead since I was thirteen and he left us—his abandoned children, according to the version I grew up with. Last summer I was given the other: Mother revised history for me. By this version he was simply thrown out. Mother ordered him to leave: his behavior—we have this in common, Jim. So I've given up; it involves too much, too many people. If you write about him, you need his sister and all the Milletts. My own

tribe, who disapprove of me—the surviving Milletts have even disowned me—should I betray them to a publisher? For once I could see
with Mother's stony gaze: You do not write up the folks.

And now only silence. Every morning I promise myself I will not read.
But I awake so frightened I am reading within an hour. Self-indulgence,
I know it for that, a total deterioration of will, but still I cannot keep
away from a book. And every morning I promise myself I will do the
mail, the piles of unopened envelopes by the door, the papers spread
over the rug. Instead I am nailed to my chair by the cold Franklin stove
and before the big windows, drugging myself with print. I have abdicated everything now.

Maybe there's a way to live on less—I try to figure it out on paper.
The rent for the studio, bills, groceries. The farm—the thought always
there, though I read to prevent it, that I will have to lose it, give it up.
A nightmare of furniture with nowhere to store it, an auction on the
lawn, closing and saying goodbye to the place. This gives me diarrhea,
an hour of discomfort for a thought.

I no longer really permit thoughts; half-formed thoughts, notions of
despair or guilt or shame or regret, are stifled before they are born,
drowned in a book. Regret—Sophie, the loss of love, the summer, the
apprentices, how wonderful it was at the farm until it went wrong. Go
on reading. Everything is to be regretted—if you go into that you will
cry . . . Read, just keep reading. Follow those thoughts and you will be
banging your fist on your thigh in self-hatred. Fool, you had it all, love
and delight and a talent, and you blew it, every last thing. Pick up your
paperback again; don't cry. Do you remember your high time?

6

I must have dragged myself here. Unable to bear it in the loft, managing to get through the streets somehow. I held out against Foreman but I can't hold out any longer. God knows how I got here, bundled on a hard chair under the watchful eyes of a security cop. A public hospital. St. Vincent's. The poor around me, visibly crazy, senile, babbling. What am I doing in this place? What propelled me really was the afternoon's exploding fear, so big it was like strangling, the heart seizing—the moment coming on the Bowery when I had to break and run. Help me any way you can—if there is help. I gather from the hard-bitten clerks and receptionists that there won't be a hell of a lot of it, and for whatever there is, they're determined you shut up and wait your turn—after you've paid. It isn't much, hardly worth the paperwork, but I can pay it. After you've paid they are a little less fierce, though still resolutely hard, mean, New York. Then you sit on a bench in a grim little waiting room with the oil portrait of the founder, the cop, a flyspecked window, three dying plants, two male relatives arguing in a phone booth, the one about to put the other away. And a woman in a chair across from me who is raving. Manic state. Is this me? Was I like that? I know I wasn't, but if I resembled this even a little it makes me die inside. Deep in depression, I quietly illustrate the opposite condition.

Finally a very young man, boyish in fact, calls my name. In the lottery of life I have drawn a kid, I think, following him. Maybe I can get a substitute; perhaps it's a different one each time. But the frenzy I bring him really doesn't discriminate. I used up Foreman's stuff. Now if I could just get more lithium from the guy here, and if the lithium works, I could climb out of this state, recover some corner of a life. Not the old life even, just a life, any kind of life—there being so many years of it to get through still. Forget about years, how many months will the depression last this time? I ask him and ask him again. "I don't know," he says. You have to admire an answer like that. But I need a deadline just to stay alive. I tell him I read in a textbook—a very discouraging experience, looking yourself up as a form of insanity—that depression can last up to nine months. "Even longer," he says, "but it's usually more like six. With antidepressants, it can be shorter still, a couple of months." "Three?" I count them—it is nearly three months already that I have endured this. I really can stand no more; it is why I am here. I stare out the window in his absence when he goes to get prescription forms, am barely able to talk in his presence. He is charming, completely without threat, even compassionate—how I love him for that, that his eyes actually seem to pity the inarticulate anguish before him.

I'm scared of him too. Of putting myself in another's hands, permitting my shameful little history of bins to come before anyone's eyes. The characters in my tale, those at whose bequest I have been busted. The times, the places: California, 1973. The occasion? Different assessments about how to produce a music festival, I want to say. Or Michael X. But forget it, you talk their language here. "Manic episode." I don't even need to mention being busted in Ireland; one institutionalization is proof of everything. And you need that to get the medicine you came for. Foreman has my records and can send them downtown. "Have you taken antidepressants before?" "Elavil: when I was first accepted into the program at the university." "What was your reaction?" "I hated it; it made me feel . . . fuzzy. But it seemed effective." "Well, we're going to try something else." His little cheerfulness. It is good he is so small as well as so young, like a boy playing doctor. So much younger than I, he is less able to bully and play the authority. They not only give out lithium here, he says, they do a bit more therapy than I've been used to—how do I feel about that? Not terribly cordial, I admit, but at this point I am very depressed, and simply grateful for his patience with me.

He saw me two or three times a week thereafter, tense dreadful sessions wherein I remained nearly speechless—wanting to reveal as little of my life as possible and in any case deprived of language by the silence of depression. Below that speechless lassitude the mind races from one imminent disaster to another, each of them a foregone conclusion, all very real. Some are financial, about which he can do nothing. And I prefer not to discuss Sophie with him, a reticence she found insulting: I saw it as a compliment.

So he hit upon writer's block and the book on my father and made enthusiastic attempts to practice his psychodynamics; he is an intern. This caused me some consternation: I regard what I'm working on as sacred or magical enough never to be discussed. The jargon of psychotherapy was the last conceivable avenue through which I would want to approach my father as a literary subject. "Why don't you bring in some manuscript, maybe sketch a bit for next week, and we'll go over it?" young Dr. Benfield suggested once. Whereupon I had to say my stuff was off limits—something that seemed to hurt his feelings, or at least perplex him.

Otherwise he was kindness personified, merely being himself and concerned. Once we argued: His theory is that depression is anger turned inward; therefore if he could get a rise out of me, there might be progress. He goaded me with a little litany of what a graduate student in psychology told me later were standard phrases: "And how do you feel about that?" "And how does that make you feel?" The little taunt went on and on, until I said I found myself getting annoyed with him. "And how do you feel about that?" "That I came here for help and not to pick a fight."

He was mollified. We got along. My days are spent, many of them, walking across town to get my blood level drawn for lithium and in the hour with Benfield, the one being who seems to care if I live or die. An odd relationship to have formed with a stranger, a good fortune that scarcely seems credible. And it isn't really, it's staged; but he is good at what he does. Sophie cares a great deal more for me, many do. But this impersonal crutch—and he is a crutch and knows it—was completely necessary at first, both of us in time cutting down on the visits, until that great moment when his mere existence in a certain room on Thursdays is no longer all there is between me and death or isolation or despair. I cannot help but be grateful, enormously grateful, and tell him so. Even that first day. He smiled. "Accepting help is the hardest thing of all."

There are a thousand things about this that I hate. I have come to depend, I realize while sitting in the hospital chair waiting for blood to be drawn, or in the vast public room waiting for the number to light up on the board signifying that my "medication" is ready at the pharmaceutical counter. And since this is free or next to free, it naturally takes forever. Entire days are consumed in this business. Accepting the drug of dependency. It was that or running toward a death which lacked even the energy of suicide. This last hope is a surrender too, even of the dignity of selfhood. I no longer go through the sophistry of I am right, they are wrong—I never was crazy, was driven crazy, misunderstood. I read the symptoms and find myself in the case histories: Middle-aged man in Ohio who had recurrent manic-depressive episodes every three years and so forth; the symptoms laid out, prognosis slightly encouraging after several months of ingesting psychopharmacological medication. Woman in her thirties, administered electroconvulsive shock therapy; showed improvement, but continuing series of relapses over a period of years.

In the corridors of St. Vincent's I am one with the mad in the texts. One of the sick and destitute waiting for the technician's ungentle bloodletting. One of the shabby who waste eternity staring at the lighted numbers and reading discarded newspapers, forbidden to smoke. The officials, fortunates who are interns or nurses or clerks, security police or janitors, the white-coated pharmacists behind their glass windows, bustle around us, a passive audience of blacks and Puerto Ricans, old white men in pajamas who have come off the wards, mothers of young children, recipients of Medicare and Medicaid. Madwomen who mumble, men who pace, nervous people who use the phone all the time to tell whomever that they are still stuck down here, won't be done for another couple hours. I chafe too and then sink back into whatever I am reading.

The reading is omnivorous now; I have given in to it completely, even telling myself at times that I am a convalescent. Beyond shame most of the time, one day reading up to and through and even after a blood sample, occupying the same chair for some four good daytime hours. Telling myself every ten pages or so that I must leave, must go home and do something. But I kept right on reading, my errand done, and still taking up space here. Perhaps taking advantage of the company, such as it is, the refuge from solitude that this alienated sea of humanity represents. You can't smoke, but it's free, and I can't afford to sit in a coffee shop, have insufficient imagination even to find one. Spending the day that way would be deliberate, a flaunting of my vice even to myself; here I can say I'll go home in just a moment, at the end of this chapter. The time goes on and on, and still I hide in a hospital corridor, hide from life itself. Mortified, shaken, helpless to stop.

When I finally emerged it was as from a debauch. I had wasted the day. Nothing that had happened from the beginning to this moment, the whole journey starting last summer—nothing caused so much inner shame as this clandestine reading. "Why not read?" Benfield says, imagining that writers read to some purpose. "You don't know what I read—I read crap." "Don't be so puritanical, you're recovering, resting." But I'm not; I'm abdicating, sloughing off, giving up. My reading chair—the big black leather Italian chair by the Franklin stove, a place I used to read after work—is where I now spend the entire day.

The book about my father sits in its sheaf of typed pages and spiral notebooks on the red table down in the kitchen. Undisturbed for weeks, no longer attempted. The inanimate paper is full of threat; there is a knot in my stomach when I pass it. But I never put it away—I never put anything away. There is some stoic impulse in keeping it there in sight to rebuke me. In case one morning I wake up sane and able.

During depression the world disappears. Language itself. One has nothing to say. Nothing. No small talk, no anecdotes. Nothing can be risked on the board of talk. Because the inner voice is so urgent in its own discourse: How shall I live? How shall I manage in the future? Why should I go on? There is nothing ahead, my powers are failing, I am aging. I do not want to continue into the future as I see it. These and other more urgent things, the crucial details of life: one specific overdue bill, an unanswered letter, a phone call that may make all the difference in an immediate emergency. And so, on the little surface of life, these deeper questions being so peremptory, there is nothing to advance by way of conversation. One's real state of mind is a source of shame. So one is necessarily silent about it, leaving nothing else for subject matter. Therefore, one listens, bullied by others' talk, that very talk an invasion. Yet one needs to have something said, something has to fly across a restaurant table, even if it's the interminable description of a conference one didn't attend and cares nothing about. Since one's field of interest is now very small. Oneself. In danger.

The loss of language is so crucial, such a bereavement. Language does not really go away, it goes inward. Downward. Shriveling in the process, becoming repetitious, as when one facing great peril repeats the same protective formulas. Yet one mourns language, sociability, cama-raderie, needing it now more than ever. And how necessary it becomes just as one observes its superficiality; the wavering of friends, the cold-ness of strangers, the essential uncaring of life itself, its monstrosity. And in the face of this evil—not even to have words to protect one from the vacuum. To grow mute as well as helpless.

7

Fumio lives just two blocks away. For eight years we have lived happily in the best-friend relationship he outlined when we came to live in separate buildings on separate streets. Two old brick lofts, by some fate situated so that we could see each other's lights, each of us knew if the other was home. We had only to lift the phone and call: Fumio knew of the perfect samurai movie at Bleecker Street, or I had too much roast beef and needed help eating it or a visitor he would get a kick out of meeting. The hour I returned from a trip the phone would ring, as if he were the watchdog of my vacant home, watering the plants sometimes, one of the few who had a key in case of trouble. All so easy, neighborly, it would be that way all our lives long. The last illusion of Sartre and de Beauvoir.

But when he stopped by after New Year's and sat wearily by the fire, he was a man without illusions, his manner that familiar insecurity of the sane before the mad. Hadn't I been locked up in Ireland? Ireland is a mystery to him, but if I was locked up I must have deserved it. He brought me a present from his visit home to Tokyo, a *han-ten,* a kimono jacket his mother had sent back with him for me. She used to sew me one every Christmas; I lived in them. A *han-ten* after all these years: I taught her how to drink gimlets, we went to baseball games together—it is twenty years since I have seen *Obaa-chan.* I looked at her son, wanting to flood him with all the love I felt for him in Ennis, still full of the total recall of the bin. His look back was one of nervous anxiety. Hardening himself, somber, withdrawn. The stone samurai side: enduring, resisting. I could see he thought me a lost soul. I could also see his boredom, his sadness, his never wanting to bother with this again, all weighing him down. The dread of the mad: didn't we feel it for the friends we had to go and see in Bellevue, the poet buddy who used to go up to Harlem on a tear and return barefoot in a taxi to be bailed out with a ten-dollar bill? Am I that to him now, a worsening condition?

I have not seen him since that January visit. Four months. Once that would have been impossible, once we watched over each other, talked every day. So when I forgot to turn on the answering machine and picked up the phone without thinking this morning, it was an explosion. For a moment I was happy: he wanted to see me. Of course, this is terrifying too—no one must see me as I am now. I'm hiding, a cockroach under a bookcase watching dust balls roll along the floor. His voice on the phone frightens me. Bad news, a hard side to it.

He must see me at once, he is going away. He has been offered a professorship at Dartmouth. My God, he'll live in New Hampshire, he'll leave town. Almost as disastrous as if he were going back to Japan forever, a fear I have lived with for twenty years. It's nine o'clock on Sunday morning. The call shatters the day. He is leaving New York. And I must come over and see his new fish sculpture.

It is, as he puts it, "pretty good—not so bad." His voice conveys infinite pride and satisfaction. I remember the first one he showed me, on a huge ceramic plate he had had specially made for it by his friend the potter. Magnificent it was, triumphant: carved clean wood, a sweep of skeleton almost magically summoning the spirit of fish itself. All his research at the Museum of Natural History in each of its hundreds of bones. Above all, the manna he had inculcated into this sculpture, this undressed series of bones, the ghost of its muscle and nerve, its scales and flesh, present even in the bare bones and jaws, the great mandibles, the whiskers shooting back from the mouth. All that strength: lovely.

I have lost writing and know I will never sculpt again—to look at art like this is an agony now. You cannot admit this. "Sure, I'd love to see it." "Okay, come over. Then we can go downstairs to Phoebe's, eat some breakfast. We gotta talk about this divorce."

Divorce? The word is strange, terrible. More powerful than absence, hostile, a deliberate removal. Now, at this moment, this nadir. My face burns. It doesn't seem possible to refuse to meet him, go to his studio, admire the new piece, sit through a breakfast where I am divorced. Impossible to call him back and tell him to go to hell, that this is not how

I want to spend the day. Even to come out and tell him I'm broken, sick unto death, I cannot cope with divorce too. This word like a knife in the heart.

No matter that we have been separated for years. Or that we were forced to get married at the behest of the state, Immigration allowing us only thirty days—it was that or deportation. So cussing and grumbling we submitted to City Hall. Marrying this way and not believing in marriage, we did not believe in divorce either. Not getting a divorce was a matter of principle for us. Perhaps of friendliness, too, having watched divorce and its animosity, bitterness, its quarreling over possessions. Now finally he has called to announce he will be divorced, rid of me, severed clean. This last connection. If only I weren't sick now with depression. He will see me broken.

He might pity me. He might hold off because of that. Forget it, I don't want that pity commingled with contempt. I must get myself together. What will I wear? Unable to deal even with that, I read the entire two hours remaining until our meeting, shutting off every humiliation this call has summoned. My husband has made an appointment to divorce me. He has a lawyer even; it must all be achieved at once because he is going away to be a professor.

At his studio I am docile, awaiting the worst. Which it seems will be postponed for Phoebe's. I have trouble with my hands, shaking from the lithium, the Elavil; actually, the Tofranil now, Elavil's substitute. Between this stuff and my fear of him, of today's interview, and my hands, which tremble continuously ever since the panic set in, I must make a big production of lighting a cigarette. I do so with great care, care with the box of cigarettes, particular care with the match, and constant care in how the cigarette is held steady lest it betray me. I turn away to light up, concentrating on the new sculptures—which are wonderful—concentrating on the tools and equipment, careful also not to smart off, remembering in dismay my last visit here.

I had come by unexpectedly just when I got home from Ireland, just before Christmas, passing his house on the way to the grocery store, shouting his name and waving, then waiting till he threw down the keys. Around our neighborhood we usually wrap them in a sock or a glove; with his delicious ingenuity, Fumio has fashioned a working miniature parachute. Banzai, I called to him, seeing this joke descend—delighted to see him—like a kid paying a visit to his very best chum. Just home from Ireland and full of grand stories: What a great country, all the artists here ought to clear out and go there to live—there are no taxes for artists. Listen, I found the greatest building over there, it's an old paint factory. I could get it for a song. I describe the mill at Ennis which I am mad to buy and turn into an arts center for the Irish people. All I need is ten thousand, the Irish Arts Council promised to pay for the rest. Lunatic schemes now that the farm is going. I remember my confidence then—we were two artists together: I could still talk him down. After my show failed I started my descent.

And here he has worked and done something wonderful. How I wish I could turn to him and tell him what has happened to me. But he wouldn't want to know; it is the last thing one admits to—barrenness. He couldn't help, he couldn't do anything about it. It would embarrass him. It would expose you entirely—are you not exposed enough? Crazy and certified. Now this too, you despair of art—the final proof you have lost your mind. And will never recover it. Mallory's idiotic phrase about a degenerative disease. He believes that too; many heads have shaken over this. The ghost of whatever I was, visiting his studio now to see his latest triumph.

Today I am no longer so special a viewer. Only one of the many who come to the studio, mostly men with six-packs. Today he doesn't particularly linger. I praise and admire, but then I have always praised and admired. When I had my show this January, he did not come to the opening and had to be persuaded to stop by at all before it closed.

Up at the farm in February, I came upon the hand-lettered invitation Fumio had made for our bridal dinner. Buried in a cupboard, still safe. I framed it and hung it, his crest at the top, his wonderful painstaking script all in celebration of a feast. The spirit, the elegance, the starving artist's particular grace and style; more aristocratic than kings. Here was quietude and loving, in these carefully formed Roman letters; twenty times he had copied this out with a brush and applied the gold paint to the four leaves of his crest. The Immigration authority was getting us hitched but we could do the thing in a style all our own. They sent the kimonos from Japan and we had a grand time, artists and relatives equally inebriated.

There is still a coffee table in this room from those years, a little stool he has kept. Among the band saws and the stored-up linden wood, the crates for exhibitions in so many places: he is getting famous, a success. Galleries and museums. Now a university. He talks like a businessman at times, or affects to; the result not very convincing, at times even annoying. But his life is this now, sculpture as an end in itself. And mine is the opposite—I can no longer write, do not care to paint, cannot conceive of the effort of sculpture. Let's go to Phoebe's; the sight of this place, its industry, defeats me.

Fumio does too. These bright red suspenders he has on; funny, charming, most attractive, the red against the faded blue of his denim workshirt, the raven black of his hair, crisp and beautiful, without a thread of gray in it—how much younger he looks and feels than do I though he is nine years my senior—these red suspenders of his have become a malign force, something vicious declaring his power over me in the interview to come. His superiority is established first by his work, by his ability to produce beauty and life in wood. As if a rank were set up between us artists which the bacon and eggs of our marital termination will only underline.

We sit down in the familiar hash house, another living room all these years, situated not quite equidistant from our two lofts, since it is on his corner and I am two blocks up. Phoebe's is the navel of the neighborhood: "Meet you at Phoebe's." We celebrated there continuously, openings and closings, arrivals and departures; if you went abroad or came home again you could not do so without a party in Phoebe's back room. Today is not a celebration, high talk, reunion, the delight of the past. Today is opposition. I am bested in every way, but I am not even trying to compete, a noncombatant. How could anyone exult over me?—pale, the damn hands shaking, tongue glued to the roof of my mouth with medication, the silence of dreary hopelessness. Watch your hands. Think of something to say. Quick, think of something. So he won't say it—so he won't start.

My grief at his leaving this world of ours downtown is overshadowed by his insistence that he go away divorced. It's about the house in Japan, he says, so that it be free of any encumbrance at his death. So that his mother and sister may inherit without my disputing them. But that's silly. The very last thing I need in the world is a house in Japan. As if the farm were not enough to worry about—imagine crossing an ocean to fix the roof. I loved his studio in Japan, was his tenant there before I was his lover, but that house has always been his alone. For the last twenty years he has given it to his sister, who lives there with her son, Fumio's nephew. His mother lives right next door. Nothing could persuade me to be a predator there.

But he explains, earnestly—so earnestly there is a rage in it—he must be legally divorced or there will be problems before Japanese law. I am registered at the consulate here as his wife; that legally entitles me in Japan as well. "Then we'll make some paper about it; surely I can just waive every claim—and I can do it so that it is made official now and it needn't wait for you to die. Anyway, man, what's this death business?" "It's possible to die; I'm over fifty now, I have to think of this." And he is going away—only for a year, thank God—but still going out of the city. Then, too, he has just spent the holidays with his family, his mother and sister, the nephew who will probably inherit the house after Fumio's sister. Fumio has been subject to pressure by all of them to clear this up and legitimize their claim. Getting rid of me formally in the process, which hurts a bit; but their own reasons are valid and their skepticism of my relinquishing claims to their property is understandable too.

"I'll ask my friend Grace again, she's in practice now; but the last time she told me I needed nothing more than that quitclaim thing you signed about the farm." "No, not enough. It's enough here, but not enough when it's Japan. Different countries, two legal systems." "I'll ask her again," I say, stalling, gaining time. The man before me in red suspenders, eating a plate of eggs. I cannot eat mine, am sick at the very look of them, nibbling at my toast, watching him recede from me. . . . What of his sculpture when I am no longer heir to any of it? His dealer will have it, of course.

I love his sculptures, his drawings; none of them will be mine now. Nor will he be the custodian of my things anymore, sculpture, manuscripts. I had always felt safer in the world because we would look out for each other's things. I don't want his house, never have, but the art, his and mine—now we are no longer linked in that way either. In no way then, our old ages lived out in separate ways and places—does he go from me now forever? That silly jargon he keeps going on in, Jacobean something or other he keeps repeating—I realize only after a moment it's some cut-rate lawyer he has already paid fifty dollars, and is planning to pay another two hundred and fifty if he can just get me to sign a paper. Sure, I say, broken like a branch, ready to inscribe anything—he wants it.

Because even when he called I knew I could not resist. How can you refuse someone a divorce? He doesn't want to be connected anymore, even for old times' sake or because being married was something we were once and did not wish to disavow—had no reason to, since we were neither planning to marry anyone else and had no paranoia about property. Nor—and this is the point, I guess—did we have any desire to sever. My own marriages to Sophie or Dakota or Sita never interfered with that. Neither did his liaisons. One could be married many times— but it was always forever. We would never be the strangers that other people became.

Marriage with us had none of the usual trappings of bondage and respectability, so maintaining it after the fact was a sweetness between us, a courtesy, a courtliness. Now it is over. Now it is the state and the lawyer he goes on about: how fast they are, how cheap, what a hurry they are in. And then we will be like everyone else. I will be a divorced woman, a statistic. Not liberated—that came slowly in the years of living apart, living on my own, living with women, in marriages that were not marriage either. But this is a divorce, the standard contract.

The windows of Phoebe's onto the street. Fumio talks for both of us—just as he did in the studio, a tyrant of energy whom I both hated and admired, a whirlwind of work there. His so justifiable pride. I am dissolved in admiration of him. How well he's working, how neat he has made his little living quarters. Pictures of his first wife everywhere: Yoshiko is adored still in death. Even a picture of me, the second and less satisfactory wife—one of the *Life* photos from 1970, the summer of *Sexual Politics*. How young I was then, such a success. I must not cry before him, carefully eating toast and pushing the scrambled eggs around. It is only the coffee I want—merely to live on coffee. And cigarettes. Eating them nearly. And I think of it as eating each time I put one in my mouth.

Jesus—has it come to this, the wonderful world we had once, this man and I? The sunny breakfasts in the old Bowery loft, the days we never even went to work but told each other stories, Fumio reciting a Tolstoy short story one whole wintry afternoon. Beginning each day with a retelling of the Genji or the Heike—"to warm up my English"— he'd laugh, like a boy with his head thrown back. The stories were still courtship when we were already years into marriage; they were to delight me and himself and either postpone working or call it off. But we didn't care. For all our diligence—and we worked like hell and a hundred times harder than everyone else—we were also the most leisurely people, the most indolently flirtatious or erotic. Whole days were canceled out just to stay in bed or to break off in the early afternoon to go there, feeling horny: "Don't you feel horny, let's take a little rest"—the wink, the perfect compliance of those years in the very best French studio on the Bowery, as we called it. Putting the greatest care into our shopping for artichokes, our invitations, the appointments of our rooms a triumph of ingenuity over poverty. Being happy, we were the center of happiness, beloved of our friends—anyone could come by with a bottle of wine or without, and the penny collection or some other seraphic source would provide.

Beloved of our friends. And now he lives alone. I do as well. He seems covered with solitude despite his occasional mah-jongg hangovers. I feel loneliness like a stone, cannot remember the names of friends, so remote all that is now, so long ago. Now it is a matter of whom to call when you feel a little better—only to find they are busy, might schedule you for some impersonal occasion two weeks hence. What happened to it, where did it go?

There in the red suspenders: I cannot perceive this as Fumio. But this semistranger is divorcing you. Your husband is divorcing you. You are crazy and he is leaving town.

But he's not your husband, he's Fumio: lover, friend—all that for a lifetime. Fuck their papers, marriages and divorces alike. Will he give me the same sales talk about how this will make us better friends? Has he a hidden agenda, a new lady, one who means business? No, that is not the point: the house in Japan is the only purpose. "I'll ask Grace again, if it's okay with you. There's probably some less complicated and expensive way to do this." "It has to be soon." "Okay."

Now there is hardly anything left to say. It is natural now that he will ask me about myself. And there is nothing to tell, only secrets of my days of nothingness, abject terror, panic alternating with inactivity of the most infantile kind—entire eighteen-hour days reading.

"What are you working on?" The dreaded familiar question, familiar as the voice of Bell Telephone's bill collector when you pick up the phone unwittingly. "The book on your father?" "Sort of. I'm having a little trouble with it." "Well, keep at it," he says, the waitress here, the money exchanged. I want to pay for this myself, even if it hurts; if it were the last dime I had, I should insist. Never mind that this could tide me over two whole days if I shopped right, if I went on not shopping longer still. You must not let him pay for his own divorce conference even if it is his. Pay or you accept humiliation—damn it, pay for this.

But he has already paid, poised to leave for half an hour now, reluctant at the same time. I am too. Part of us yearns for something gone past regretting but regretted still, glimpsed, nearly understood, then eluding us. Like a figure half recognized passing before the big windows onto the street. Where we always see our friends walking by—that is the charm of Phoebe's. Certainly not the food. You can sit there with Ruth and see Fumio go by, or sit with Sophie and see Ruth. Certain afternoons everyone I know crowds around one table, picked up off the street. You see one and rap your knuckles on the glass, but you rarely need to because everyone passing Phoebe's is already looking through the window for their chums, even when they are busy with errands, even carrying the laundry as Fumio often is. So the laundry can wait—have a beer. Or a salad.

Or these eternal eggs, the hopeless toast, the coffee brought shaking to my lips. "I'm taking the lithium now." The confession. The penance said after receiving absolution. "That's good." Absolution after the fact, cold now. I am doing what he wanted, what they all wanted. But they no longer care. It is a little too late. At the table to the left of me I told Sophie some months ago that I had gone back on lithium and she cried for happiness, as if I were an alcoholic joining AA. Now that I was taking lithium I had a chance of being saved. I hold the lithium up in front of me now: the word, the strange heavy word. Offering it like a curtsy, like a prayer. Fruitlessly.

The man in the red suspenders is profoundly embarrassed, uncomfortable. He has had to deal with a woman he is getting rid of, and that is never fun, always difficult, puts one in a bad light. Even for that I am sorry. How little did I want to be a broken old female on his hands, I whom he once admired, his brown-haired scholar in her brisk French roll, her neat wool dresses, her good shoes and gloves. The sculptor in the work shirt under the red suspenders was my buddy when I, too, wore a twenty-five-cent work shirt from the pawnshop downstairs below the old Bowery loft, and built sculpture in the heat of summer, the windows open to the screaming street of bums and Joey the Junkman's rabid obscenity. Fat David at the hardware store across the street gave us credit.

"Miltie had to give up his shop," Fumio says, out of nowhere. Miltie was David's partner, and when David sold the building and the business to devote himself full-time to his two mistresses and to being the pillar of his temple, Miltie, whose hardware specialty was fishing tackle, opened his own store on Astor Place. But couldn't make a go of it between booze and money. "He's working for Shapiro now; they made him a clerk. His hands shake a lot—I don't think he'll live long.'' I stare at Fumio in a frenzy of sadness. Is everything like this, does it all come down to this, are we predestined in this kind of stuff, is it all this relentless and we never knew it till now?

Fumio knows it; the very set of his shoulders is informed with that knowing. That's why he's leaving. That's why he's working so hard, why the show next year in Soho is so important: he knows that there is nothing but work and death. That is what his very being announces under the deceptive peacockery of the red suspenders. The truth is in the hard cast of his flesh within the shirt . . . death, death, death. And loneliness, solitude until death. Only the work; if you can throw up a little barricade of work, then there is something before the end—otherwise nothing.

But I can't work. It is the thing I can never tell him. If I were going along with the shrink line, I could say I am ill and must recover, that is my work now, healing, merely healing. But to work itself—make, do, achieve, create—forget it. I may have to live out my life unable ever to do that. Having to accept those terms is what causes me such anguish all day—since my instinct would rather die than stop being an artist, cease to make, to write, to paint. It may be like that. It may be that I will just have to adopt a lay existence, no longer of the favored, the truly alive. For I see now, from without, being outside that state, how bright the artists look—crystalline lives above this mundane existence.

When I say that I will miss him, Fumio just grins: he'll be back in no time. Entreated, he concedes he may come down at Thanksgiving for the big annual party with our old gang of painters. When I say that I will miss him, he hears none of the passion in its panic, the adulation and the tenderness behind the dependency he understandably despises. Going from me, in every way going from me. That Phoebe's, this dumb bar, its harsh big windows looking onto the desolation of the Bowery, should be our end, the TV on, the waitresses hurrying around, people with their Sunday papers and their Sunday talk . . . The old-time leisure of it in contrast to the empty bleakness between us, the yellow of the scrambled eggs, the coffee being topped up since we have paid but still don't leave, I squirming in my chair to tell him my love, my terrible grief at his loss, at the loss of myself, my dying in life, the loss of us—all we were, the promise, the fun. In fact, Fun was Fumio's nickname, the only English word close to Fun-chan, the standard diminutive for Fumio in Japanese. In English the syllable had a whole new connotation, exquisitely suited to his being then, for he was joy itself, the boy lover of those years. That life, that time. The very central passage of my life was Fumio. That marriage now dissolved upon this stupid café table. Ostensibly about a question of a house and a law, property and legality. But it isn't that, and I know it; he wants a divorce in order to be divorced. "Completely independent," he keeps saying, as if he were a minor petitioning for his rights.

It is not autonomy he wants. Or even freedom. Only to be disencumbered, unburdened, forever disassociated. He is one of the people "responsible," he says, and he doesn't want it. "Fine, you can just refuse to exercise that power. It's crummy anyway—it's the power to have me imprisoned," I'd told him when he came by after New Year's. "Of course, it's a burden, Fumio. It's also a stupid patriarchal custom. I'm not your property to have jailed or not." "But it's more than that, it's any and all responsibility, legal, financial, whatever." "If you want me to pay for the two collect phone calls from Ireland I will." "I don't care about phone calls and you've loaned me plenty of money always. But I don't want responsibility." "So don't cooperate with the machine," I said, manic or confident or full of mental patients' liberation and madness network rhetoric.

I believe it still, but now I'm back on the stuff, reduced to dosages, to hope of recovery someday if I cooperate absolutely. The victim of my disease. And its priests and theorists, doctors and clinics and textbooks joining hands with the cabal of the beloved in a semicircle before me as I stand on the edge of the world. One step back and I fall into death and suicide, hundreds of steps forward and I join them in reintegration. The looks on their faces do not welcome me; they shun me. I've abdicated, surrendered my point of view, am no longer in conflict with them over the nature of my experience or its validity, abjectly agreeing to my madness, its distasteful, ridiculous, soul-searing humiliation, its odious otherness—now returned to them, willing, cringing. A creep. They look on with a pity that withers.

The shame I walk home in has a novelty: I'm now one of the millions of discarded women, a cast-off wife. The companion of my heart this distant and embarrassed man, my fellow artist of twenty years this bullying guy in suspenders, his very successes rubbing me out. There is not even room to be glad for him—he is so glad himself it defeats me. One sees it going on, the weeks and months ahead conferring with his goddamn attorney, losing him. For he need no longer communicate with me at all. Losing him to distance and divorce—when I could have kept him after all as friend and beloved—losing even his friendship, that very bond in the blood that was us, our twinhood. Ten years married, then another eight years as friends, living apart but close in the way that one would call his name in Iran if arrested or in Ireland if jailed, know it on the lips if one died suddenly of a heart attack or a bullet or as a truck bore down, and there was as much as an instant. So well, so long, so utterly have I loved this man that he is a sinew in my chest, a memory in my nipple, a muscle still in my cunt or along the inside of my thigh that will stay or recall or remember and never begin to forget. So that one need not even swear to it. All swearing and forswearing are nothing, like the idiot legalisms of this paperwork which now absorb his so short span of attention. Because that sensitive skin along the inner thigh now or when I am eighty will know and bear witness even in the last capacities of sense—it is all there still, as the history of a tree is traced in its rings. Don't you remember? You who taught me the life of the tree, how each of its years and moments was in those rings, as people we have loved would be rings within ourselves, if we were split open. Split open.

8

Like most people carried along through this drama, Sophie has experienced a good deal of strain herself, a smaller but parallel unraveling which she claims is still affecting her, the reason for her short temper and general irritability. I must put up with her moods; she has with mine. She cannot return to me yet—if ever—because it is still so fresh. She can never trust in me again; of course she could not endure a recurrence. And my disease is all recurrence. "Not if I take lithium," I say. "You'll go off it again." "No I won't." "You say that now, but you did before." "I learned—I hardly need to learn that again." We actually argue about something as fugitive as whether on some future date I will or will not swallow four capsules of lithium a day. They are bitter quarrels. So much is bitterness; we knew too much, have seen too much. I am too used and flawed in her eyes for her ever to return to me. The pain of it swells inside me; if she knew the degree of remorse in this mute creature. If I could cry. My whole being is dedicated to hiding emotion, covering the defeat.

If Sophie did return to me I am aware that I would be locked in forever with someone who knows just which cue would remind me that I am a patient in remission, with a shameful past that can be rerun at any moment. Relationships invaded by psychiatry become prisonlike, a symbiotic intertwining of keeper and parolee, an uneasy combination of suspicion and resentful dependency. Wouldn't it be better to find someone who didn't know? To take the damn lithium and shut up about it all? Of course, any new lover would hear in no time, the well-meaning taking the trouble to explain—stories poured into Dakota's ears when she met me; Sophie's too. But at least there'd be a clean slate, and you could engineer the presentation and ensure that there was some ironic version of it all they'd hear first from you.

So there are moments when I think I am well off without her, for all her loyalty; since it is Benfield and Sophie who have saved my life these months. She is the only one to visit, calls every day. But such lifelines are also dependencies. Maybe if I were to be free, which is to be well, I should be free of her as well. She has the goods on me. Not only that, she has run through me, exhausted me; I am an empty well to her now.

These days she goes on in the teeter-totter of a night with Marcy, a night with me. Sometimes a night for herself, rid of both of us. And then the cheery voice comes through on the phone, the only phone call I ever answer, screening them first on this dishonest and contemptible machine that preserves me in limbo, wasting time and reading junk while numbed out on imipramine or whatever antidepressant Benfield has decided is the thing. He gives me the choice of taking or not taking the stuff; what happens when he says it's time to go off them and take life straight? "How are you?" Sophie asks. "Fine," I invariably answer, detesting this word more than any other. Yet what else does one say? "Fine and dandy, never better," I elaborate grimly. She laughs. "But really, how are you? What are you doing?"

"Reading, I never do anything else." I have confessed to this vice already, but she has no idea how serious it is. "Have you finished working?" "Nearly." Also a lie. "How about some dinner?" "Sure." The package of soda crackers is by the chair, almost empty; it is eight-thirty. She has just quit work, will come and pick me up in my car, which she has borrowed to haul Sheetrock. I empty an ashtray, make the bed, wash several days' dishes before I hear her ring and then, since she still has her keys, her step on the stair, bounding up five flights in her sleek boots and jeans, an invasion of life into this loft-sized coffin.

Now I must put on a face, go to the door, greet her—a meek little hug that parodies our past. We still sleep side by side, my nights. Marcy's are probably breathless passion. On my nights things are tame enough. She doesn't want to, or so it seems. I don't want to either: deep down I do not want to make love, the effort of it, the exertion, the damp and smell and trouble of it. It is too difficult to interest oneself in the flesh. On the surface, however, I do. Or rather, I do not want to make love but I want her to want to. I want to be loved; I even want to love—but only from the heart, emotions not glands: the eyes, the mouth, words, feelings and cravings for feeling, for passion, for the surge and music of it all, the breast torn with tenderness and longing. But no resort to the flesh. And since there is no resort to it, there is only an unfulfilled fantasy, on occasions determined beforehand: tonight I will go down on her—as if it were a task to be performed, something to be got through for the sake of the connection it would create between us, the restoration of feeling, the return of eroticism. And when the time comes, I don't want to, following instead another cue into a quarrel. They are so hard to avoid now. And argument prevents sex. I can take exception to her own lack of enthusiasm for making love, or go about it unconsciously in a way to provoke no enthusiasm. Then I am angry. Rejected, unfulfilled—the rejection food for thought for three days, further evidence of how hopeless my situation in life is. How impossible it is to write or do any work. How my condition worsens and admits of no improvement—it is months now. I keep seeing her on her knees on those dark blue sheets with the little white flowers, in the blue barn those first years, laughing with lust and delight.

But I no longer live with this tall slim figure I see in silhouette in the little office room on Fifteenth Street, watching her talk on the phone: the motion of her new life will carry her away, right out of my ken. And she will finally be someone I hardly know anymore—I want to cry this aloud, interrupt her phone call, shout her back to me. Part of it is Marcy, the pressure that Marcy's demands put on her.

Or, looked at another way, the pressure that my continued existence puts her under. If there were no Marcy, she could deal with me perhaps. But if she were with Marcy only, it would be easy. For all the strain of this triangle, for all the tension Marcy's existence brings on, the problem is actually my existence. Within this half-life of depression. Following upon the spectacle of my madness, a thing that must have harrowed Sophie a great deal, her sense of correctitude, the notion she had of me before I exploded into so many shredded bits. Now, of course, I am tamed and contrite. But what good is it if I carry it so far as to disintegrate, to presage a whole lifetime of incompetence, dependency, the long face of grief, the abysmal dullness of depression?

What prognosis anyway? The disease is cyclical. It will return. Health is merely remission. Even with lithium as a prophylactic, who can say she'll stay on it, who can say it will always work if she does? There are cases . . . Sophie is full of the wisdom of pamphlets from Marcy's brother the medical student, the number of times Martha Ravich has gone off it, the theories of some new guy with vitamins. Or another lithium guy uptown I should see—he's put out a brochure. Sophie with her hopefulness, putting up with me. At the crack of dawn when I've stayed overnight Sophie fetching me coffee from the deli after she has moved my car off the street and into a parking lot to avoid a ticket. Sophie letting me rest or carry on my vulture's reading habit at her place on the days I go to Benfield or have blood drawn at the hospital around the corner from her. Sophie keeping tabs on me, bawling me out if the visits to Benfield discourage me. Sophie keeping me alive. At that minimum level of vitality that is still breathing. Perhaps even her tempers are an attempt to force some life back into me.

And perhaps in a curious way we are healing each other. After the cataclysm, if we could survive this we would be able to survive much else . . . that "we" which is so dubious now, so in the balance.

9

Sophie and I sit in the car in front of my building on the Bowery; she's in the driver's seat. She will let me off here and go on to her construction job. She's late in fact, and my speechless dithering is holding her up. "Look, do you want me to drop you off *here* or somewhere else?" "Ah . . ." "Say something, for God's sake, tell me." Mutual embarrassment. "I don't know." But I do know for sure that I cannot climb those stairs, face the mail, the chair by the window where I read—and go on doing nothing all day. Sophie is borrowing my car as she often does now—my little Volkswagen has become an adjunct of her construction company. Work she does with others: Chris, Donna, even Marcy. Having spent last night with me, Sophie will spend this night with Marcy. Or in working late: the job begins to eat into the little time I see her. "Hurry up, decide—what do you want? I'm late." The harshness of her now, her scorn covering me, undermining my determination to have her back, to last this out. Why stay with someone who treats you like this?

Paradoxically, her extraordinary patience these months, her kindness and tenderness, her solicitude: even leaving me, she has not left me to rot. I am such a far cry from the person she loved once, loves still—how the memory of who I used to be must dismay her, looking at the faded creature in a raincoat coming from her shrink, held together with medicine, supported by antidepressants, without the gumption or sanity to get out of the car. Pleading—I am pleading for something: some other day, some place to go, some different existence from the one ahead of me for the next forty-eight or seventy-two hours till I see her again.

Sophie is the only person I see, my single outside force, stimulus, contact. Gently she says it this time: "I really have to get to the job." "Sure. It's just that . . ." "What?" Finally bringing it out—"Could I come with you?" A silence. "Maybe I could help." And she says yes. I run upstairs for a change of clothes, a painting shirt, some old jeans we found the other day.

Within an hour I am on a scaffold, painting a ceiling with a spray gun, huge machinery around me and below on the floor. Saying to myself, through the din of the compressor and the deluge of fine drifting paint, Look, you are someone painting a ceiling, you are a construction worker at five dollars an hour, a worker not a boss, mind you, because you can no longer write, don't even know who you are anymore, and can't cope at all. So you are glad to paint ceilings, put up Sheetrock—anything rather than stay alone in that loft, unable, for the rest of your life. Somewhere in the middle of life you got lost.

With a spray gun on scaffolding, muddling after the thread of life in section after section of cement ceiling, suspended above the big ground-floor space we are converting to—of all things—a bookstore. Science fiction books. The owners of the place people I dislike intensely; as the hireling of their hireling I am invisible to them, a drone. They approve or fail to approve of the ceiling and it gets still another coat; they walk all over the varnish we have laid down over the newly sanded floors and Sophie rages. As a hired hand, I have only to keep on, relieved of responsibility but permitted to do the work. How healing it is, when good for nothing else, to be able to plaster a wall. The sculptor's craft of it, the experience in restoring the farm and building the studios. Construction—the very constructiveness of it. Never mind the little British peacock for whom we are creating the store, his inspections, his sensational entrances and exits: the radio announces that the second Irish hunger striker has died today. I listen to the proprietor interview his clerks, his hustle about the big commissions they'll get, the grandiosity of his line of "collector comic books." This guy has no idea—but he's saving my life. Thanks to him I'm a working stiff.

Thanks to Sophie, really. Changing into work clothes in the basement of this store every morning, with its dusty cement floor, the naked new Sheetrock walls, the cracked little toilet, the primitive hooks where our jeans and shirts hang; changing into street clothes for lunch or at the end of the day—another number of hours without pain, or with less pain. My own predicament put aside awhile for the nice little problem of how to tape that left-hand wall perfectly, how to sand the plaster into invisibility. Even hard cases, like how to fix this rather hopeless staircase, how to get the old newel post to be strong enough to carry traffic—these problems are a blessing compared to last month's fears that I would never be able to finish the book on my father, that the summer ahead alone at the farm would be hell.

Taping Sheetrock, I forget that I am wasting my life doing this. Then I remember, remembering, too, that I am lucky to have the work today and will lose it when this job ends. Fortunately, there is a floor to sand in the Village next; a guy came in off the street and, seeing a group of women running floor sanders, asked for a bid. Probably thinks we're cheaper. We were elated. More work. My grief lifts little by little: the work is restoring me. Maybe the construction company will succeed—could I spend my life this way, older and older, at five dollars an hour? Nothing else in sight. It would be good for Sophie; in no time she would be an administrator and designer over a team. Once, I could have contributed capital and made a place for myself in such a scheme. Now I am grateful, not only for the work to divert me from the burden of self—I'm grateful for the wage. After the creditors' share, I'll still have a hundred dollars, enough to live on for a week or two. This time I'll buy food, eat again. My terror of the future recedes into the day-to-day of physical labor, the success of the here and now.

Sophie is pleasant to work for. The first week she even took me to lunch, walking out with me to one café after another until we had tasted all the hamburgers in the area, waiting kindly through these meals, through my silences, my clinging to the job. In this work I begin to feel worthwhile, occupied, competent. It is crazy to be doing this, I think, sweeping the dirty, long-abandoned floors over and over again. Sure it's crazy, but at least it's something. It might astonish certain people—the long story of how I got here, how this is what my life is now. And I am glad of it, almost selfish about the sanding machine, taking turns on it with Marcy. For, of course, Marcy is here; there is that to live with too.

When she arrived the evening of the first day, I realized she came here after work to earn the extra money, stayed to have dinner with Sophie, spend the night at her place. We are all very civilized about it but there are the inevitable moments when Marcy begins to change clothes to go home alone. Or with Sophie. Or when Sophie, being nice to me, stays longer, thereby announcing that I am the one chosen tonight. And

Marcy is in tears in the ugly little toilet. I must give way, listen while Sophie explains how difficult this all is for her, for Marcy as well; so I must be understanding, take my car and leave. They were to see a film together after all. By inviting myself into the job I am intruding, perhaps even taking work away.

I am good at the job. And it is infinitely good for me. Days when I can be a construction hand are good days. The others are not good: slow days on the job, Marcy's days, days between jobs. I did the mail finally. Even cleaned the loft and restored the plants. After that there was nothing to do but read, stare, and remember. How much better to work. Any work. Because I live for the work now, that apartment we're doing in the Village. Pear trees in blossom all along the street, easy old stucco buildings. Working in the smell of stain and varnish, even the strange personal smell of this tiny apartment, its unique soul: we are employed by two swish antique dealers who are using us to spruce it up so they can collect an inordinate rent. I relish the tenor and hue of every single one of its oak boards as we sand and polish, taking more time than we should. Losing money on the job, one of Sophie's tendencies since she never bids high enough—the usual mistake of tyro contractors. But the blossoms on the trees, the heat of the sidewalk, the insistence of spring in the warmth of the stucco, the push of the new leaves . . . I am getting better.

10

And then one day the farm was paid for; one day in late April I wrote the last check. A great weight lifted off me. I had lived five months under the shadow of an auction. The horses are safe, taken on by a riding stable, but the colony will disappear. I tried the bank; they'd give a mortgage on the farmhouse, but without an income I could not meet the payments and so would lose even the homestead. Sell off a few acres? Standing in the road with a realtor, trying to imagine house sites in a thicket of locust trees, I realized it would take a year or two to get permission from the planning board, the board of supervisors, and the health board. Then time to find a buyer. I didn't have that much time before foreclosure. So I would have to save it as a writer. The miracle was that I could. Paying in dribs and drabs with each small sum that came in from abroad, everything I could get my hands on; firing the money off without pausing to consider living on it or paying other debts; doing construction work and stinting on groceries, on life itself, I have paid every debt now except Page's, and even that is cut in half.

And now the farm, or rather the land to make a woman's art colony at the farm, is solid, paid to the last cent. Europe did it, the little advances from Italy, France, Germany, Scandinavia for this or that book not yet translated—my agents did a wonderful job. The Germans paid early, the Swiss got it there on time. The last bit. Writing is impossible, art seems unimportant, there is just the farm left. The lavender barn remains half-completed, a reminder of the summer. In a way, if I could finish it—alone, without apprentices—in a way with that single heroic act I could redeem everything, every folly, every loss, even the loss of myself.

An ordeal, like the ordeal of fairy tales where one prolonged effort produces justification, redemption, unlocks the riddle, awards the prize. If I can build a house alone, unaided, or aided only by Sophie on the occasions when she visits to do the more arcane types of carpentry: framing openings, installing casements and French doors. But all the drone work: the Sheetrock, mudding and taping, painting and sanding, insulating, moldings and baseboards, trim; and all the work on the floors: sanding and varnishing—that will be mine. Virtually unaided. Alone there. Months of solitude with nothing but this task—how will I stand it? And having to live in the place, too, since I must keep the tenant in the farmhouse—there is no other way to pay next year's taxes. Living in the shell of an unfinished house without a toilet, bath, sink, all those things one comes to miss. There will be no apprentices because there is nowhere decent for them to live. Because I am too ashamed after last year to ask another bunch and haven't advertised or spread the word. I cannot really bear company, still can hardly talk, would feel foolish in their presence.

There are days it takes me eight hours to climb a ladder and paint a few boards. There are July afternoons when I cannot even take measurements in the heat, trying to put on the trim boards—it is finally time for them—perfectly. On a tall ladder and in the glare and my own despair, I spend forty minutes getting one set of figures. Then down into the shade of the shell—the ground floor, which still looks like a boy's clubhouse: Sophie's term, though we have finally made the floor, a whole month of it, the month of June. And it is perfect: the floorboards sing into the stone wall, cut exactly to match its irregular line; the whole thing is level as water. Four of us built it: Sybille, Gloria, Sophie, and I. They are back in town and I am alone again, alone for weeks at a time. Finding refuge in the shade of the main room, away from the sun and the impossibility of taking readings from one ladder when two are needed and someone to hold the other end of the tape measure. Make coffee. Read for a moment or just close your eyes and rest them. Have a cigarette and then go out there and try again. Today you put up those boards: it's your job today. You have to. Shirker, get back to it; force yourself.

Forcing myself, the ladder shaking; one day and then another. Then weeks of mudding and taping. Volunteers arrive magically on certain days from the city: women from a theater conference who have come from all over America and Europe and noticed a little card on a bulletin board that asked for help up here. I am their cook, their carpenter, their hostess—grateful for their companionship, acquaintance, unbelievable hard work. Especially Barbara George, who makes theater against nuclear arms and comes up time and again, bringing others: women who ride motorcycles, an Italian woman doctor, a French actress, a Greek woman who owned a cargo boat that the CIA or the Shah's sister or some sinister force commandeered and sank. Long tales and stories around the big table on the ground floor, the windows in finally, the floor laid, the lamps hung, a provisional sink rigged up—the place becoming a home for anyone who would stop by and lend a hand in return for sunshine, good dinners, and French wine.

Another week would pass before any visitors come and in that time I must finish mudding a ceiling, install all the woodwork, insulate around all the windows. Fall is here: by the time I should have finished I haven't yet. It must be perfect, it must be beautiful—this handmade, handcrafted house. So loving in each detail, the thing taking on a great and special beauty now, a look of its own—part chalet, part something unique: a house of casements and beams. The light in here, particularly the reflected light of the snow, has a clarity and beauty I have never seen anywhere else. There are nights I walk the place, watching the stars from its many windows, imagining myself staying here, writing here, doing the book on my father finally. Almost happy again, happy with work, that happiness. Loving it almost too much to leave.

And the last day, I wished I were writing here in the library instead of just paying bills, with the vast winter sun like music or gold across the floor and the rug and the cushions—for it is finished now, elegant. That last day it hurt a little to give up the place to the tenants coming in. A nice pair of students, brother and sister: they would take good care of it and their rent would pay the school taxes and save the farm one more year.

Next year there would be apprentices again and the colony would go on. We had made it—we had seen it through. Sophie and I. For this is our story too. And it has no conclusive ending. The rupture of the "mad" summer, its devastation, has never healed. Though years have now gone by. Nor do we sever either, preparing again for yet another summer of the colony. Four or five summers more until the first harvest and we enter upon the second stage and begin building the cottages for the full-time writers and painters. I never know if Sophie will be there still, nor does she. We seem to have become a habit with each other: comrades beyond mates. There are new lovers in her life, probably always will be. I have surrendered both hope and expectation but enjoy my new independence. I lived alone on the Bowery last winter and liked it. We seem to do better as friends, seem to do better living separately in the winters. Still sharing the summers, the farm, the colony. But something broke in that fatal summer that can never be repaired in either of us—some essential trust.

The lavender house was finished that February; in the spring I went to Paris for two weeks. Away from America, I felt the desire to write beginning to return again; hesitantly, tentatively, I conceived a book on the terrorism of the state against the individual, which runs through our century, transforming the nature of polity and civil life, its victims creating a new genre, the testimony of the political prisoner. I read Arthur London in a cheap Paris hotel room and dared to make a few shaky notes, placing my terror and claustrophobia next to his, resolution forming again.

But back in New York I couldn't go on with it. I stopped reading the Amnesty International report on the methods of the Greek junta and began pacing the floor on the Bowery. Already understanding that it was this book or none, *The Loony-Bin Trip* or nothing. For it stood like a boulder in the middle of the room, demanding to be attended to—it could no longer be ignored.

The next day I was visited by an old friend, a former lover, Rae, long institutionalized and broken in those places, a painter once, but dependency and self-doubt had left her a family ward, an empty husk. I had to write something. So I made a short story of that visit. What had been broken in her, in me, struggling to heal or hide the fractures.

And the next day I began *The Loony-Bin Trip*.

CONCLUSION

I wrote *The Loony-Bin Trip* between 1982 and 1985. The last section was written first, in a hangover of penitence and self-renunciation, that complicity with social disapproval which is depression. Now, when I reread it, I find something in it rings false. True, it describes depression: the giving in, the giving up, an abnegation so complete it becomes a false consciousness. But typing it over I want to say, Wait a moment—why call this depression?—why not call it grief? You've permitted your grief, even your outrage, to be converted into a disease. You have allowed your overwhelming, seemingly inexplicable grief at what has been done to you—the trauma and shame of imprisonment—to be transformed into a mysterious psychosis. How could you?

I was trying to find my way back. Out of the unendurable loneliness of knowing. Acceptance. I could not bear to be the only one anymore. I could not pit my truth against so many, against the power of science, nor could I live without other people. I surrendered my understanding, lost myself trying to survive and accommodate. And I went on taking lithium. It seemed a condition of parole: if I stopped taking it and were found out I might be confined again. A sort of Pascal's bet: I was terrified that without the drug I could plummet again. What if they were right after all? My own mind was too dangerous.

For years the urge to break free of lithium tugged at me, but my fear of consequences was too great: another fall, another capture? Then I was invited to attend a conference of the National Association for Rights, Protection, and Advocacy, professionals recently authorized by the federal government to protect the rights of persons with "mental illness." There is a liberal faction within the Association that has consistently permitted the veteran organizers of the anti-psychiatric movement to attend and speak out. I met them and was able to connect finally with others of my own persuasion, to discover their energy and support. I went to a few more conferences, still on lithium, deploring aloud the system and its drugs but in secret taking lithium, hedging my bets, maintaining my crutch, aware of bad faith, but frightened.

Finally my comrades Paul and Dayna asked me if I was on drugs. The movement attitude is tolerant: take them if you like; if you want to withdraw there is help and support. Dayna had withdrawn from lithium several years before. She told me to "drink lots of milk, don't get over tired, have faith, and tell no one." Paul and Dayna would be the only ones to know; they'd call me every Sunday night and I'd report.

In fact there was never anything to report. In 1988 on my birthday, September 14th, I took 600 mg of lithium instead of the usual 900, going below the therapeutic level for the first time. On January 1st, I reduced it to 300 mg, and on March 15, daring the Ides of March, I went to sleep for the first time in seven years having taken no lithium at all. Nothing happened. Nothing ever happened. None of the anger I had feared; indeed it seemed that lithium had created a stifled fury in me for years which abated and then fell away. To my surprise I had a new patience now, and serenity, was more tolerant and open, even able to fall in love again. And this time I kept my secret.

Over a year went by without incident. I still kept mum. Then one day when Sophie was visiting the farm—a flourishing place now, our trees full grown and our harvest at last able to support the art colony—it seemed the right moment; there was a great harmony between us. "I've been off lithium for over a year now, Sophie." The astonishment in her face, then relief. "What happened?" "Nothing, that's it, nothing." And then we laughed and the laughter freed us. She shook her head: had it all been for nothing?

The psychiatric diagnosis imposed upon me is that I am constitutionally psychotic, a manic-depressive bound to suffer recurrent attacks of "affective illness" unless I am maintained on prophylactic medication, specifically lithium. For a total of thirteen years I deadened my mind and obscured my consciousness with a drug whose prescription was based on a fallacy. Even discounting the possible harm of the drug's "side effects," it may seem little consolation to discover that one was sane all

along. But to me it is everything. Perhaps even survival: for this diagnosis sets in motion a train of self-doubt and futility, a sentence of
alienation whose predestined end is suicide. I have been close to that
very death, remember its terror and logic and despair. One struggles to
forgive the personal betrayals, just as one must come to analyze the
forces that hemmed one in. But it is essential not to forget. In the
remembering lies reason, even hope and a saving faith in the integrity of
the mind.

It is the integrity of the mind I wish to affirm, its sanctity and invi-
olability. Of course there is no denying the misery and stress of life
itself: the sufferings of the mind at the mercy of emotion, the circumstances which set us at war with one another, the divorces and antag-
onisms in human relationships, the swarms of fears, the blocks to
confidence, the crises of decision and choice. These are the things we
weather or fail to, seek council against, even risk the inevitable dis-
equilibrium of power inherent in therapy to combat—they are the grit
and matter of the human condition. But when such circumstances are
converted into symptoms and diagnosed as illnesses, I believe we enter
upon very uncertain ground.

The entire construct of the "medical model" of "mental illness"—
what is it but an analogy? Between physical medicine and psychiatry:
the mind is said to be subject to disease in the same manner as the body.
But whereas in physical medicine there are verifiable physiological
proofs—in damaged or affected tissue, bacteria, inflammation, cellular
irregularity—in mental illness alleged socially unacceptable behavior is
taken as a symptom, even as proof, of pathology. (There are exceptions
to this: brain tumors, paresis [tertiary syphilis], Huntington's chorea,
and Alzheimer's disease—in each of these there is indeed physical
evidence of cellular damage. However, these conditions are not what we
mean by mental illness. What we generally mean—schizophrenia,
manic depression, paranoia, borderline personality disorders, and so
forth—are all illnesses which are established upon behavioral and not
physical grounds). Diagnosis is based upon impressionistic evidence:
conduct, deportment, and social manner. Such evidence is frequently
imputed. Furthermore, it may not even be experienced by the afflicted
party, but instead may be observed by others who declare such a one
afflicted.

For in the case of "mental illness," the petitioner for treatment is
very often not the one said to be afflicted, but someone else altogether.

Commitment laws are so written that the afflicted shall be deprived of judgment on the application of next of kin in conjunction with psychiatry. Their purpose is to deny the allegedly ill person the legal entitlement of any and all rights, civil, constitutional, or human. This is unlike anything we know of in physical medicine, where the prevailing attitude is compassion and respect. In fact, the mental hygiene code, modeled originally upon the criminal code, binds the afflicted party under every method of legal restraint. The afflicted is in a sense one accused, hospitalization constituting a type of arrest, accompanied by police power and physical force both in seizure itself and in detention, where escape is prevented by locks and bars and prohibited by statute as well. Having committed no crime, one can—while drugged and unable even to comprehend the proceedings, without even counsel of one's own choosing—within a routine five-minute hearing lose one's liberty for an indeterminate period, even for life. Without the right to refuse "treatment," a human being is defenseless before such proceedings.

Indeed the involuntary character of psychiatric treatment is at odds with the spirit and ethics of medicine itself. The historic brutality of the methods of psychiatric treatment is well known—chains and manacles. It continues today in routine therapeutic treatments, such as "four-point restraint" (whereby a person is bound with leather wrist and ankle cuffs to a bed or table for days at a time) and the solitary confinement of "isolation" or "quiet" rooms. Such involuntary treatment takes on the character of control, even of punishment. Even worse are the stupefying effects of drugs and of fearsome devices like electroshock machinery. It is difficult to discount the hostility inherent in such courses of "treatment," used on people who are, after all, incarcerated and helpless. Together with the shame and stigma felt on all sides, the general embarrassment and ridicule associated with the affliction of "madness," it makes the pretense that we are dealing merely with illness and healing quite untenable at last. Far more obvious is the fact of social control, the threat and consequence of a divestiture of human rights and the use of force.

Ethically, and eventually legally as well, there is finally the issue of the Hippocratic Oath: one shall do no harm. The "medical model" of mental disease has taken a terrible toll on the bodies of its victims as well as on their minds and emotions. Throughout the world millions of persons now suffer from tardive dyskinesia, an iatrogenic disorder of the central nervous system brought on by the ingestion of toxic substances, the neuroleptic and antipsychotic drugs prescribed as medication. Tardive dyskinesia is an irreversible condition, resulting in (among other injuries) involuntary spasms—physical disfigurements that stigmatize and often isolate the sufferers, minimizing social interaction and opportunity. Tardive dyskinesia is produced by the entire family of neuroleptic drugs: Thorazine, Stelazine, Haldol—substances derived ultimately from chlorine and coal tar. Lithium presents a threat to the kidneys and the heart. The Physician's Desk Reference, by merely reprinting the warnings of the pharmaceutical companies themselves, makes grim reading about any psychotropic drug. It is difficult to understand how anything this physically harmful could continue to be prescribed, even for an offending mind. *Mens sana, in corpore sano.*

Why should one of the thousands and hundreds of thousands who have known the pit and the betrayal—the fear of madness or madness itself—not tell of it? Break the taboo of respectability which has been broken so seldom. Challenge the system that keeps millions in line. Try to explore the region from whose bounds only silent and censured travelers return. I wrote *The Loony-Bin Trip* in part to recover myself, my mind, even its claims to sanity. But in hope as well that I might relinquish that conundrum—sanity/insanity. Somehow avoid that trap while trying to find out the truth: what did happen that summer—the summer at the farm in 1980—and that autumn in Ireland? What light from there back to that other time, the first time, in 1973; that summer, that autumn? The winter following in each case the nadir of depression, the hope of suicide, the death in life. I wrote *The Loony-Bin Trip* to go back over the ground and discover whether I did go mad. Went mad or was driven crazy—that differentiation. But it is not so cut and dried, cannot be. And if I did go mad, even acknowledging latitude and overlap, then what was madness, the irrational, what was it like? Experientially, rolling back the secret and shame, remembering.

Writing these last words in Paris, sitting before the perfect window, number 60, rue de Seine, looking out over the tile roofs of the city, my eyes delight in the spire of the Sainte Chapelle, chapel of the medieval kings of France, an amazing ornate sculpture, a great work of imagination. Focusing upon it I bring together my own experience and that of the multitude who like me have known the cruelty and irrationality of this system, that I may plead for a new respect for the human mind itself, its reason, intelligence, perception, acumen, and logic. Let there be no more forced hospitalization, drugging, electroshock, no more definitions of insanity as a crime to be treated with savage methods. No more state intervention into grief or ecstasy. Let sanity be understood to be a spectrum that runs the full course between balancing one's checkbook on the one hand and fantasy on the other. Possibly higher mathematics as well. At one end the humdrum but exacting work of the mind, at the other, surrealism, imagination, speculation. In the center there is occasionally a balance between logic and the creative forces, which generally tend to fall upon the wilder side: metaphor, simile, parallelism, abstraction, all along a median range. To one side reasoning, equations, expository prose. To the other, theater, painting, déjà vu, recollection. A spectrum. A rainbow. All human. All good or at least morally indifferent. Places within the great, still-unexplored country of the mind. None to be forbidden. None to be punished. None to be feared. If we go mad—so what? We would come back again if not chased away, exiled, isolated, confined.

It is well we say "go" mad, for it is a place—inasmuch as it exists, what little "madness" there is, what has not simply been manufactured out of other things: social controls, family disagreements, lovers' quarrels, professional interests and advantages, the state's ambition to control private life. What little madness one can still extract from simple eccentricity, the "inappropriate" offenses of deportment—like hippies at high mass or punk costume at state functions—since what passes for crazy in one situation is only "crazy" in another. Say then, that there is still "another country" in consciousness. Visited in drugs. Willingly and for fun. Or unwillingly and for nightmares: for we are in technique only at the beginning of negative pharmacology, and its nefarious uses still only in the "seminal" stage and not yet the plague they can surely become among us in an age when torture is revived and institutionalized—unless they are stopped. Forced hallucination, forced delusion. Enforced "insanity," insanitas itself, because a deliberate sickening of consciousness and perception.

But madness? That small remnant of altered consciousness, pure or in response to circumstances. Circumstances of life, even those of the body itself and its chemistry. How cruel and stupid to punish this as we do with ostracism and fear, to have forged a network of fear, strong as the locks and bars of a back ward. This is the jail we could all end up in. And we know it. And watch our step. For a lifetime. We behave. A fantastic and entire system of social control, by the threat of example as effective over the general population as detention centers in dictatorships, the image of the madhouse floats through every mind for the course of its lifetime. More mysterious than the thief in the night, the hit-and-run driver. It is death, but death in life, entombment, burial while alive. Only the fortresses of the ancien régime rivaled the entirety of this capture. Or certain places nowadays, private houses on certain streets in certain countries we know not of. But the madhouse lives for us all.

It waited for Jonathan Swift's great mind to ''break,'' to ''crack,'' to be lost. I have escaped his imprisonment, but I have no more lost my mind than he did. Only my freedom. How tragic that he never recovered his, the great mind in chains for years, a dog collar around his neck. We do not lose our minds, even "mad" we are neither insane nor sick. Reason gives way to fantasy—both are mental activities, both productive. The mind goes on working, speaking a different language, making its own perceptions, designs, symmetrical or asymmetrical; it works. We have only to lose our fear of its workings. I do not speak of Alzheimer's disease or any other condition where the mind's function itself appears to be hampered. I mean plain old ''insanity.'' And I say it doesn't exist.

Madness? Perhaps. A certain speed of thought, certain wonderful flights of ideas. Certain states of altered perception. Why not hear voices? So what? If you break a window, you pay for it; break a law and you see a cop, a lawyer, and a judge, pay a fine or go to jail. But surely it is the law of Thought Crime to forbid, punish, or incarcerate different thoughts. Mental activity at the margin. Or over the line. We do not know the mind. Yet. We have forbidden much if not most of human activity, from sexuality to science and learning or thinking aloud, through the greater part of our history. Now we have, through technology, the capacity to forbid and enforce still more.

Unless we stop. And jump—actually jump—right past our superstitions. Craziness. Insanity. Still worse, psychosis, episodes, disorders, and so forth. Let the mind be free. Thought. Talk, expression, exploration. That at least, where so little else is free in this short and so often miserable life. Bring down the madhouse, build theaters with its bricks, or playgrounds. Let us leave each other ''alone.'' No longer meddled with, we can muddle through without interfering relatives or state psychiatry. The human condition is helped best by being respected.

Let us stop being afraid. Of our own thoughts, our own minds. Of madness, our own or others'. Stop being afraid of the mind itself, its astonishing functions and fandangos, its complications and simplifications, the wonderful operation of its machinery—more wonderful because it is not machinery at all or predictable. As ingenious and surprising and uncertain of result as the first stroke of a painting, as various in possibility. As full of ornament and invention as the spire of the Sainte Chapelle outside my window, a really crazy steeple full of frills, and balls, and cuckoos.

ACKNOWLEDGMENTS

THIS WASN'T AN EASY BOOK TO DO: eight years went into writing and rewriting it. It wouldn't have seen the light of day without my editor, Jenny Cox, who believed in it, took the vast pile of manuscript, reduced it by half, and gave it what strength and coherence it has. I wouldn't have been at liberty to write at all were it not for Margueretta D'arcy, who rescued me from confinement in Ireland with the help of Deirdre McCarten, Sylvia Meehan, Nell McCafferty, Maere Rountree, and Ivor Browne. I am just as grateful to Donald Heffernan for restoring my liberty years before by winning my sanity trial in St. Paul.

During the years I worked on the manuscript many friends encouraged me, particularly Alexandra Chapman and Marie-Pierre Bey in Paris and Linda Clarke in New York. Well-wishers read the manuscript when I circulated it for a few years in photocopied "samisdat." I am grateful to the members of my own family, my mother and two sisters, who, having listened to doctors once, could, over the years, come to listen to me as well. That understanding grew into reconciliation and a vital support. Most of all, my thanks to Sophie Keir, who started out hating this book but has come to like it, her gift for friendship and her own sense of fairness transforming opposition into affirmation: above everything, her great courage in letting me use her name in telling this story.

Finally, I would like to honor a number of people whose long service in the civil rights movement against psychiatric abuse has made them heroes to me, as well as friends: Dayna Caron, Paul Dorfner, Peter Breggin, M.D., Rae Unzicker, George Ebert, Huey Freeman, and Leonard Frank. Also, I want to express my great admiration for Sally Zinman and Judi Chamberlin and others with them who, in creating the model for the self-help center for expatients, have created hope, support, and healing for those wounded by the system.

University of Illinois Press
1325 South Oak Street
Champaign, IL 61820-6903
www.press.uillinois.edu